HIGHER EDUCATION OF SC/ST GIRLS IN ORISSA

HIGHER EDUCATION OF SC/ST GIRLS IN ORISSA

A Study of Participation and Attainment

Prof. (Dr) Bijoya Mishra

GYAN

The Publication was financially supported by the ICSSR. The responsibility for the facts stated, opinions expressed, or conclusions reached, is entirely that of the author and that the ICSSR accepts no responsibility for them.

Consultant Prof. Susheela Bhan, Executive Director, Institute for Peace Research and action, Gagan Vihar, Delhi.

Higher Education of SC/ST Girls in Orissa : A Study of Participation and Attainment

ISBN: 978-81-212-1133-8

Published in 2011 in India by
Gyan Publishing House
23, Main Ansari Road, Darya Ganj,
New Delhi-110002
Phones : 23282060, 23261060
Fax : 011-23285914
E-mail: books@gyanbooks.com
Website: www.gyanbooks.com

Laser Type Setting by: Square Vision, New Delhi
Printed at: Chawla Offset Press, Delhi

*to my SC/ST girl students,
who are the source of inspiration
for my research*

CONTENTS

PREFACE

The research project on "Higher Education of SC/ST Girls. A Study of Participation and Attainment was commissioned in Rama Devi Women's Autonomous College, Bhubaneswar (2004–2006) associating a group of researchers from different fields like Sociology, Political Science, Women's Studies, etc. with Prof. Bijoya Mishra, former Principal, Rama Devi Women's Autonomous College as Project Director and financial support from ICSSR.

This study is mainly a comprehensive enquiry into the reasons for the low enrolment of girls from deprived sections of the society in institutions of higher learning. It also addresses the related questions about the obstacles and hurdles that the students encounter, specifically because of their gender, class, caste and insularity. The study also attempts to determine the impact of special hostel facility for SC/ST girls and to analyse their attainment in regard to their performance in examination. Finally, the study has policy implications, for it suggests policy changes needed to improve their access to and achievement in higher education.

There was a study on the educational problems of the SC/ST students in colleges in 1975 carried out in twenty-five states in the country including Orissa. This study, supported by ICSSR, was limited only to a few SC/ST students in six districts of Orissa and a very insignificant number of girl students were included. Given its limited scope and coverage, it was not intended to study in depth the problems of SC/ST girl students in the State as regards their participation and performance in higher-education. Moreover, it did not extend to post graduate and technical/professional education. The present project vastly expanding the ambit of the earlier study in the current socio-economic environment, follows a relatively un-trodden path and reveals various facets of impediments, specially in the context of the social-cultural environment of these communities. It also reveals the attitudes of SC/ST girls, their parents and communities and their response to current challenges of higher learning. The project is a sincere attempt to diagnose policy and implementation constraints and provide a framework for formulation of alternative strategies.

The ten chapters included in the book present the analysis of secondary and primary data collected by the researchers from different records of educational institutions, examining bodies and Government papers and primary data through interview of students, teachers, parents, people's representatives, policy makers and eminent SC/ST personalities. Their suggestions regarding educational development of SC/ST girls have been recorded and analyzed separately. Although the selection of respondents was based on random sampling techniques, care has been taken to ensure that they represented their population in different institutions. They were drawn from colleges in Bhubaneswar (the capital of Orissa), Mayurbhanj district (district with largest tribal population in the State) and the largest medical college in Cuttack. One hundred and fifty-seven tribal girls and one hundred and thirteen girls from scheduled caste communities (altogether 270 SC/ST students) from twenty-two institutions (starting from higher secondary to post-graduate and technical courses) have been interviewed and their problems assessed. Through inter-relation data, different factors influencing their enrolment and performance were analyzed. Eighty-five college teachers including ten Principals/Vice Principals were interviewed and their opinions regarding attitude and performance of the girls in the institutions have been recorded and analysed. Thirty tribal and twenty scheduled caste parents with daughters pursuing higher education have also been interviewed using separate schedule to assess their views on higher education of girls.

A seminar was held in Utkal University at the beginning of the project to seek guidance from experienced research personnel in this field prior to preparation of interview schedule. A social matrix was prepared initially so that all the objectives of research project could be incorporated in the interview schedule. About twenty questions for personal data, twenty-six questions on educational problems, forty on economic problems, fifteen on social and forty on cultural constraints were prepared. To assess the efficacy of Government policies, twenty-five questions were asked to obtain their views regarding policy changes they felt should be brought about.

There were several sensitive issues for discussion with student respondents such as their role in taking decisions about their own future, apprehension about their future after higher education, perception of their service to their community (if any), their changing attitude towards customs and traditions of the community, feeling of alienation from community due to education, etc. These were discussed with the help of interview guide and not through direct questions.

At the final stage of research, seminars were held in different colleges and the preliminary findings were discussed with the educationists before finalizing the analyses. Low performance, high drop out rate and lack of confidence were the main impediments. Many suggestions were offered by the teachers like arranging special coaching, extra tutorial classes and spoken English classes, etc. In the process, some of the failures of the educational policies in addressing the special needs of the SC/ST students have been observed. Particularly, shortcomings were observed in implementation of 'Upgradation of Merit Scheme' of Central Government which is meant for providing special coaching to meritorious students for entry into technical courses.

While arriving at the conclusions as to what can be done to attract more SC/ST girls to higher education, to enhance their performance and to integrate them into the mainstream, suggestions from different stakeholders, policy makers and many important personalities have been included in this research. This study is very significant in providing information on the educational aspiration and hurdles and difficulties faced by women from the vulnerable sections. An understanding of their special problems is necessary for the formulation of suitable policies on education that will take into account the multiple burdens of vulnerable women.

Prof. Rita Ray
Dept. of Sociology: Utkal University

ACKNOWLEDGEMENT

As the Principal of the largest Women's College in Orissa, Rama Devi Women Autonomous College, in the State Capital, I had the opportunity of close association with SC/ST girls studying in the college (20% of about 4000 seats reserved for them), particularly boarders of a special Adivasi hostel, named Indira Gandhi Women's Hostel, accommodating about 250 of them. This special hostel, only of its kind in the State at college level, is run by SC/ST Development Department, with a view to attracting SC/ST girls from different parts of the State to higher education. From my regular and close interaction with them, I was painfully aware of their educational deficiencies and nourished a sincere desire to take an indepth study of their underlying educational and social constraints and derive ways to address them. This dream was fulfilled after my retirement only because of financial assistance from ICSSR for a research project. Finally, this publication, aiming at dissemination of the result of the research was possible because of sanction of a publication grant. I am indebted to ICSSR for both the research and publication grant.

I am grateful the then Principal of Rama Devi Women's College, Dr. Kalpana Das, for extending all necessary help, which I continued to receive from all her successors throughout my project. The help and co-operation from Vice-Principals, Administrative Bursar, Controller of Examination and all the staff members of college including librarians have been invaluable. I am grateful to them.

I owe a special debt of gratitude to Prof. Rita Ray, Head of P.G. Department of Sociology, Utkal University, who guided the present research work from the very beginning till the end, always sparing time for me whenever I needed. She offered suggestions at every point and helped me finally in this publication. Without her support, this publication would not have been possible. I am thankful to the-then Director of School of Women's Studies, Prof. Asha Hans for providing me all necessary help in her department. I am grateful to Directors of various institutions, who have unhesitatingly permitted me to use their libraries and resources for the study. I would like to make special mention of National Institute of Social Work and Social Sciences (NISWAS), Naba Krushna Choudhury Centre for Development Studies (NKCCDS) and Schedule Caste and Schedule Tribe Research and Training Institute (SCSTRTI). I have also benefited from National Library, Calcutta and the Libraries in Utkal University, Rama Devi Women's College and Orissa Branch of Indian Institute of Pubic Administration.

In course of my field work in Mayurbhanj district, I have received ungrudging support from the District authorities including the District Welfare Office. I would like to place on record my sincere thanks to Ms. C.T.M. Suguna, I.A.S. the-then Collector in the Tribal District of Mayurbhanj.

I am grateful to Vice-Chancellors and Registrars of Utkal University, North Orissa University and Biju Pattnaik University of Technology and Chancellor of Kalinga Institute of Industrial Technology (Deemed University) for providing me all necessary help in data collection. My thanks are due to the authorities of all colleges/institutions covered under the study for the unsparing efforts they made to retrieve data from old records and for their valued suggestions.

In course of interactive seminars/workshops we undertook, principals teachers and educationists offered valuable suggestions for which I am immensely grateful.

I had sought the views of many prominent personalities including Minister SC/ST Development Department, Minister, Women and Child Development Department, Principal Secretary, SC/ST Development Department, State Information Commissioner, ex-Chief Minister, ex-Ministers, M.L.As and many noted community leaders. They have been very kind and generous in giving their views candidly. I am grateful to them.

I am very thankful to Superintendents of all five Women's Hostels in Utkal University and of the Adivasi Hostel of Rama Devi Women's College for the group discussions and extensive interactions with the inmates. I place on record my special thanks to authorities of Kalinga School for Socially Challenged (KSSC), a fully residential school for tribals and of the hostel of Sacred Heart Organisation for offering opportunity to interact with their students. I profusely thank the SC/ST girls to whom I dedicate this work, for providing free and frank views in all matters and enriching the research project.

I offer my appreciation and gratitude to friends associated with me in the project, namely, Dr. Madhumita Das, Dr. Jugal Mishra and Dr. Anita Panda for their support and help whenever needed. My special acknowledgement and thanks are due to my young researchers, Sri Lalatendu Sahoo, Ms. Sheetal Tripathy, Ms. Ameeta Kanungo and Ms. Sailaja Nandini for their dedication and sincerity in collection and compilation of data and other related work. I thank Sri Parida for providing me the facilities of SPSS package of software and Ms. Mamata for her efficient DTP work.

Finally, I am deeply grateful to my husband and daughter, without whose constant support during my very busy schedule, I could not have completed this work.

Dr. Bijoya Mishra

1

INTRODUCTION

1.1 Women and Education

Education is the key to empowerment, dignified survival and social wellbeing of women. As a UNICEF report puts it, "In the long term, almost every other aspect of progress, from nutrition to family planning, from child health to women's right is profoundly affected by whether or not a nation educates girls". Girls' education has a direct impact on infant mortality, morbidity and life expectancy. Most important is the fact that education empowers women with a basic knowledge of their rights as individual and citizens of their nation and the world. University Education Commission under the Chairmanship of Dr. S. Radhakrishnan, which was set up by Government of India in 1948 immediately after independence, has underlined the importance of women's education. The report says: "There can not be educated people without educated women. If general education had to be limited to men or women, the opportunity should be given to women for, then only it would most surely be passed on to the next generation". Yet, it is the education of women which, for various historical reasons, did not receive required attention in the past.

It is also observed that development in India is not uniform. Imbalance exists between males and females, one region and another and among communities. The National Council of Education (established in 1963) constituted committees from time to time to recommend suitable measures for development of women's education and to bridge the existing gap between men's and women's education. In order to conduct a comprehensive investigation of all questions relating to the rights and status of women in the country and to provide suitable guidelines for formulation of social policies including education, The Ministry of Education and Social Welfare (now Human Rescources Development Dept.). Government of India, had constituted a **Committee on the Status of Women (1971-72)**. The report of the Committee titled **Towards Equality** (submitted in December, 1974), was the real Magna Carta for women. This report was the real eye-opener to the prevailing stark inequalities between men and women and contained many recommendations to improve women's education.

The National Policy of Education (NPE-1986) and the **Programme of Action (PoA-1992)** were policy instruments in search of equality and accorded high priority to the education of women.

Despite constitutional provisions and several measures adopted in the successive Five Year Plans, the level of literacy among women has always been lower than that of men.

1.2 Educational Status of SCs/STs

Education, as an important input for human resource development, has special significance for Scheduled Castes and Scheduled Tribes. It not only improves prospects for employment and economic well-being but also promotes self confidence and helps in building up capacity to meet

STATE WISE TRIBAL POPULATION IN INDIA

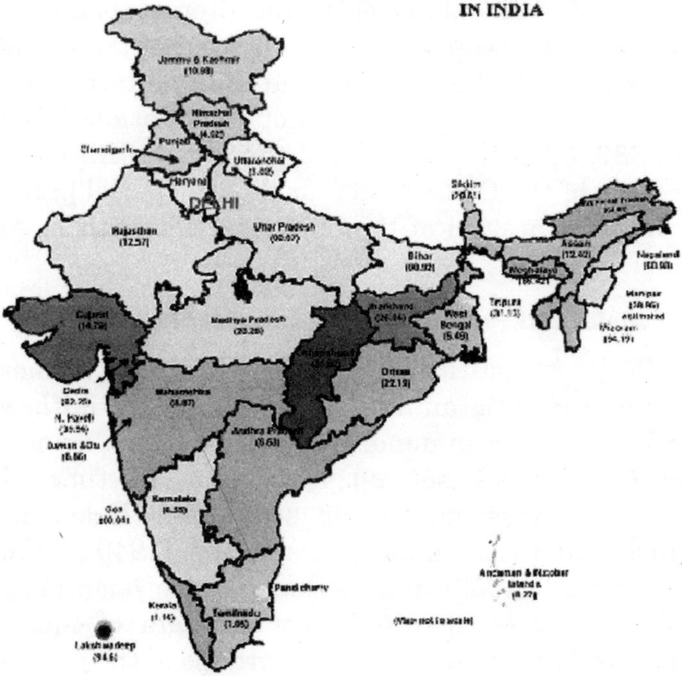

the challenges of changing times. It also helps curbing economic exploitation and social oppression of the SCs and STs going on for centuries.

Although programmes to promote welfare and encourage education among SCs/STs date back to the period prior to independence, the efforts were strengthened and legitimatised by making special provisions in the Constitution. Article 46 of the Directive Principle of State Policy provides: "The State shall promote with special care the educational and economic interests of the weaker sections of the people and in particular, of the Scheduled Castes and Scheduled Tribes and shall protect them from social injustices and all forms of exploitations". Articles 330, 332, 335, 338 to 342 and the entire fifth and sixth schedule of the Constitution deal with special provisions for implementation of the objectives set forth in Article 46.

1.3 Policies and Provisions for Educational Equality

While Constitution provides the basic framework, policies and programmes in education are initiated on the basis of recommendations of various Commissions and Committees set up from time to time. Three major Commissions set up soon after Independence, namely, Radhakrishnan Commission (1949), Mudaliar Commission (1952) and Kothari Commission (1964-65) endorsed the constitutional commitment of equality of opportunity in education for all groups of the society.

Government of India mandated establishment of National Commission for Scheduled Castes and Scheduled Tribes, which would monitor implementation of provisions of the Constitutions relating to safety and welfare of SCs/STs. One of the regular activities of National Commission is monitoring progress in the matters of economic and educational development of SCs and STs.

In addition to establishment of National Commission on Scheduled Castes and Scheduled Tribes, Government of India dedicated the Ministries of Social Justice and Empowerment and Tribal Welfare to continuously plan and monitor the development and welfare of SCs/STs. The Ministries have launched a number of schemes for the upliftment of Schedule Cases and Schedule Tribes such as universal literacy of SCs/STs, free education at all stages, establishment of Navadyoya Vidyalaya, reservation of seats in educational institutions, etc. Despite constitutional provisions and several measures adopted in successive Five Year Plans such as Special Component Plan for SCs and Tribal Sub-Plan for STs, the level of literacy among SCs and STs continues to remain low.

1.4 Disparity in Education

Out of several forms of educational inequalities two need special attention. First is the wide disparity between education of boys and girls at all stages in all sectors of education. Second is the disparity in educational development between general category and backward sections - Scheduled Castes and Scheduled Tribes. A girl from SC/ST family is doubly disadvantaged; firstly because she is a girl and secondly for belonging to the deprived section of the society. Though sustained efforts by Government have led to some significant improvements in literacy and educational development for weaker sections, the gap between general literacy and SC/ST literacy, especially between man and women, is still significantly skewed.

1.4.1 Disparity in Literacy Rate

The table shows gap in literacy rates of general and SC/ST population and also a large gender gap in literacy in all classes. For SC/ST, though the rate of increase in

Table: 1.1 – General and SC/ST Literacy Rate of India (in percentage)

	General Literacy		SC Literacy		ST Literacy	
	Male	Female	Male	Female	Male	Female
1961	40.40	15.35	10.27	3.24	8.54	3.16
1971	45.96	21.97	14.67	6.49	11.30	4.85
1981	56.38	29.76	21.38	10.93	16.39	8.44
1991	64.13	39.29	49.91	23.12	40.65	18.19
2001	75.85	54.16	66.38	41.31	59.34	34.75

Source: (1) Census of India, 1991-2001; (2) Scheduled Tribe Atlas of India – Census of India, 2004.

literacy and particularly, the rate of increase in female literacy, is very encouraging, yet, it is far from being at par with general literacy. Between the SCs and STs, literacy rate of SCs shows a better picture than STs.

Fig. I-A – Female Literacy Rate in India

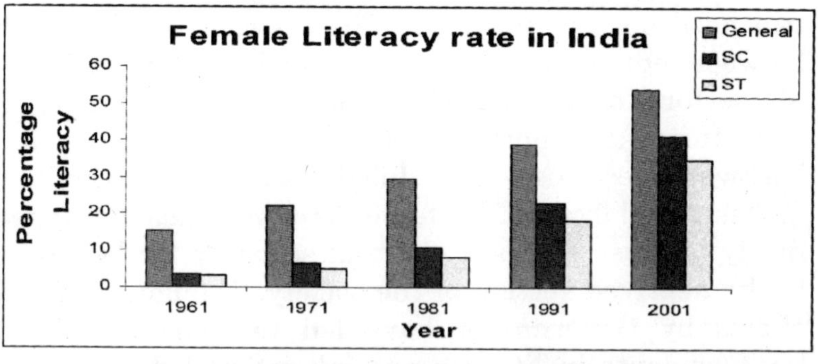

Looking at basic data and educational statistics of SC/ST, the National Commission for SCs and STs has remarked: "In spite of all constitutional frame work and efforts put in successive plan periods, it appears that SC/ST have still to go a long way to come to general level in the field of education. Special measures to improve literacy and educational level should be taken up so that the gap in literacy rates between SC/ST on one hand and non SC/ST population on the other, can be bridged". (Third Report of National Commission for Scheduled Castes and Scheduled Tribes, 1995-96, Vol.I). With regard to female literacy, the Commission has remarked: "The low level of literacy among SC/ST women is a cause of grave concern and is largely responsible for their marginalization in socio-economic fields".

1.4.2 Disparity in Higher Education

Considering the enrolment of children belonging to SC/ST in schools, 28th Report of Commission for Scheduled Castes and Scheduled Tribes notes that though the proportion of SC/ST students corresponds to their population at primary level, there is a sharp decline at middle level, which continues and becomes more prominent as one proceeds to secondry and higher education. According to Government of India Statistics, in 1988-89, SC and ST students enrolled in Higher Education constituted only 9.8% and 2.7% of total enrolment respectively. SC women formed 2.13% and ST women only 0.8% of total enrolment (Selected Educational Statistics, 1989, Studies in Education statistics No.1, Ministry of HRD, Government of India). Moreover, in the field of Higher Education, the proportion of SC/ST students enrolled in Science and Technology subjects is very low compared to those in Humanities (Arts and Education) and among them the percentage of girl students is insignificant.

The table 1.2 shows that at higher level, traditionally less competitive and simpler disciplines like Humanities have comparatively better SC/ST enrolment. Science education rests more.

Table: 1.2 – SC/ST Students in Higher Education (in Percentage)

Subject	SC (All Students)	ST (All Students)	SC (Women)	ST (Women)
Arts, Humanities, Social Sciences	9.87	2.79	1.61	0.19
Science	5.71	0.80	0.67	0.14
Commerce	4.55	2.14	2.41	0.65
Teacher's Training	7.67	2.62	3.15	0.60
Engineering/ Architecture	5.88	1.32	0.39	0.80
Research (All Subjects)	2.91	0.60	0.60	0.19

Source – Selected Education Statistics, 1988-89 in Education Statistics, No.1(1990) Ministry of H.R.D. Department of Education, Planning, Monitoring and Statistics Division, Government of India, 1990, Table-VIII, pp.36-45.

1.5 Orissa Scenario

A study of demographic composition of Orissa shows the State has sizable number of SCs and STs, i.e. 16.5% and 22.13% respectively of the total population of 36,804,660 (2001 Census). More than 11% of country's tribal and 3.7% of SC population residents in Orissa. Thus, SC/ST population of Orissa comprises 38.65% of its total population, which is the second highest among all major States the first being Chhatisgarh at 43.37%. The literacy rate of SC/ST is lower but their sex ratio is higher than the general category population.

General literacy rate for the State is 63.1% whereas for SC it is 55.5% and for ST only 37.4% according to 2001 Census. However, sex ratio for the entire population is 972 and for SCs and STs, it is 979 and 1003 respectively. Low educational level of SC and ST girls is a matter of grave concern.

DISTRIBUTION OF TRIBALPOPULATION IN ORISSA

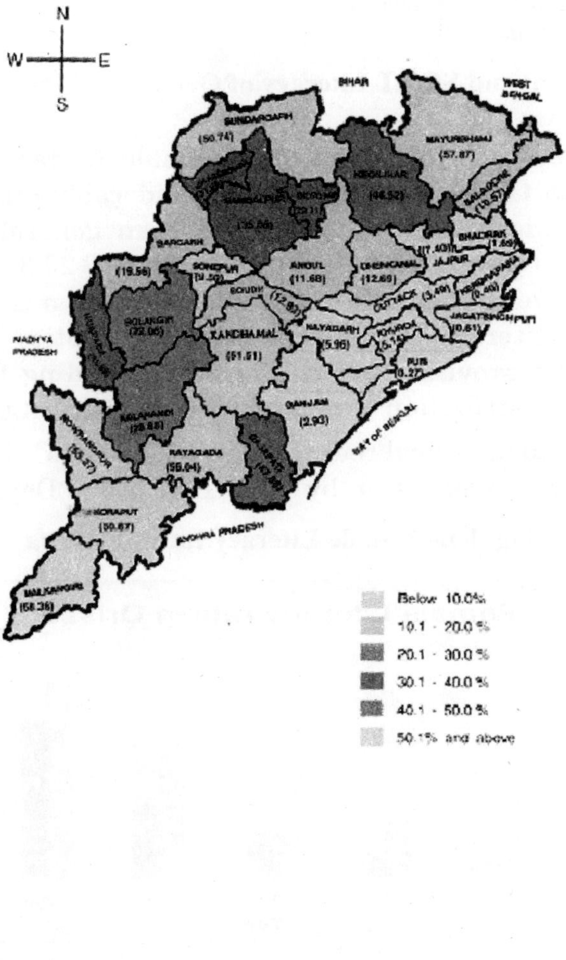

Table: 1.3 General and SC/ST Literacy Rate of Orissa in Percentage

	General Literacy		SC Literacy		ST Literacy	
	Male	Female	Male	Female	Male	Female
1961	34.68	5.65	19.8	3.4	12.05	1.77
1971	38.29	13.92	25.9	5.2	16.39	2.38
1981	47.10	21.90	35.5	11.32	23.27	4.76
1991	63.09	34.68	52.42	20.74	34.44	10.21
2001	73.35	50.31	70.47	40.33	51.48	23.37

Source : Census of different years, Scheduled Tribe Atlas of India Published by Census of India, 2004.

1.6 General and SC/ST Literacy of Orissa

It is seen that though the female literacy rate of SC/ST in Orissa has increased considerably during the last decade; it is still much less than general female literacy (General-50.31%, SC-40.33%, ST-23.37%). The State Government has undertaken various measures to improve literacy status of these communities through steps like provision of scholarships, boarding facilities and free distribution of text books and garments, etc.

Due to historical reasons, education for SC/ST people has been looked after by both Education Department

Fig. I-B- Female Literacy Rate of Orissa

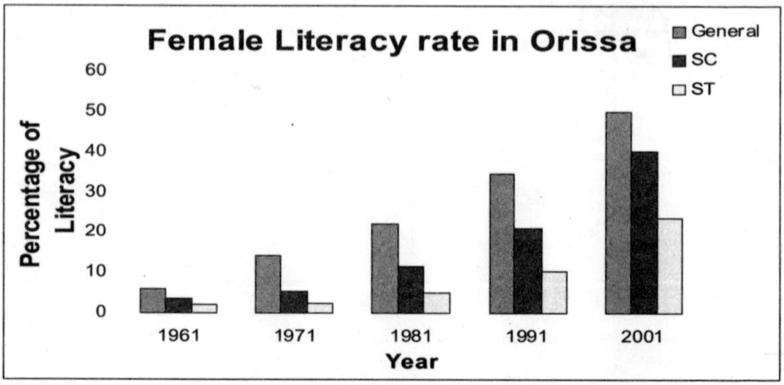

as well as SC/ST Development Department of State Government. Special types of residential and non-residential schools are run by ST and SC Development Department such as Sevashrams, Ashram Schools, Kanyashrams and Tribal High Schools. This Department also maintains 7 Special Adivasi Hostels including 2 for women in under to accommodate SC/ST students pursuing studies (4 Post-matric and 3 Pre-matric hostels).

1.7 Dropout Rate at Different Levels

The dropout rate at different levels of school education is found declining gradually in respect of general castes as well as SCs/STs.

As observed from the Table 1.4, although the drop out rate is declining, it is still very high, particularly in case of SCs and STs. The drop out rate is maximum at

Table: 1.4 – Dropout Rates in Schools in Orissa

Types of Schools	Year	All Category			Scheduled Castes			Scheduled Tribes		
		Boys	Girls	Total	Boys	Girls	Total	Boys	Girls	Total
Primary Schools	2002-2003	32.3	36.5	34.4	35.8	38.7	37.2	49.3	57.4	53.3
	2003-2004	31.9	35.4	33.6	34.6	36.6	35.6	48.2	56.6	52.4
	2004-2005	31.4	32.7	32.0	34.0	35.6	34.8	48.0	56.0	52.0
Upper Primary Schools (Middle)	2002-2003	57.7	60.5	59.1	45.7	49.2	47.5	75.0	80.3	77.7
	2003-2004	56.5	58.6	57.5	60.9	65.3	63.1	73.0	78.5	75.8
	2004-2005	48.2	50.1	49.1	47.0	63.0	55.0	67.0	72.0	69.5
Secondary Schools	2002-2003	65.9	68.5	67.2	74.1	76.5	75.3	78.0	76.5	77.3
	2003-2004	62.5	66.7	64.4	74.3	73.7	74.0	76.3	74.9	75.8
	2004-2005	61.0	66.0	63.5	72.0	73.0	72.5	76.5	74.0	75.3

(*Source* – Economic Survey, Government of Orissa, 2005-06)

the High School stage, followed by Upper Primary and then Lower Primary levels. It seems very few children, enrolled in primary classes, make it to Matriculation Examination (only about 15%). It is observed that the drop out rate among SC/ST boys is higher than SC/ST girls, while in general category, the drop out rate among the girls is higher than boys. Particularly for tribal girls it is observed that their drop out rate is much lower than that of boys (Boys-76.5%, Girls-74%). This interegsting trend may perhaps be ascribed to the need for engagement of tribal boys for supplementing family income.

1.8 Education beyond High School

Table: 1.5 – Percentages of SC/ST Students Appearing in H.S.C. Examination

	SC Students		ST Students		Others	
	Boys	Girls	Boys	Girls	Boys	Girls
2000	8.3	5.2	6.3	3.3	42.6	34.3
2001	8.2	5.2	6.5	3.7	41.9	34.5
2002	7.8	5.2	6.6	4.0	41.9	34.6
2003	7.5	5.1	6.8	4.2	41.2	35.2
2004	8.03	5.3	7.2	4.5	40.6	34.9

Source – Board of Secondary Education, Orissa.

Fig. I-C - Average percentage of students appearing in H.S.C. Examination, 2004

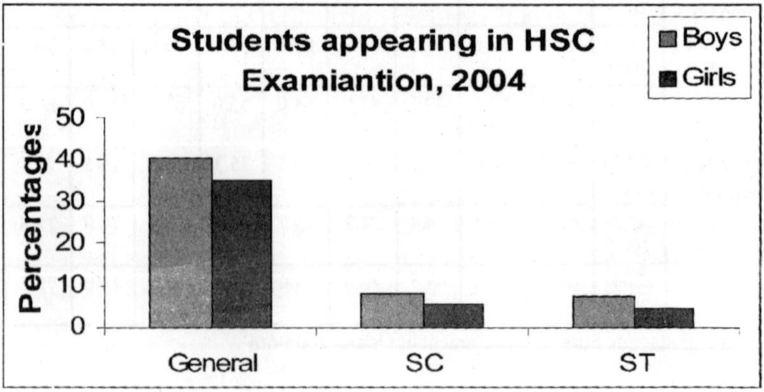

The Board of Secondary Education (BSE), Orissa, conducts High School Certificate Examination and looks after academic standards of High Schools. When participation of SC/ST students all over the State at the Secondary level (Class-X) is considered, it is found to be quite low compared to general caste students.

It is seen that a disproportionately low percentage of SC/ST students are enrolling and appearing in final examination in High School. The number is extremely low for SC/ST girl students (on the average over 5 years it is 5.2% for SC girls and 3.2% for ST girls).

1.8.1 Higher Secondary Education

The Council of Higher Secondary Education (CHSE) regulates, controls and develops higher secondary education in the State. As per recommendation in the National Policy of Education (NPE, 1986), the +2 wing (Higher Secondary Class) has been separated in all Government Colleges since 2001-02. After separation, there are facilities for Higher Secondary education in 1,112 general colleges in the State including 49 Government Colleges. However, the proportion of SC/ST students in these colleges is very low. Moreover, their proportion in

Table: 1.6 – Percentages of SC/ST Students in Higher Secondary Examination

	Arts			Science			Commerce		
	Gen	SC	ST	Gen	SC	ST	Gen	SC	ST
2000	84.17	8.87	6.96	88.26	6.6	5.14	88.22	6.01	5.77
2001	80.4	10.43	9.17	87.87	6.69	5.44	88.19	6.09	5.72
2002	80.16	10.25	9.59	88.32	6.32	5.36	88.28	6.17	5.55
2003	80.47	9.91	9.62	88.26	6.16	5.58	90.18	5.00	4.82
2004	80.12	10.14	9.74	87.39	6.64	5.97	89.76	5.28	4.96

Source – Council of Higher Secondary Education, Government of Orissa.

Science and Commerce seems to be much lower than in Arts. It appears that more SC/ST students qualify for Arts stream, where number of seats is more and cut-off mark for admission is lower.

As seen from Table 1.7, between 2000-2003 the percentage of SC girls to boys increased from 26% to 32% in Science, 50% to 66% in Arts and 6.5% to 10.4% in Commerce. Corresponding percentage of ST girls is 33.5% to 40% (Science), 52.5% to 66% (Arts) and 11% to 17% (Commerce). Thus, in every stream, the percentage of SC/ST girls has been increasing. However, it is far from

Table: 1.7 – Percentage of SC/ST Girls appearing Higher Secondary Examination

Stream	Year	SC			ST		
		No. of Boys	No. of Girls	% of Girls to Boys	No. of Boys	No. of Girls	% of Girls to Boys
Science	2000	2647	684	25.8	1943	652	33.5
	2001	2695	795	29.4	2115	724	34.2
	2002	2515	808	32.1	2002	818	40.8
	2003	2164	696	32.1	1806	729	40.3
Arts	2000	12018	5995	49.8	9246	4860	52.5
	2001	10102	5342	52.8	8684	4897	56.3
	2002	8129	4608	56.6	7275	4637	63.7
	2003	5994	3592	59.9	5602	3708	66.1
Commerce	2000	888	58	6.5	813	95	11.6
	2001	818	61	7.4	724	101	13.9
	2002	723	88	12.1	624	106	16.9
	2003	586	61	10.4	532	92	17.2

(*Source* – Council of Higher Secondary Examination)

being equal to that of boys. Only in Arts, girls comprise more than 50% of boys; otherwise their number is much lower than boys. Thus, girls' education is yet to get due importance in SC/ST families.

1.9 Higher Education in Orissa

(i) Degree Colleges

During 2004-05, 1680 general colleges were functioning in the State out of which 97 were Government colleges and 448 were aided colleges. Out of Government colleges, 49 colleges have facilities for Degree courses. Similarly in private sector, 1064 and 522 colleges were imparting education for higher secondary courses and Degree courses respectively. Besides the above, Post Graduate courses in 27 subjects were available in 25 Government colleges and M.Phil facilities in 11 subjects in 3 Government colleges. Out of these Government colleges, 17 Junior colleges (+2 level) and 16 Degree colleges (+3 level) are meant only for girls. In private sector, there are 152 women colleges in the State (Source – Department of Higher Education, Government of Orissa).

According to Government Order [G.O. No. IXE. MGC.57/77-37782 (2)-EYS dated 1st December 1977], twenty per cent of seats in all colleges are reserved for Scheduled Castes/ Scheduled Tribes (ST-12%, SC-8%). Again, there is a provision that if all seats reserved for SC/ST candidates are filled up and it is found that there are still a number of candidates in that category, the principal of the college has the discretion to admit additional 10% of students belonging to SC/ST category (6% ST and 4% SC). However, after careful consideration, these discretionary seats have been raised to 18% of total strength (10% ST and 8% SC) since 2004 (letter No.III, H.E. Adm. 47/04-36979/HE, dated 23rd September, 2004 of Secretary H.E., Government of Orissa to Director, Higher Education, Orissa). But National Commission of Scheduled Tribes has urged the State Government that there should be 22% clear-cut reservation for ST students for admission in +2, +3 and P.G. Course according to the ST population percentage in the State (letter No.7/7/2004-

Gen of National Commission for Scheduled Tribes to Secretary, Department of Higher Education, Government of Orissa).

Despite such reservation, SC/ST enrolment is found very low, particularly at degree level.

Table: 1.8 – Enrolment of SC/ST Students at Degree Level (+3)

Academic Session	Percentage of Students Enrolled		
	General	SC	ST
1999-2000	82	11	7
2000-2001	82.33	10.84	6.83
2001-2002	81.76	10.97	7.27

(*Source* – Directorate of Higher Education, Government of Orissa).

Not only the enrolment was not proportional to their population, but even the reservation of 12% for ST and 8% SC was never filled up.

(ii) Universities

The State has ten Universities including one Sanskrit University, one Agriculture University, one Culture University, one Deemed University, and a University of Technology (imparting only Technical courses). The reservation procedure is followed in all the Universities. Enrolment in three Universities, (1) Utkal University in the State Capital, (2) North Orissa University in Tribal District of Mayurbhanj and (3) Biju Pattnaik University of Technology have been investigated in detail in this study.

1.10 Technical Education

Technical Education in the State is imparted at various levels through Engineering Colleges, Engineering Schools, Polytechnics, Industrial Training Institutes (ITIs), and Industrial Training Centers (ITCs) and in some general colleges and Universities. The Directorate of Technical Education and Training (DTET) functions as the nodal agency to plan and implement technical education programmes in the State. Biju Pattnaik University of Technology (BPUT) has been established and started functioning in the State since July, 2002. At present 5 Government Engineering colleges and 35 Private Engineering colleges are functioning under the University.

In the Government sector, there are 13 Engineering Schools/Polytechnics out of which four Polytechnics (with total capacity of 535) are meant exclusively for women.

In the field of Medical Sciences, the State has three Medical colleges (another private college has come up recently), one Dental college, one Pharmacy college, three Ayurvedic colleges and four Homeopathic colleges.

1.11 Conclusion

In all General and Technical colleges, 12 per cent seats are reserved for STs and 8 per cent for SCs. In addition to this, 30% seats in Engineering colleges (both Government and Private) are reserved for girls. In spite of all these efforts, participation of SC/ST girls is low, specially in Technical Education, where it is extremely low.

2

SURVEY OF LITERATURE

The Scheduled Caste and Scheduled Tribe population of Orissa comprises about 38.41 per cent of the State's total population (SCs 16.53% and STs 22.13%) according to 2001 Census. Orissa's ST and SC population comprises about 10 per cent of the total Tribal population and 3.7% of the total Scheduled Caste population of the country. Socio-economic status of the SC/ST population lags far behind others. Educational levels in SC/ST community are low, specially among women. Scheduled Caste literacy at 56.5% (2001) and Scheduled Tribe literacy at 37.41% (2001) lagged far behind the State average of 63.1% (2001). Only 23.49% of Scheduled Tribe women and 40.3% of Scheduled Caste women were literate compared to 50.51% female literacy in the State (Census of India – 2001). At higher levels of education, participation of Scheduled Castes and Scheduled Tribes, specially SC/ST women, has been negligible. Research work in the field of education for SC/ST women has been mostly confined to literacy of SC/ST women and educational status of SC/ST girls only at lower level. Extensive survey of literature has been done before and after the project was prepared to locate documentation, if any, on higher education of SC/ST girls.

1. **Shils (1961), Misra (1963),** Kamat and Deshmukh (1963), Desai (1953) and Shah (1964) have discussed the significance of caste and its close link with education. They have shown that it is usually the children from relatively higher castes that are able to take advantage of higher educational opportunities.

2. **Suma Chitnis (1974)** aimed at finding whether the investment made by both the Centre and States helped the Scheduled Castes to gain economic/ social mobility. Though findings revealed that Scheduled Castes lagged behind in literacy and educational enrolment, study was not done in gender perspective.

3. **H. Chatterji (1975)** conducted a study to analyse causes of school drop out syndrome among Harijan children. It found that it is largely poverty coupled with other factors (like domestic responsibility, inability to attend school, discrimination and ill treatment by classmates) that forces Scheduled Caste children to give up schooling. Study was limited to finding cases of dropout.

4. There was a study on the educational problems of the Scheduled Caste and Scheduled Tribe students in colleges in 1975 carried out in twenty-five States. The study was sponsored by the ICSSR. In Orissa, it was limited to a few SC/ST students in six districts and a very insignificant number of girl students were included in the study. It did not extend to post graduate and technical/ professional studies. Our study may be considered as a contuniation of the above project.

5. **U.D. Tribhuban (1977)** studied the role of education in bringing about the desired changes

to help educated Scheduled Caste women in their upward movement. The findings revealed that due to education, Scheduled Caste women are able to achieve higher status unknown in their family and community. This indicates need of a study of ways to attract more girls to higher education.

6. **B.V. Shah (1979)** has shown that attitudes of tribal people towards education are governed by the ideas of economic return. They wish to achieve this in a short time span. They do not like to have long gestation and waiting periods. This only provides one reason of low enrolment of tribals in higher education.

7. **R.K. Bhandari (1982)** has shown that enrolment of women at secondary and tertiary stages in different States demonstrates uneven progress across the country. In Secondary stage i.e. Class IX-XII, U.P. and Bihar have the lowest enrolment of women, followed by M.P., Rajastan and Orissa. So detailed study regarding the cause was indicated.

8. **S. Ram Sharma (1984)** has conducted survey in five selected States and has opined that the amount of stipend for Scheduled Caste and Scheduled Tribe students was not sufficient and the procedure for release of the grant needed to be simplified. He has given several suggestions for modification of schemes for improvement in education. So a study in detail for economical constraint in education is needed.

9. On the basis of the report of the Education Commission of 1982, **S. Ram Sharma (1984)** has shown the relative growth of enrolment of girls as compared to that of boys. He has shown that one of the problems in higher education of women has

been the large drop-out rate. So, a study of ways to check dropout rate is needed.

10. **Vimal P. Shah (1984)** and Tara Patel in their book "Tribal Education" have discussed about literacy among different categories of tribals in the State of Gujarat in detail and district-wise variation thereof. Such study is needed for Orissa.

11. **S. Ram Sharma (1984)** in his paper on "Need for Technical and Vocational Education for Scheduled Caste Women" has examined the situation of SC/ST students in vocational education, their enrolment in different courses and impact of reservation. (He has studied the enrolment in five States but not in Orissa, which is attempted in this project).

12. **Anil Kishore Sinha (1985)** in his study on tribals in Chhotanagpur University has pointed out that the tribal studies need a special focus in University education. He has also stressed on the need for change in curriculum in University education to utilize the talents and energies of tribal students. This kind of study in Orissa is very much needed.

13. **Shyam Lal (1987)** has analysed constitutional safeguards for the Scheduled Tribes and also important measures to improve tribal education under different Five Year Plans. He has shown how representation of SCs and STs in jobs under the Union Government is negligible in higher ranks.

14. **Sarita Manna (1990)** has made a study of literacy, discontinuity of education, etc of tribal girls in three States; West Bengal, Orissa and Bihar. She has also studied mothers' awareness of and encouragement for daughters' education. However, no study was done regarding higher education.

15. **S.K. Chatterjee (1990)** in his book "Educational

Development of Scheduled Castes" has analysed the schemes sponsored by Central Government and State Government for educational development of Scheduled Caste and Scheduled Tribe students. He has reported about many students benefiting from scholarship schemes and different grants. This does not include study of their shortcomings.

16. **Lewis Xavier (1990)** has shown, that though due to reservation policy more students from disadvantaged sections get admitted to colleges, but they are unable to cope with the curriculum offered.

17. **S.K. Ghose Mallik and Anita Ghose Mallik (1990)** have analysed the drop out rate of tribal children in Orissa and found it to be about 76% in 1977-79. They have found poor economic condition and lack of realization about importance of education, to be responsible for this. Other reasons should also be studied in detail.

18. **T. Lakshmiah (1991)** was of the view that at Secondary stages of education, where the tribal children are expected to compete with the non-tribal children, the former should be given special coaching. The same arrangements may continue further for higher levels of education.

19. **N.N.G. Mathur (1991)** has made an in-depth study of educational problems of tribal students in Rajastan. He has come to the conclusion that family background and parental co-operation for education was not favourable for those students. He has also said that the majority of tribal girls expressed their dissatisfaction about hostel arrangements. Such study for Orissa would be useful, particularly for higher education.

20. **B. Suguna (1992)** in her paper "Women in Higher education: Issues and Challenge" has analysed growth of female literacy as well as enrolment of women in University education and women's colleges on the basis of U.G.C. Annual Report, 1988-89. (But no study in respect of SC/ST students has been done separately).

21. **Prof. Veena Shah (1992)** in her paper on "Tribal Education, Prospects and Prospective" has analysed several sociological studies conducted in different parts of India and tried to find out the barriers to education in spite of several incentives. She has also analysed the factors which facilitate education among tribals. No separate study for higher education was done.

22. **M. Rehman and K.K. Biswal (1994)** have analysed census data and have brought age-wise, sex-wise gross enrolment ratio (GER) and school attendance, etc. They have shown that the relative educational status of girls indicates clear sex disparities and these disparities are more pronounced in rural areas, and particularly among SC, ST and other disadvantaged groups.

23. **S.N. Tripathy and D.N. Padhy (1995)** have provided district-wise distribution of tribal population, literacy rates for SC/ST in different States and ST/SC students' enrolment at school. (But no analysis has been made for higher education).

24. **Chitrasen Pasayat (1995)** has analsyed district level literacy in Orissa and has shown that literacy situation among tribal population, particularly among women, is dismal. He has analysed the cause of such low literacy and made some suggestions for improvement. The study was not extended to higher education.

25. **Dr. B.C. Mishra (1996)** has analysed the reasons

for increasing drop out among tribal children and has narrated some interesting case studies. But this is not about higher education.

26. **Dr. I. Satya Sundaram (2000)** has opined that educational facilities provided for SCs should take into account their special needs. He has stressed that "Employment-oriented education and diversified vocational training should receive special attention".

27. **Karuna Chanana (2000)** has shown that despite careful articulation of education for equality for women, as is reflected in the educational policy discourse, the disparities still continue. She has made an in-depth study of the enrolment of women (a) across faculties or subjects and (b) across levels such as under-graduate, graduate and doctoral research level. This indicates need for detailed study about the problems.

28. **Geeta B. Nambissan and Mona Sedwal (2001)** have discussed the educational scenario in 1990s and effectiveness of DPEP and SSA (announced in 2000) in expanding educational facilities for Dalit (Scheduled Caste) children. The study does not include higher education.

29. **Karuna Chanana (2001)** has shown that though the proportion of enrolment of women in Higher Education increased considerably, it continues to be much lower than that of men. The study was in general for India.

30. Analysing Annual Education Report, **Karuna Chanana (2001)**, has shown that in 1988-89, the proportion of enrolment of SC students in total enrolment in different faculties in higher education varied from 9.87% in Humanities to 2.91% in Research.

31. **Karuna Chanana (2001)** has found that there are hardly any studies which link the two stages of education (Secondary to Higher Education), that too with focus on women.

32. **K. Sujatha (2001)** has pointed out that in tribal majority states, a host of welfare measures have been initiated through the Tribal Sub-Plan approach. As a result, enrolment of tribal students has gradually increased. No special study was done regarding higher education.

33. **Karuna Chanana (2001)** has tried to ascertain whether expansion of opportunities for women's education has actually had the desired equalizing effect or has merely remained restricted in terms of social and economic status. Her data showed that college education was the monopoly of students from traditionally superior castes. Women from lower castes constituted barely 2.7 per cent.

34. **Sarita Sahay (2002)** has shown that while the proportion of tribal women at lower educational levels is appreciable, there is a gradual decrease in the percentage of women having higher educational qualifications. This was with reference to India in general.

From this long list of reference, it is found that there is very little published data on the extent of SC/ST girls at different levels of higher and technical education in the State. It was felt that little in-depth and comprehensive analysis of participation of girls from SC/ST communities in higher education and the underlying socio-economic constraints has been attempted. Particularly, the attitudes, pressures and constraints inhibiting their participation and the attainment/performance compared to others were not adequately investigated. Thus, the review of research literature in the relevant area indicates inadequacy of work done in the field of higher education for SC/ST girls in the State of Orissa. So it was felt necessary to undertake an in-depth investigation and analysis into the problems of limited access of SC/ST girls to higher education and their indifferent performance. Attempts should also be made to find solutions to these intractable problems, specially in Orissa with very high SC/ST population.

REPORTS

1. Annual Report, Government of India, Ministry of Tribal affairs, 2003-04.
2. Annual Report of Scheduled Tribes and Scheduled Castes Development Department, Government of Orissa, 2003-04.
3. Annual Report of the Administration of Scheduled Areas (1993-9), Government of Orissa.
4. Economic Survey – Government of India, 2003-04.
5. Economic Survey – Government of Orissa, 2003-04.
6. India: Human Development Report (1999) – National Council of Applied Economic Research – p.115.
7. (a) National Human Development Report – Planning Commission.

   (b) Census of India – (2001).
8. Report on Development of Tribal Area – National Committee on the Development of Backward Area – (1981) – Planning Commission.
9. Report of the Working Group on Tribal Development – Sixth Plan – 1980-85.
10. Report on Development of Female Education among Tribal Communities – National Commission for Women, New Delhi – November, 1994.

11. Selected Educational Statistics (1989) – Studies in Educational Statistics No. 1, 1990, Ministry of Human Resources Development, Department of Education, Planning, Monitoring and Statistics Division, Government of India, New Delhi, 1990 – Table VIII – pp. 36-45.

12. Special Component Plan for Scheduled Castes, 10th Five Year Plan, 2002-07 – Scheduled Caste and Scheduled Tribe Development Department, Government of Orissa.

13. Twenty-Eighth Report of the Commission for Scheduled Castes and Scheduled Tribes, 1986-87, Government of India, New Delhi – p. 33-34.

14. 'University Grants Commission Report, 1972' – Pocket Book of University Education – p. 116.

3

RESEARCH DESIGN AND METHODOLOGY

3.1 Research Rationale

Orissa has a land mass of 1,55,707 sq.km comprising 3.68 crore population. As per 2001 population census, 44.7% of the land mass belongs to Schedule Areas and 38.66% of the total population comprises Scheduled Tribes and Scheduled Castes. Majority of Scheduled Communities are poor and live below poverty line. All round development of the State can't be achieved by ignoring these classes of people. Therefore, the State Government is committed to ensure speedy development of these communities through effective implementation of economic, social, cultural and welfare measures.

The ST and SC population together in the State in 1991 was 121.61 lakh, which increased to 142.27 lakh in 2001, showing a growth rate of 16.99% (growth rate for total population was 15.94%). The Sex Ratio among ST and SC Community was 1003 and 979 respectively, while it was 972 for all communities. It is acknowledged that education is the most important instrument for human development and girls' education has great impact on national wellbeing. That is why the principle of gender equality is enshrined in the Indian Constitution, in its Preamble, Fundamental Rights, Fundamental Duties and Directive Principles. The Constitution not only grants equality to women, it also empowers the State to adopt measures of positive discrimination in favour of women (Article 15[3]). Moreover, Article 46 of the Constitution of India envisages that the State shall promote, with special care, the educational and economic interest of weaker sections of the people and in particular that of Scheduled Tribes and Scheduled Castes. After independence, the Government has taken a number of steps to raise the educational level of SCs and STs which was extremely poor at that time.

Although sustained efforts of government have led to some significant improvements in literacy and educational development for the weaker sections, the gap between general literacy and SC/ ST literacy, especially between men and women, is very significant. In 1991, overall female literacy percentage of Orissa was 63.09% for male, and 34.68% for females. It was 52.4% for SCs and 20.74% for STs. In 2001, general literacy increased to 73.35% for male and 50.31% for female, whereas in case of SCs it became 70.47% and 40.33% and for STs 51.48% and 23.37% respectively. Despite considerable improvement, female literacy for SCs/STs lags far behind. National Commission for SCs and STs has remarked, "In spite of all the Constitutional framework and efforts put in during the successive plan periods, it appears that SCs/ STs have still a long way to go to come to the general level in the field of education. Special measures to improve literacy and educational level should be taken through a timebound programme so that the gap can be bridged in the next 5 to 10 years" (Third Report of National Commission for Scheduled Castes and Scheduled Tribes – 1995-96 Vol-I). With regard to female literacy, the Commission remarked – "In spite of the fact that there are Constitutional provision and several measures have been adopted in the successive five year plans, the level of literacy among women in general and particularly among SC/ ST women, is deplorably low. The pace of development cannot be sustained if it bypasses women, who not only comprise half of the population but provide catalytic force for bringing about social change. The low level of literacy among SC/ ST women is a cause of grave concern and is largely responsible for their marginalization in socio-economic fields."

Considering enrolment of children belonging to SC/ ST, the 28th Report of Commission on Scheduled Castes and Scheduled Tribes notes that though at primary level the proportion of SC/ ST children corresponds to their population, there is sharp decline at middle level, which continues and becomes more prominent as one proceeds to higher education. According to Government of India Statistics, in 1988-89, SC students and ST students enrolled in Higher Education constituted only 9.8% and 2.7% respectively of total enrolment; SC girls formed only 2.13% and ST girls only 0.8% of total enrolment (Selected Educational Statistics, 1989 – Studies in Educational Statistics, 1990, No.1, Ministry of H.R.D., Government of India). Due to persistent efforts in recent years, there are significant signs of improvement of education at primary and secondary level. However, no significant breakthrough is discernible at higher levels of education. According to VIth All India Educational Survey (published by NCERT in 1998), as on 30th September, 1993, the percentage of SC/ST students studying in class XI and XII attached to degree colleges was only 12.19 and 6.59 respectively. In order to look at actual representation of SC/ST in Arts, Science, Commerce, Education, Engineering and Technology, Medicine, Law and other courses, the National Commission for SC/ST issued instructions to all Universities/ Deemed

Universities and National Universities to furnish the data of actual representation of SCs/STs in the above-mentioned courses. From the information received from 34 Universities for 1993-94 and 23 Universities for 1994-95, the Commission came to the conclusion that the enrolment of SC/ST students in Universities is extremely poor. The Commission suggested that, "The U.G.C., the Ministry of Human Resource Development and the State Government should periodically review the causes of poor intake of SC/ST in various courses and initiate steps to improve the competitive skills for ensuring adequate representation." (National Commission for Scheduled Castes and Scheduled Tribes – Third Report – 1994-95 and 1995-96-Volume-I, p.24). Besides, low participation of SC /ST girls in higher education and their attainment in terms of performance in examination has also been very low. Current policies and incentives have not adequately addressed the problem.

Accordingly, it was felt necessary to undertake an in-depth investigation and analysis into the problem of limited access of SC/ST girls to higher education and their indifferent performance and to find solutions to this intractable problem specially in Orissa with very high SC/ST population. This research project mainly aims at addressing this important issue.

3.2 Research Objectives

The objectives of research project were –

(i) To assess and analyse the trends and disparities in enrolment of SC/ST girls students in post secondary higher educational institutions.

(ii) To investigate the reasons of disproportional participation of SC/ST girls in higher education through a review of economic, social, cultural and institutional constraints.

(iii) To investigate the impact of special hostel facilities provided to SC/ST girls on pursuit of higher education.

(iv) To study the attainment of SC/ST girls in higher educational institutions with regard to their performance vis-à-vis performance of girl students of other castes in different examinations.

(v) To examine the current policies of Government for promotion of educational development among girls of SC/ST communities, their implementation and their efficacy in achieving the desired goal.

(vi) To evolve and recommend policy changes and other remedial measures for increasing access of SC/ST girls to higher education.

3.3 Research Hypothesis

The study was based on the following hypothesis:

(i) The participation of Scheduled Caste and Scheduled Tribe girls falls rapidly and disproportionately at higher levels of education.

(ii) It is acknowledged that the performance of SC/ST girl students falls sharply as compared to girl students from other castes at higher levels of education.

(iii) Apart from economic factors, sociological and cultural factors also inhibit participation and performance of SC/ST girls in higher learning.

(iv) Policies including reservation of seats (8% for SCs and 12% for STs) in all educational institutions in the State, provision for reservation of posts in Government sector (ORV Act, 1975 – 16.25% and 22.50% for SCs and STs respectively) and provision of special training programmes have been found inadequate, since most of the time, the quota is not filled up due to non-availability of suitable candidates.

(v) Policies of financial support have been found inadequate and disbursement of assistance irregular.

(vi) Special hostel facilities for SC/ST girls need some improvement for attracting more and more girls to higher education.

Accordingly, a thorough review of current policies and their implementation was called for to identify weakness and deficiencies and evolve suitable modifications and alternatives.

3.4 Research Design

This was a participatory research, which included SC/ST girls in the institutions of higher education, their family members, teachers and heads of the institutions. Leader of communities including elected women from SC/ST community were also included in the study.

3.5 Locale of Research – Orissa State

Sample Selection

1. Selection of Districts:

(i) State Capital of Bhubaneswar, with the largest and oldest University, the largest Women's College of the State and many prominent institutions of higher education;

(ii) Mayurbhanj District, with the largest tribal population of the State, a new University catering to needs of tribal students, and many educational institutions;

(iii) Cuttack, with the largest and oldest Medical College in the State.

3.5.1 Selection of Institutions

(i) UtkalUniversity(intheStateCapital,Bhubaneswar, representing students from all districts).

(ii) Rama Devi Women's College (Autonomous), Bhubaneswar.

(iii) Rama Devi Junior Women's College, Bhubaneswar.

(iv) B.J.B. Autonomous College, Bhubanswar. (co-educational);

(v) B.J.B. Junior College, Bhubaneswar. (co-educational);

(vi) College of Engineering and Technology (C.E.T.) – Government Engineering College.

(vii) Institute of Technical Education and Research (I.T.E.R) Private Engineering College.

(viii) Koustuv Institute of Self Domain (KISD) – the only Women's Engineering College (Private sector).

(ix) Kalinga Institute of Industrial Technology (K.I.I.T.) – Deemed University in the State Capital in private sector.

(x) Biju Pattanaik University of Technology (BPUT);

(xi) S.C.B. Medical College, Cuttack (in Cuttack District);

(xii) North Orissa Univrsity, Baripada (Mayurbhanj);

(xiii) M.P.C. (Autonomous) College, Baripada;

(xiv) M.P.C. Junior College, Baripada;

(xv) Mayurbhanj Law College (Mayurbhanj);

(xvi) Seemanta Engineering College, Mayurbhanj (Private);

(xvii) Sree Maa Mahavidyalaya, Baripada.

Altogether 17 institutions were studied.

Seminars on the Theme

In Utkal University (School of Women's Studies)

In Rama Devi Women's (Autonomous)

3.5.2 Selection of Respondents

(i) Respondents in institutions were chosen by random selection method, their number being almost proportional to number of SC/ST girl students supposed to be present in a class in the institutions. Sometimes this number is less due to unavailability of adequate number of students in a class. The total number of ST students interviewed is 157 and that of SC students 113;

(ii) Family members and parents in villages/homes were interviewed, their number being 30 for ST and 25 for SC;

(iii) 75 College Teachers and 10 Principals/Vice-Principals were contacted for interview;

(iv) Some important personalities/educationists were interviewed and their suggestions recorded;

3.6 Tools Used in Collection of Data

Data was collected from various sources:

(i) Primary data was collected by carefully designed semi-structured, open-ended interview schedules. Three types of separate interview schedules were used, for students, for teachers and for parents [Annexure – I(A), I(B), I(C)]. The questionnaires for students were carefully designed to ascertain;

(a) The economic and social background of their communities and families;

(b) The problems they have to face while entering the institution and while pursuing studies;

(c) Their performance in examinations and self assessment;

(d) Their feelings about attitude of teachers and other caste students towards them;

(e) The efficacy of reservation system for SC/ST and capability of applicants to meet the minimum standard for availing of such reservation;

(f) Their opinion about special hostel facilities available for them;

(g) Their suggestions for improvement of their educational standards in the institutions;

(ii) Their attitude in different matters and related details were found out through informal discussions using interview guide [Annexure-I(D)];

(iii) Data was also collected by interviewing some educated and professionally-qualified women from SC/ST communities and obtaining first hand information about the challenges faced by them;

(iv) In each community, the research team held group discussion as well as conducted individual interviews focusing on life stories or case studies of girls who have taken advantage of higher education;

(v) Secondary data regarding enrolment of students, their performance in examinations and disbursement of scholarships was found out from the corresponding institutions by using Specific Proforma. Letters were sent to Principals/Heads of the Institutions regarding this prior to the visit of research team;

(vi) Data was also obtained from Higher Education and SC/ST Development Departments, Board of Secondary Education, Council of Higher Secondary Education, Annual Reports of different Department of Central/State Governments, Economic Surveys, Human Development Reports, Census Reports, India Education Reports; etc.

3.7 Seminars

In the beginning of the project, a seminar was held in Utkal University attended by prominent educationists, retired professors and researchers working in the field of SC/ST issues. Government officials associated with SC/ ST Development Programmes were also invited to the seminar.

The objective of the Seminar was to get a wide range of suggestions for research design and methodology and to use their experiences in preparation of questionnaire/ interview schedules.

At the end of the project, seminars were held in different colleges with participation of teachers, about the problems of SC/ST girls in educational institutions. Opinions and suggestions were invited from different teachers regarding improvement of SC/ST girls' participation in Higher Education and improvement of their performance.

3.8 Social Matrix

For preparing the interview Schedule, a Social Matrix was prepared so as not to miss any part of the objectives. (Annexure-II).

3.9 Focus Group Discussion

Focus group discussions were held in girls' hostels, so that problems and views of SC/ST girls could be recorded through informal discussions.

3.10 Data Analysis

Statistical Package for Social Sciences (SPSS) was used as the main tool for data analysis. The data collected from students of different institutions was tabulated separately for SCs and STs using Microsoft Excel spread sheet after proper coding and then analysed by using

SPSS package. In certain cases, comparison was made with general students and SC/ST students through inter-relation data and bar graphs or pie graphs drawn as and when necessary.

4

SC/ST GIRLS IN INSTITUTIONS OF HIGHER LEARNING: STUDY OF ENROLMENT PATTERN

4.1 Introduction

Before entering the college (+2 level), students have to pass High School Certificate Examination conducted by Board of Secondary Education (Class-X). Unlike in other States, in Orissa, +2 level courses (Class-XI, XII) are imparted at college level, termed Junior colleges. Matriculation (class X) examination is a big hurdle for SC/ST students to get into colleges. As shown earlier, proportion of SC/ST students appearing in class X (HSC)

Table: 4.1 – Enrolment of SC/ST Students in H.S.C. Examination (In Percentage)

Year	SC Students		ST Students	
	Boys	Girls	Boys	Girls
2000	8.3	5.2	6.3	3.3
2001	8.2	5.2	6.5	3.7
2002	7.8	5.2	6.6	4.0
2003	7.5	5.1	6.8	4.2
2004	8.3	5.3	7.2	4.5

Source: Board of Secondary Education, Orissa.

Table: 4.2 – Percentage of SC/ST Students Passed in H.S.C. Examination

Year	SC Students		ST Students	
	Boys	Girls	Boys	Girls
2000	29.2	26.1	28.1	23.3
2001	28.3	24.1	26.2	22.7
2002	32.2	28.9	30.3	25.6
2003	40.4	35.0	38.0	32.6
2004	44.3	37.2	41.6	37.3

Source: Board of Secondary Education, Orissa

examination is low and their pass out rate is still lower. Out of the students appearing in H.S.C. examination, SC girls constitute only about 5% and ST girls about 4%. Again, the success rate of ST/SC girls is much lower compared to that of SC/ST boys. Before the study was undertaken in different colleges, the result of High School Certificate Examination was analyzed.

As seen from Table 4.1 and Table 4.2, the percentage of pass for SC/ST students is quite low compared to that of general students. In different years, the pass rate in case of STs is lower than that of SCs. Moreover, both for SCs and STs, the trend shows that the pass rate of girls is lower than that of boys. Such low performance of SCs/STs at H.S.C. level can be considered a very important cause for their low enrolment at college level. Moıeover, as revealed from the data, most of SC/ST students, particularly girls, pass only in third division and as such, find it difficult to avail seats in co-educational colleges, despite reservation.

4.2 Profiles of Institutions under the Scope of the Project

4.2.1 Institutions in the State Capital

1. **Utkal University** – Utkal University, the oldest and largest of Orissa's ten Universities and the

second largest in the country, has been a representative institution of higher learning in the State. It offers M.A., M.Sc., M.Phil and Ph.D. Courses in fourteen Social Sciences and Humanities subjects (referred to as 'Arts' in the report), six Science subjects and also five Professional courses, besides Commerce and Law in its own campus. It is the largest affiliating University in the country. It also offers twenty other self financing job-oriented courses leading to P.G. Diploma or P.G. Degree.

Admission to Post Graduate/M.Phil classes is granted on the basis of career and entrance tests. The minimum qualification for entrance is a second class (50% marks) in Bachelor's/Master's Degree which bars many SC/ST students entering the University in spite of reservation. As per rule of Orissa Government, in each subject, 8% of the seats for SC and 12% for ST students are reserved (inter-changeable). In case of non-availability of candidates in one of these categories, seats are filled up from the candidates of the other category. There are six boys' hostels for 1220 boarders and five girls' hostels for 600 students. Special accommodation is provided to SC/ST students in these hostels. Therefore, SC/ST students from all parts of the State aspire to enter this prestigious University.

2. **Rama Devi Autonomous Women's College**– Rama Devi Women's College, one of the premier women's institutions of Orissa, started functioning as the first government women's college in the State Capital, Bhubaneswar, in 1964. From the academic year 1999-2000, this premier institution was declared by the U.G.C. as an autonomous college. From 2001-2002, Post graduates and Degree classes are functioning as Rama Devi Women's Autonomous College and the Higher Secondary classes under Rama Devi Women's (Junior) College. Together, it is the largest women's college in the State.

The autonomous college imparts postgraduate teaching in Hindi and Home Science. All seats at Graduate level are Honours seats. There are twelve Honours subjects in Arts, six Honours subjects in Science and two Honours subjects in Commerce.

3. **Rama Devi Junior College** – The Higher Secondary course of erstwhile Rama Devi Women's College have been separated in 1999 and are functioning under Rama Devi Junior College in the same premises as the Autonomous college. All the three streams, Arts, Science and Commerce with 512,256 and 128 seats respectively, are always filled up. In all, about 2000 girls study in this junior college.

As per rules of State Government, 8% and 12% seats in each class are reserved for SC and ST students respectively. A striking feature of Rama Devi Women's College is that there are three hostels for general students and a special Adivasi hostel for SC/ST students, namely, Indira Gandhi Women's Hostel. It is the only hostel of its kind in the State and has a capacity of 320 students with 10% reservation for SC and 90% for ST students. This is the reason for which SC/ST girls from different parts of the State came to this college.

Special teaching is imparted to SC/ST girls enrolled in Higher Secondary classes, under 'up-gradation of merits of SC/ST students' scheme by Government of India, for entry into Medical/Engineering Courses.

4. **Buxi Jagabandhu Bidyadhar (B.J.B.) Autonomous College** – The College, established in 1957, is the oldest and largest co-education college in the State Capital. Since 2000-2001, the Higher Secondary Classes were separated and function under Junior College. The college offers Honours Courses in 6 Science subjects, (236 seats) and in 14 Arts subjects (512 seats). Besides, it has two Honours Courses in Accountancy and Marketing Management in Commerce (176 seats).

Unfortunately, there is no girl's hostel in this college for which intake of girls is limited to only local areas. However, women applicants opting for a subject for which teaching facility is not available in any of the local women's colleges are given weightage for admission.

The college provides accommodation for boys in two hostels, namely, General Hostel and B.R.Ambedkar Hostel. The later is meant only for SC/ST boy students.

5. **B.J.B. Junior College** – The Higher Secondary classes in B.J.B. College have been separated from Degree classes and B.J.B. Junior College was established in 2000-2001. It has three streams, Arts (512 seats), Science (512 seats) and Commerce (256 seats). Most bright students of the State aspire to come to this prestigious college since this college has the distinction of producing almost 15 toppers among first twenty in the State every year. So there is very keen competition for admission into this prestigious institution. As such, the number of girls is less compared to boys and number of SC/ST girls is negligible, though the reservation procedure of government is followed.

6. **College of Engineering and Technology (CET)** – This constituent college of Biju Pattnaik University of Technology, the premier Engineering College in the State Capital, offers B.Tech. Degree programme in almost all branches of Engineering. Bachelor of Architecture and MCA programmes are also offered in the college.

As this is the only Government Engineering College in the State Capital, it occupies the top position in the list of most preferred colleges. 8% and 12% seats are reserved in each discipline for SCs and STs respectively. Besides, 30% of the seats in all categories are reserved for women candidates. Due to low fee structure of Government College and 30% reservation for girls, many SC/ST girls are expected in this college. But the enrolment in the college is done on the basis of Joint Entrance Examination, which is a hurdle for them.

7. **Institute of Technical Education and Research (ITER)** – This institute, one of the private engineering colleges in the State Capital, was established in 1996-97 and is affiliated to Biju Pattnaik University of Technology. It offers B.Tech. Degree in almost all Engineering subjects and in Computer Application; it also offers MCA Degree. It has 85% of seats as free seat (without donation) in which 30% are reserved for women candidates; 8% and 12% of free seats are reserved for SC and ST candidates respectively.

8. **Kalinga Institute of Industrial Technology (KIIT)** – Established in 1996, it has expanded very fast and has now acquired the status of Deemed University. It offers B.Tech. Degree in six disciplines. Its total annual intake capacity is 480. It also offers MBA, MCA and Diploma Courses in all Engineering branches. The same reservation procedure for girls as well as SC/ST is followed as in other private Engineering Colleges.

9. **Kaustuv Institute of Self Domain (KISD)** – This is the only Women's Engineering College in the State established in the year 2001. The institute offers B.E. Degree in Computer Science andEngineering, Electrical Engineering and Electronics and Tele-Communication Engineering. According to Government rule, 8% and 12% seats are reserved for SC and ST candidates respectively. Being the only engineering institution for girls, more SC/ST girls are expected to study here.

10. **Biju Pattnaik University of Technology (BPUT)**–Biju Pattnaik University of Technology (BPUT) has been established by Government of Orissa in June 2002. All colleges in the State offering Engineering, Pharmacy, Architecture and most of the colleges offering MCA and MBA programmes are affiliated to

this University. The objective of the University is to bring all technical (except Medical) Institutions in the State under one umbrella providing all institutions with uniform curricula and syllabi. It conducts JEE (Joint Entrance Examination) in the State for admission into different courses in Engineering/Technology, MBBS/BDS, B.Pharma and MCA. There are five government engineering colleges and 30 private engineering colleges under the University.

11. **S.C.B. Medical College, Cuttack** – This is the first Medical College of the State. It is situated at Cuttack and is affiliated to Utkal University. It has 144 seats for M.B.B.S. and 20 seats for B.D.S. course. The same reservation procedure (8% for SC and 12% for ST) is followed, as in Engineering Colleges, but there is no special reservation for women candidates.

4.2.2 Mayurbhanj District: A Profile

Mayurbhanj district, lying on the northern border of the State of Orissa, is the largest district of the State (6.69% of total area of the State). The percentage of Scheduled Tribe population is 56.6 (second highest in the State, first being Malkangiri with 57.4%) and the percentage of SC population is 7.7% according to 2001 census. Thus, the total SC/ST population of the district is 64.3% of total population. The entire district of Mayurbhanj is a Scheduled Area. Female:male sex ratio of the district is 980 (more than State average of 972). In case of SC it is 990 and in case of ST, 994. Thus, SC/ST female population is almost equal to male population. However, their literacy rate is quite different. Though literacy rate of the district is 51.9% (for Orissa it is 63.1%), it is only 38.28% for women as compared to male literacy of 66.36%. The percentage of female literacy among Schedule Tribes and Schedule Castes is 24.1 and 37.79 respectively. Low rate of literacy of women in SC/ST population does not permit them to access many welfare and development programmes of Government intended for them.

4.2.3 Institutions Covered by the Project in Mayurbhanj

1. North Orissa University –

North Orissa University at Baripada was established in 1998 with jurisdiction extending over predominantly tribal districts of Mayurbhanj and Keonjhar. There are 79 affiliated colleges, both general and professional, catering to the demands of higher education.

Being a new University, it was compelled to start a series of self-financing courses for the benefit of students and for future development. Keeping in mind the local requirements and conditions in view, the courses offered are M.Sc. in Bio-Technology, Environmental Sciences, Wild Life and Conservation Biology, M.A. in Tribal Studies and Education and also LL.M. Subsequently, subjects like M.C.A., M.B.A., Physics, Computer Science, and M.L.I.S. (Master in Library and Information Science) were also introduced. However, participation of Tribal girls seems to be low in the University.

2. Maharaja Purna Chandra (M.P.C.) College (Autonomous)

M.P.C. Autonomous College, Baripada, is one of the prestigious institutions for higher education in the State and the most sought after college in the tribal district of Mayurbhanj. Established in 1948, it was declared Autonomous by U.G.C. in 2000-2001 and since then the Higher Secondary classes were separated.

The college offers Post Graduate degree in Science in four subjects and in Humanities (Arts), six subjects and also M.Com. It offers Honours courses in four Science subjects and in Arts stream, there are eight subjects for B.A. (Hons.). In Commerce, it offers Honours in four subjects. Being situated in a tribal district and having hostel facilities for girl students with 12% reservation for STs, it is a preferred choice for many tribal girls.

3. M.P.C. Junior College

This college along with Graduate and Post Graduate classes together was earlier known as M.P.C. College. After the Degree and Post Graduate classes were separated and shifted to a new campus as M.P.C. Autonomous College, Higher Secondary classes function under the name M.P.C. Junior College, since 2001. The college offers Higher Secondary education in all the three branches of Arts, Science and Commerce. Being the largest and oldest college in the district located at district headquarters and having hostel facilities, a large number of tribal girls should find place here. However, the number was found to be quite low as compared to general students.

4. Government Women's College, Baripada

The college was started with a view to attracting tribal girls for higher education since they do not normally prefer co-education colleges. Initially, it had Higher Secondary as well as Degree courses with Honours in different subjects. But after separation of +2 college, the Higher Secondary classes merged with M.P.C. Junior College and all the Honours subjects merged with M.P.C. Autonomous College. So at present, it offers general degree courses in pass subjects only in Arts. It is situated in the same campus as M.P.C. Junior College (old palace of Maharaja of Mayurbhanj). However, it is useful for SC/ST girls, who wish to pursue higher education in a women's institution staying in a girls' hostel.

5. Sree Ma Mahavidyalaya

Initially, it grew from an English Medium School to a Higher Secondary Girls' School. Then on public demand, degree classes were opened, but only with pass subjects. It has succeeded in attracting many SC/ST girls.

6. Mayurbhanj Law College

Located in the vicinity of North Orisa University campus, it offers LL.B. degree. Extra remedial classes are being taken up for SC/ST students. As such, it has been successful in attracting many SC/ST girl students.

7. Seemanta Engineering College, Baripada

Seemanta Engineering College, Mayur Vihar, Mayurbhanj, is the premier private technical institution in the North Orissa region offering B.Tech Degree in several disciplines and also M.C.A. It is at present affiliated to Biju Pattnaik University of Technology (BPUT). It is located by the side of National Highway, 35 kms. from Baripada, the district head quarters of Mayurbhanj. It is well connected by road with neighbouring tribal dominated Sates of Jharkhand and with West Bengal and Bihar. Following 30% reservation rules for girls of Orissa Government (only for free seats) and 12% and 8% reservation for STs and SCs, many SC/ST girls come to this institution. Moreover, there is a large women's hostel with very good residential facilities, which attracts girls.

4.2.4 Institutions Offering Diploma Courses (Polytechnic)

In the government sector, there are 13 Engineering Schools/ Polytechnics, which offer diploma courses in both engineering and non-engineering discipline. Out of the above institutions, four Polytechnics at Rourkela, Dhenkanal, Bhubaneswar and Berhampur with an intake capacity of 535, are exclusively for women. In addition, there are 17 private Polytechnic/Engineering Schools functioning in the State.

Institutions taken up under the Research Project were (i) Kalinga Institute of Industrial Technology (KIIT),

Bhubaneswar, (ii) Bhubanananda Orissa School of Engineering, Cuttack, (iii) Industrial Training Institute, Cuttack. Surprisingly, many SC/ST girls were found in these institutions.

Thus, altogether 22 educational institutions have been included in the research project where the enrolment pattern was studied in different courses separately.

4.3 Enrolment Pattern in different Institutions under the Study

The enrolment of SC/ST students in all the above institutions under study was collected by researchers for five consecutive years and then analysed. It was very difficult to trace the past records in different Colleges and Universities. In Utkal University, centralized data was not available and thorough searching of old files had to be done. In some colleges, old records were not available, and these were searched out from the old files. Data on the average of five years of enrolment recorded from different institutions are enclosed in this report.

4.4 Utkal University

To analyse the enrolment of Utkal University, the data of 27 departments were grouped into five categories.

1. Arts – Analytical and Applied Economics, Ancient Indian History, Culture and Archaeology, Anthropology, English, Geography, History, Oriya, Philosophy, Political Science, Public Administration, Psychology, Sanskrit, and Statistics (14).
2. Science – Botany, Chemistry, Geology, Mathematics, Physics, and Zoology (6).
3. Professional Courses – Bio-Technology (M.Sc.), Business Administration (MBA), Computer Science (MCA), Library and Information Science (B.Lib., M.Lib.), Personal Management and Industrial

Table: 4.3 – Enrolment of SC/ST Students in Utkal University

Sl. No.	Name of the Institution	Year	Total	General		SC		ST	
				Boys %	Girls %	Boys %	Girls %	Boys %	Girls %
1	Utkal University (Arts)	1999	793	178 (22.4)	439 (55.4)	62 (7.8)	38 (4.8)	59 (7.4)	17 (2.1)
		2000	657	173 (26.3)	360 (54.8)	37 (5.6)	34 (5.2)	31 (4.7)	22 (3.3)
		2001	648	167 (25.8)	367 (56.6)	32 (4.9)	33 (5.1)	24 (3.7)	25 (3.9)
		2002	649	161 (24.8)	380 (58.6)	28 (4.3)	33 (5.1)	27 (4.2)	20 (3.1)
		2003	646	141 (21.8)	381 (59.0)	38 (5.9)	37 (5.7)	26 (4.0)	23 (3.6)
2	Utkal University (Science)	1999	239	110 (46.0)	88 (36.8)	20 (8.4)	4 (1.7)	14 (5.9)	3 (1.3)
		2000	228	106 (46.5)	87 (38.2)	18 (7.9)	3 (1.3)	10 (4.4)	4 (1.8)
		2001	233	107 (45.9)	97 (41.6)	11 (4.7)	5 (2.1)	7 (3.0)	6 (2.6)
		2002	243	112 (46.1)	93 (38.3)	10 (4.1)	9 (3.7)	10 (4.1)	9 (3.7)
		2003	252	106 (42.1)	102 (40.5)	15 (6.0)	8 (3.2)	13 (5.2)	8 (3.2)
3	Utkal University (Commerce)	1999	49	25 (51.0)	13 (26.5)	5 (10.2)	0 (0.0)	4 (8.2)	2 (4.1)
		2000	48	18 (37.5)	26 (54.2)	3 (6.3)	1 (2.1)	0 (0.0)	0 (0.0)
		2001	48	19 (39.6)	21 (43.8)	2 (4.2)	3 (6.3)	3 (6.3)	0 (0.0)
		2002	48	23 (47.9)	14 (29.2)	3 (6.3)	2 (4.2)	6 (12.5)	0 (0.0)
		2003	48	20 (41.7)	17 (35.4)	4 (8.3)	0 (0.0)	6 (12.5)	1 (2.1)

4	Utkal University (Prof. Courses)	1999	142	79 (55.6)	30 (21.1)	17 (12.0)	1 (0.7)	10 (7.0)	5 (3.5)
		2000	139	75 (54.0)	40 (28.8)	9 (6.5)	3 (2.2)	6 (4.3)	6 (4.3)
		2001	139	57 (41.0)	54 (38.8)	7 (5.0)	7 (5.0)	9 (6.5)	5 (3.6)
		2002	143	57 (39.9)	63 (44.1)	7 (4.9)	6 (4.2)	8 (5.6)	2 (1.4)
		2003	148	70 (47.3)	49 (33.1)	12 (8.1)	5 (3.4)	9 (6.1)	3 (2.0)
5	Utkal University (Law)	1999	26	11 (42.3)	10 (38.5)	3 (11.5)	0 (0.0)	2 (7.7)	0 (0.0)
		2000	26	13 (50.0)	10 (38.5)	2 (7.7)	0 (0.0)	0 (0.0)	1 (3.8)
		2001	25	11 (44.0)	9 (36.0)	3 (12.0)	1 (4.0)	0 (0.0)	1 (4.0)
		2002	25	12 (48.0)	8 (32.0)	2 (8.0)	1 (4.0)	2 (8.0)	0 (0.0)
		2003	25	6 (24.0)	14 (56.0)	1 (4.0)	1 (4.0)	3 (12.0)	0 (0.0)

Relations (PMIR) (5).

4. Commerce (1)
5. Law (1)

Fig.IV-A

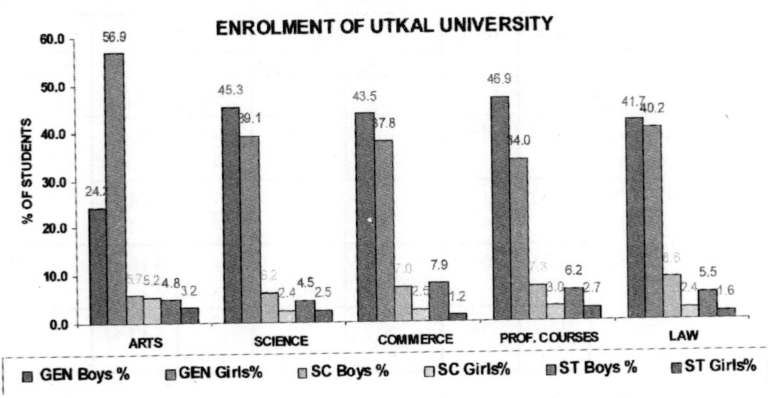

Analysis

1. It was found that though the percentage of reservation is 12% for STs and 8% of SCs, the total number of SC Students always exceeded that of ST students. During last five years, the 12% reservation quota for ST students in the University was never filled up. It varied from 7% to 8% and always boys were more than girls.
2. The total number of girls in the University is much higher than the number of boys. But it is just the reverse in case of SC/ST students (Fig. IV-A).
3. The number of SC/ST girls is much less than general girls and also less than SC/ST boys. SC girl enrolment is slightly better than ST girls enrolment.
4. Comparatively more SC/ST girls are found in Arts course than in other courses, i.e. they seem to choose comparatively easier and less expensive courses.
5. In Law stream, record reveals that there were only 3 SC and 2 ST girls during the last five years.
6. For M.Phil courses, in 2003, out of 198 seats available in 24 subjects in the University, only 18 SC and 8 ST students took admission and among them SC girls were only 5, but there was no ST girl.

Table: 4.4 – Enrolment of Rama Devi Women's (Autonomous) College

Sl. No	Name of the Instistution	Year	Total	General		SC		ST	
				Boys %	Girls %	Boys %	Girls %	Boys %	Girls %
6	Rama Devi Women's College (PG)	1999	49	- -	39 (79.6)	- -	3 (6.1)	- -	7 (14.3)
		2000	47	- -	41 (87.2)	- -	4 (8.5)	- -	2 (4.3)
		2001	60	- -	52 (86.7)	- -	4 (6.7)	- -	4 (6.7)
		2002	48	- -	40 (83.3)	-	2 (4.2)	- -	6 (12.5)

		2003	60	- -	51 (85.0)	- -	5 (8.3)	- -	4 (6.7)
7	Rama Devi Women's College (UG) +3 Arts	1999	312	- -	274 (87.8)	- -	24 (7.7)	- -	14 (4.5)
		2000	426	- -	380 (89.2)	- -	29 (6.8)	- -	17 (4.0)
		2001	405	- -	356 (87.9)	- -	27 (6.7)	- -	22 (5.4)
		2002	473	- -	419 (88.6)	- -	36 (7.6)	- -	18 (3.8)
		2003	462	- -	339 (73.4)	- -	62 (13.4)	- -	61 (13.2)
8	Rama Devi Women's College (UG) +3 Science	1999	105	--	80 (76.2)	--	9 (8.6)	--	16 (15.2)
		2000	94	--	74 (78.7)	--	12 (12.8)	--	8 (8.5)
		2001	95	--	76 (80.0)	--	9 (9.5)	--	10 (10.5)
		2002	101	--	78 (77.2)	--	12 (11.9)	--	11 (10.9)
		2003	98	--	77 (78.6)	--	5 (5.1)	--	16 (16.3)
9	Rama Devi Women's College (UG) +3 Commerce	1999	64	--	64 (100.0)	--	0 (0.0)	--	0 (0.0)
		2000	64	--	63 (98.4)	--	1 (1.6)	--	0 (0.0)
		2001	64	--	59 (92.2)	--	3 (4.7)	--	2 (3.1)
		2002	80	--	71 (88.8)	--	6 (7.5)	--	3 (3.8)
		2003	80	--	74 (92.5)	--	1 (1.3)	--	5 (6.3)

Table: 4.5 – Enrolment of Rama Devi Women's (Junior) College

Sl. No	Name of the Institution	Year	Total	General		SC		ST	
				Boys %	Girls %	Boys %	Girls %	Boys %	Girls %
10	Rama Devi Women's College +2 Arts	1999	520	- -	371 (71.3)	- -	76 (14.6)	- -	73 (14.0)

		2000	537	- -	378 (70.4)	- -	72 (13.4)	- -	87 (16.2)
		2001	517	- -	352 (68.1)	- -	79 (15.3)	- -	86 (16.6)
		2002	515	- -	365 (70.9)	- -	70 (13.6)	- -	80 (15.5)
		2003	526	- -	336 (63.9)	- -	93 (17.7)	- -	97 (18.4)
11	Rama Devi Women's College +2 Science	1999	260	- -	202 (77.7)	- -	30 (11.5)	- -	28 (10.8)
		2000	265	- -	208 (78.5)	- -	24 (9.1)	- -	33 (12.5)
		2001	260	- -	202 (77.7)	- -	24 (9.2)	- -	34 (13.1)
		2002	279	- -	213 (76.3)	- -	33 (11.8)	- -	33 (11.8)
		2003	280	- -	212 (75.7)	- -	29 (10.4)	- -	39 (13.9)
12	Rama Devi Women's College +2 Commerce	1999	128	- -	112 (87.5)	- -	7 (5.5)	- -	9 (7.0)
		2000	125	- -	110 (88.0)	- -	12 (9.6)	- -	3 (2.4)
		2001	131	- -	112 (85.5)	- -	16 (12.2)	- -	3 (2.3)
		2002	108	- -	99 (91.7)	- -	3 (2.8)	- -	6 (5.6)
		2003	126	- -	107 (84.9)	- -	13 (10.3)	- -	6 (4.8)

Fig. IV-B

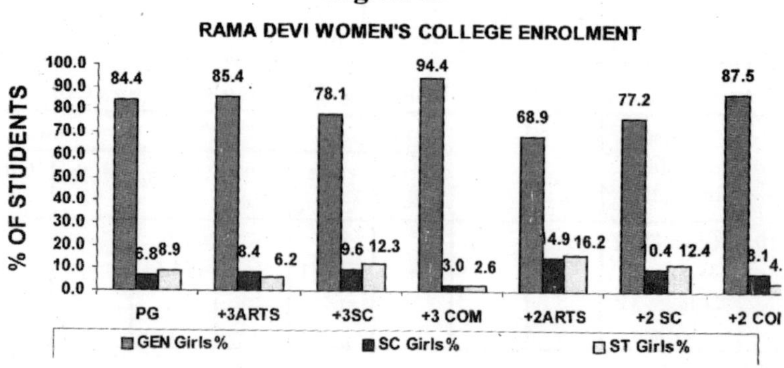

Therefore, our analysis confirms the apprehension that despite reservation of seats and financial incentives, SC/ST girls do not come forward to avail higher (Post Graduate) education.

Analysis

4.5 Rama Devi Women's College (Autonomous) +3 and P.G. Courses)

In Post Graduate classes (Home Science and Hindi), enrolment of SC/ST students is very low, average for 5 years (1999-2003) being 6.7% for SC and 8.8% for ST.

1. Contrary to Higher Secondary classes, at +3 level, the percentage of SC/ST girls is maximum in Science (9.5 for SC and 12.7 for ST), then in Arts (8.4 for SC and 6.2 for ST) and lastly in Commerce (3 for SC and 2.6 for ST). Thus, SC/ST girls seem to prefer Science stream at +3 stage.

2. In Science stream, ST students out number SC students, which is opposite in case of Arts and Commerce.

3. But many Science students drop out at the middle of the course to join professional courses like Engineering and Medical and at the end of three years, very few SC/ST girls were left.

4.6 Rama Devi Women's College (Junior) (Higher Secondary Classess)

In Rama Devi Women's College, the enrolment of SC/ST girls is comparatively better than other colleges, since there is special hostel facility to accommodate them and since this is a girls' college. The enrolment records reveal that –

1. Their number is more in Arts stream (14.9% for SCs and 16.1% for STs than in Science stream (10.4%

for SCs and 12.4% for STs). In Commerce stream, it is much less (8.1% for SCs and only 4.4% for STs) (Fig. IV-B).

2. Many SC/ST girls were admitted on their merit without availing the reservation provided for them. Sometimes even seats had to be increased using the Principal's discretion to accommodate left out SC/STs applicants.

Analysis

Table: 4.6 – Enrolment in B.J.B (Autonomous) College

Sl. No	Name of the Institution	Year	Total	General		SC		ST	
				Boys %	Girls %	Boys %	Girls %	Boys %	Girls %
13	B.J.B. college +3 Arts	2000	392	152 (38.8)	196 (50.0)	12 (3.06)	10 (2.6)	9 (2.3)	3 (0.8)
		2001	465	198 (42.6)	265 (57.0)	17 (3.66)	12 (2.6)	8 (1.7)	4 (0.9)
		2002	492	181 (36.8)	274 (55.7)	20 (4.07)	12 (2.4)	12 (2.4)	3 (0.6)
		2003	487	127 (26.1)	219 (45.0)	7 (1.44)	17 (3.5)	11 (2.3)	6 (1.2)
14	B.J.B. College +3 Science	2000	159	111 (69.8)	33 (20.8)	6 (3.77)	2 (1.3)	6 (3.8)	1 (0.6)
		2001	96	29 (30.2)	36 (37.5)	16 (16.7)	2 (2.1)	13 (14)	0 (0.0)
		2002	159	93 (58.5)	38 (23.9)	16 (10.1)	3 (1.9)	9 (5.7)	0 (0.0)
		2003	117	47 (40.2)	41 (35.0)	16 (13.7)	1 (0.9)	11 (9.4)	1 (0.9)
15	B.J.B. College +3 Commerce	2000	157	83 (52.9)	57 (36.3)	9 (5.73)	1 (0.6)	4 (2.5)	3 (1.9)
		2001	154	78 (50.6)	63 (40.9)	3 (1.95)	3 (1.9)	4 (2.6)	3 (1.9)
		2002	159	87 (54.7)	58 (36.5)	4 (2.52)	2 (1.3)	4 (2.5)	4 (2.5)
		2003	173	96 (55.5)	59 (34.1)	14 (8.09)	1 (0.6)	3 (1.7)	0 (0.0)

Table: 4.7 – Enrolment in B.J.B. (Junior) College

Sl. No	Name of the Institution	Year	Total	General		SC		ST	
				Boys %	Girls %	Boys %	Girls %	Boys %	Girls %
16	B.J.B. Junior College +2 Arts	2000	281	94 (33.5)	129 (45.9)	25 (8.9)	11 (3.9)	19 (6.8)	3 (1.1)
		2001	565	196 (34.7)	232 (41.1)	55 (9.73)	33 (5.8)	42 (7.4)	7 (1.2)
		2002	563	205 (36.4)	244 (43.3)	23 (4.09)	28 (5.0)	58 (10)	5 (0.9)
		2003	579	143 (24.7)	287 (49.6)	52 (8.98)	48 (8.3)	41 (7.1)	8 (1.4)
17	B.J.B. Junior College +2 Science	2000	536	354 (66.0)	114 (21.3)	24 (4.48)	1 (0.2)	38 (7.1)	5 (0.9)
		2001	552	307 (55.6)	131 (23.7)	40 (7.25)	32 (5.8)	33 (6)	9 (1.6)
		2002	549	292 (53.2)	145 (26.4)	46 (8.38)	7 (1.3)	54 (9.8)	5 (0.9)
		2003	550	257 (46.7)	178 (32.4)	50 (9.09)	7 (1.3)	51 (9.3)	7 (1.3)
18	B.J.B. Junior College +2 Commerce	2000	142	89 (62.7)	36 (25.4)	8 (5.63)	2 (1.4)	7 (4.9)	0 (0.0)
		2001	140	80 (57.1)	36 (25.7)	13 (9.29)	1 (0.7)	10 (7.1)	0 (0.0)
		2002	143	74 (51.7)	34 (23.8)	14 (9.79)	2 (1.4)	18 (13)	1 (0.7)
		2003	155	80 (51.6)	45 (29.0)	17 (11.0)	3 (1.9)	3 (1.9)	2 (1.3)

Fig. IV-C

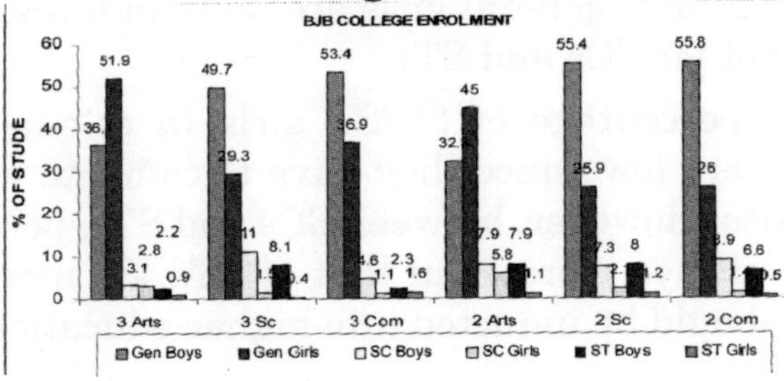

4.7 B.J.B. College (Autonomous)

In +3 classes, the number of SC/ST girls is much less than general girls and SC/ST boys. In Science, percentage of general girls is 24.8% whereas that of SC girls is 1.5% and ST girls only 0.8%. In Arts, though percentage of girls is more than boys (for general boys it is 37.1% and for girls 53.4%), for SCs and STs their percentage is as low as 2.9% and 0.9% respectively (Fig. IV-C).

Table: 4.8 - Average Enrolment in +3 Classes – B.J.B. Autonomous College (1999-2003)

Steam		Percentage of Students					
		General		SC		ST	
		Boys	Girls	Boys	Girls	Boys	Girls
Arts	459	37.1	53.4	3.2	2.9	2.2	0.9
Science	133	49.6	29.3	11.0	1.5	8.1	0.5
Commerce	160	53.4	37.0	4.6	1.2	2.3	1.5

Thus, enrolment of SC/ST girls in B.J.B. College is extremely low. However, SCs enrolment is better than that of STs and the percentage seems to increase over the years.

4.8 B.J.B. College (Junior)

Since this is the largest co-education college in the State Capital and consistently shows good result all good students aspire to get admission in this college and competition is very tough. In Science, the average percentage of general girls is less than boys and also for SCs/STs. In Arts, general girls are more in number than boys but not for SCs and STs.

Thus, percentage of SC/ST girls in co-educational college is very low, since they have to compete with SC/ST boys also. However, between SCs and STs, percentage of SCs is always more than that of STs. So more tribal students should be inducted into higher education.

Table: 4.8 A – Average Percentage of Students in +2 Classes B.J.B. Junior College (1999-2003)

Steam		Percentage of Students					
		General		SC		ST	
		Boys	Girls	Boys	Girls	Boys	Girls
Arts	497	32.1	44.9	7.8	6.0	8.0	1.0
Science	547	55.3	26.0	7.3	2.2	8.0	1.1
Commerce	145	55.9	26.2	8.9	1.4	6.9	0.7

Table: 4.8 B Enrolment of SC/ST Girls in Technical Institutions in State Capital, Bhubaneswar

Sl. No	Name of the Institution	Year	Total	General		SC		ST	
				Boys %	Girls %	Boys %	Girls %	Boys %	Girls %
19	Institute of Technical Education and Research (ITER) (B.Tech.)	1999	233	187 (80.3)	36 (15.5)	7 (3.0)	2 (0.9)	1 (0.4)	0 (0.0)
		2000	305	238 (78.0)	52 (17.0)	10 (3.3)	2 (0.7)	3 (0.9)	0 (0.0)
		2001	352	222 (63.1)	98 (27.8)	11 (3.1)	5 (1.4)	12 (3.4)	4 (1.1)
		2002	361	273 (75.6)	57 (15.8)	14 (3.9)	3 (0.8)	11 (2.9)	3 (0.8)
		2003	474	317 (66.9)	101 (21.3)	30 (6.3)	8 (1.7)	15 (3.2)	3 (0.6)
20	Kalinga Institute of Industrial Technology (KIIT) (B.Tech)	1999	380	271 (71.3)	80 (21.1)	7 (1.8)	3 (0.8)	15 (3.9)	4 (1.1)
		2000	430	284 (66.0)	113 (26.3)	13 (3.0)	5 (1.2)	14 (3.3)	1 (0.2)
		2001	550	387 (70.4)	112 (20.4)	19 (3.5)	6 (1.1)	19 (3.5)	7 (1.3)
		2002	550	396 (72.0)	104 (18.9)	19 (3.5)	6 (1.1)	20 (3.6)	5 (0.9)
		2003	550	345 (62.7)	136 (24.7)	28 (5.1)	7 (1.3)	24 (4.4)	10 (1.8)

21	College of Engineering and Technology (CET) (B.Tech)	1999	109	61 (56.0)	31 (28.4)	7 (6.4)	0 (0.0)	8 (7.3)	2 (1.8)
		2000	155	83 (53.5)	38 (24.5)	12 (7.7)	3 (1.9)	7 (4.5)	2 (1.3)
		2001	161	101 (62.7)	33 (20.5)	10 (6.2)	0 (0.0)	10 (6.2)	7 (4.3)
		2002	279	195 (69.9)	35 (12.5)	14 (5.0)	2 (0.7)	16 (5.7)	7 (2.5)
		2003	287	193 (67.2)	37 (12.9)	13 (4.5)	4 (1.4)	14 (4.9)	8 (2.8)
22	Kaustuv Institute of Self Domain (KISD) (B.Tech)	1999	- -	- -	- -	- -	- -	- -	- -
		2000	- -	- -	- -	- -	- -	- -	- -
		2001	108	- -	105 (97.2)	- -	2 (1.9)	- -	1 (0.9)
		2002	126	- -	122 (96.8)	- -	2 (1.6)	- -	2 (1.6)
		2003	- -	- -	- -	- -	- -	- -	- -

Fig. IV-D

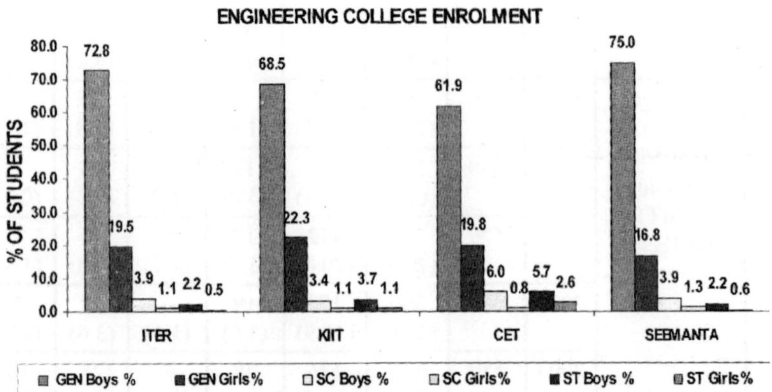

Table: 4.9 – SC/ST Students Admitted in Different Technical Courses under Biju Pattnaik University of Technology (BPUT), 2004

Sl. No.	Courses	No. of Seats	No. of SC Boys(%)	No. of SC Girls(%)	No. of ST Boys(%)	No. of ST Girls(5)
1.	Engineering	10295	248	58	146	51
			2.4	0.56	1.41	0.49
2.	Medical	327	15	06	13	15
			4.58	1.83	3.97	4.58
3.	Pharmacy	665	08	02	06	00
			1.2	0.3	0.9	0
4.	M.B.A.	1177	18	01	07	01
			1.52	0.08	0.59	0.08
5.	M.C.A.	2607	16	03	10	02
			0.61	0.11	0.38	0.07

4.9 Enrolment in Engineering Colleges

As seen from the records of individual Engineering Colleges as well as from the total enrolment in B.P.U.T. (Biju Pattnaik University of Technology), the enrolment of SC/ST girls was extremely low. In spite of the fact in State Government 30% in all categories of Engineering College seats are reserved for girls, for SC girls the enrolment in Engineering colleges was only 0.56% and for ST girls it was merely 0.49%, in 2004. Even in Kalinga Institute of Industrial Technology (KIIT), which has now become a Deemed University, percentage of SC girls was only 1.1% and ST girls 1.06%. It appears that SC/ST girls probably fail to qualify for Engineering. Even in K.I.S.D., the only women's engineering college in the State started since 2001, only two SC and one ST girl took admission in 2001 and in 2002, the number was two in each category. Obviously, SC/ST girls need special coaching at +2 level for entry into engineering colleges (Fig. IV-D).

Table: 4.10 – Enrolment of SC/ST Girls in Medical Institutions

Sl No	Name of the Institution	Year	Total	General		SC		ST	
				Boys %	Girls %	Boys %	Girls %	Boys %	Girls %
23	Shriram Chandra Bhanj Medical College, Cuttack (MBBS)	1999	107	61 (57.0)	28 (26.2)	7 (6.5)	0 (0.0)	8 (7.5)	3 (2.8)
		2000	107	64 (59.8)	24 (22.4)	7 (6.5)	1 (0.9)	8 (7.5)	3 (2.8)
		2001	107	66 (61.7)	22 (20.6)	6 (5.6)	2 (1.9)	7 (6.5)	4 (3.7)
		2002	107	73 (68.2)	16 (15.0)	5 (4.7)	2 (1.9)	8 (7.5)	3 (2.8)
		2003	107	91 (85.0)	27 (25.2)	8 (7.5)	2 (1.9)	6 (5.6)	10 (9.3)
24	Shriram Chandra Bhanj Medical College, Cuttack (BDS)	1999	15	7 (46.7)	6 (40.0)	0 (0.0)	0 (0.0)	2 (13.3)	0 (0.0)
		2000	14	5 (35.7)	7 (50.0)	1 (7.1)	0 (0.0)	0 (0.0)	1 (7.1)
		2001	18	12 (66.7)	4 (22.2)	1 (5.6)	0 (0.0)	1 (5.6)	0 (0.0)
		2002	9	5 (55.6)	3 (33.3)	0 (0.0)	0 (0.0)	1 (11.1)	0 (0.0)
		2003	17	11 (64.7)	4 (23.5)	0 (0.0)	0 (0.0)	1 (5.8)	1 (5.8)

Analysis

4.10 Enrolment in Medical College

From the record of S.C.B. Medical College, it was found that the percentage of ST girls was more then that of SC girls. In last five years, only 23 tribal girls and 6 SC girls were enrolled in S.C.B. Medical college, Cuttack, the average enrolment for ST girls being only 4.3% and for SC girls only 1.3% (over five years period from 1999-2003). The percentage of tribal girls is slightly higher because 50% of seats are reserved for outside State students, which are usually filled up by students from tribal dominated north-eastern States of the country.

In BDS, in last five years, only 2 tribal girls and no

SC girl took admission. Thus, intake of SC/ST girls is minimum in BDS course.

4.11 Enrolment in Diploma/Certificate Courses

(i) Kalinga Institute of Industrial Technology

In five years, only 27 SC girls and 7 ST girls took admission in KIIT, which makes average intake only 1.6% and 0.4% (over the period 1999-2003). Thus, SC/ST girls are not very interested for Diploma Course, since their intake is more in regular Engineering Degree Course than in Diploma Course.

Table: 4.11 - Enrolment in Diploma Courses

Sl No.	Name of the Institution	Year	Total	General		SC		ST	
				Boys %	Girls %	Boys %	Girls %	Boys %	Girls %
25	Kalinga Institute of Industrial Training (KIIT) (Diploma)	1999	260	170 (65.4)	42 (16.2)	20 (7.7)	1 (0.4)	25 (9.6)	2 (0.7)
		2000	316	189 (59.8)	66 (20.9)	32 (10.1)	6 (1.9)	23 (7.3)	0 (0.0)
		2001	314	214 (68.2)	45 (14.3)	21 (6.7)	7 (2.2)	24 (7.6)	3 (0.9)
		2002	309	208 (67.3)	47 (15.2)	33 (10.7)	6 (1.9)	14 (4.5)	1 (0.3)
		2003	351	220 (62.7)	49 (14.0)	62 (17.7)	7 (2.0)	12 (3.4)	1 (0.2)
26	Bhubananda Orissa School of Engineering (Diploma)	1999	240	185 (77.1)	55 (22.9)	28 (11.7)	8 (3.3)	43 (17.9)	13 (5.4)
		2000	240	180 (75.0)	60 (25.0)	30 (12.5)	6 (2.5)	46 (19.1)	10 (4.1)
		2001	280	208 (74.3)	72 (25.7)	33 (11.8)	6 (2.1)	51 (18.2)	9 (3.2)
		2002	335	257 (76.7)	78 (23.3)	45 (13.4)	9 (2.7)	56 (16.7)	7 (2.1)
		2003	335	277 (82.7)	58 (17.3)	41 (12.2)	7 (2.1)	66 (19.7)	8 (2.3)

27	Industrial Training Institute (ITI), Cuttack	1999	467	268 (57.4)	26 (5.6)	66 (14.1)	5 (1.1)	100 (21.4)	2 (0.4)
		2000	604	343 (56.8)	27 (4.5)	148 (24.5)	10 (1.7)	73 (12.1)	3 (0.5)
		2001	360	219 (60.8)	21 (5.8)	45 (12.5)	5 (1.4)	68 (18.8)	2 (0.5)
		2002	582	385 (66.2)	22 (3.8)	92 (15.8)	4 (0.7)	75 (12.8)	4 (0.6)
		2003	513	332 (64.7)	29 (5.7)	73 (14.2)	5 (1.0)	73 (14.2)	1 (0.2)

Analysis:

(ii) Bhubananda Orissa School of Engineering

Comparatively higher percentage of SC/ST girls are seen in this government institution. The average intake of SC girls for five years is 2.3% and for ST girls 3.7%. Thus, comparatively higher intake of ST girls then SC girls was observed in this institution. But over the years, a steady decline in percentage of ST girls was observed which came down from 5.4% in 1999 to 2.3% in 2003. However, enrolment of ST boys did not show this trend.

(iii) I.T.I. Training Institute, Cuttack

In ITI course also, a steady decline is observed in SC/ST girl students' enrolment. In 1999, the percentages of SC/ST boys were 14.1% and 1.1% and those of girls at 21.4% and 0.4% respectively. In 2003, the percentages for SC/ST boys were 14.2% and 1%, but that of girls was 14.2% and 0.2% respectively. This of course shows very low enrolment of ST students in ITI courses, in spite of reservation.

Table: 4.12 - Enrolment of SC/ST Students in Institutions of General Education in Tribal District Mayurbhanj

Sl No	Name of the Institution	Year	Total	General		SC		ST	
				Boys %	Girls %	Boys %	Girls %	Boys %	Girls %
28	MPC (Autonomous College) Baripada P.G. (Arts)	1999	155	71 (45.8)	53 (34.2)	12 (7.7)	2 (1.3)	13 (8.4)	4 (2.6)
		2000	126	38 (30.2)	63 (50.0)	6 (4.8)	4 (3.2)	9 (7.1)	5 (4.0)
		2001	144	41 (28.5)	65 (45.1)	9 (6.3)	8 (5.6)	14 (9.7)	7 (4.9)
		2002	145	46 (31.7)	59 (40.7)	7 (4.8)	10 (6.9)	15 (10)	8 (5.5)
		2003	145	27 (18.6)	81 (55.9)	14 (9.7)	7 (4.8)	12 (8.3)	4 (2.8)
29	MPC (Autonomous College) Baripada P.G. (Science)	1999	52	21 (40.4)	21 (40.4)	3 (5.8)	1 (1.9)	4 (7.7)	2 (3.8)
		2000	50	21 (42.0)	22 (44.0)	0 (0.0)	1 (2.0)	4 (8)	2 (4.0)
		2001	64	26 (40.6)	29 (45.3)	1 (1.6)	1 (1.6)	4 (6.3)	3 (4.7)
		2002	53	31 (58.5)	14 (26.4)	2 (3.8)	0 (0.0)	3 (5.7)	3 (5.7)
		2003	64	25 (39.1)	32 (50.0)	2 (3.1)	2 (3.1)	2 (3.1)	1(1.6)
30	MPC (Autonomous College) Baripada P.G. (Commerce)	1999	55	41 (74.5)	3 (5.5)	3 (5.5)	1 (1.8)	7 (13)	0 (0.0)
		2000	27	19 (70.4)	6 (22.2)	1 (3.7)	0 (0.0)	1 (3.7)	0 (0.0)
		2001	39	25 (64.1)	6 (15.4)	3 (7.7)	0 (0.0)	5 (13)	0 (0.0)
		2002	41	31 (75.6)	6 (14.6)	2 (4.9)	0 (0.0)	1 (2.4)	1 (2.4)
		2003	37	20 (54.1)	14 (37.8)	0 (0.0)	0 (0.0)	3 (8.1)	0 (0.0)

31	MPC (Autonomous College) Baripada +3 (Arts)	1999	245	96 (39.2)	82 (33.5)	23 (9.4)	3 (1.2)	32 (13)	9 (3.7)
		2000	232	96 (41.4)	84 (36.2)	13 (5.6)	3 (1.3)	34 (15)	2 (0.9)
		2001	167	79 (47.3)	57 (34.1)	11 (6.6)	3 (1.8)	14 (8.4)	3 (1.8)
		2002	163	50 (30.7)	76 (46.6)	9 (5.5)	3 (1.8)	21 (13)	4 (2.5)
		2003	169	61 (36.1)	72 (42.6)	16 (9.5)	9 (5.3)	8 (4.7)	3 (1.8)
32	MPC (Autonomous College) Baripada +3 (Science)	1999	131	72 (55)	36 (27.5)	3 (2.3)	2 (1.5)	16 (12)	2 (1.5)
		2000	144	83 (57.6)	32 (22.2)	7 (4.9)	2 (1.4)	16 (11)	4 (2.8)
		2001	161	78 (48.4)	53 (32.9)	5 (3.1)	3 (1.9)	17 (11)	5 (3.1)
		2002	225	110 (48.9)	87 (38.7)	4 (1.8)	1 (0.4)	17 (7.6)	6 (2.7)
		2003	194	106 (54.6)	51 (26.3)	20 (10.3)	7 (3.6)	8 (4.1)	2 (1)
33	MPC (Autonomous College) Baripada +3 (Commerce)	1999	230	181 (78.7)	18 (7.8)	4 (1.7)	0 (0.0)	23 (10)	4 (1.7)
		2000	196	151 (77)	20 (10.2)	4 (2)	0 (0.0)	20 (10)	1 (0.5)
		2001	56	38 (67.9)	13 (23.2)	1 (1.8)	2 (3.6)	1 (1.8)	1 (1.8)
		2002	250	176 (70.4)	34 (13.6)	11 (4.4)	1 (0.4)	25 (10)	3 (1.2)
		2003	111	78 (70.3)	16 (14.4)	9 (8.1)	2 (1.8)	6 (5.4)	0 (0.0)
34	MPC (Junior College) Baripada +2 (Arts)	1999	249	84 (33.7)	82 (32.9)	22 (8.8)	6 (2.4)	45 (18)	10 (4)
		2000	213	78 (36.6)	78 (36.6)	12 (5.6)	11 (5.2)	29 (14)	5 (2.3)
		2001	439	102 (23.2)	210 (47.8)	17 (3.9)	16 (3.6)	53 (12)	41 (9.3)
		2002	487	101 (20.7)	201 (41.3)	17 (3.5)	21 (4.3)	94 (19)	53 (10.9)
		2003	456	103 (22.6)	196 (43)	18 (3.9)	22 (4.8)	74 (16)	43 (9.4)

35	MPC (Junior College) Baripada +2 (Science)	1999	276	158 (57.2)	73 (26.4)	14 (5.1)	3 (1.1)	23 (8.3)	5 (1.8)
		2000	243	130 (53.5)	60 (24.7)	16 (6.6)	3 (1.2)	23 (9.5)	11 (4.5)
		2001	256	142 (55.5)	61 (23.8)	16 (6.3)	5 (2)	19 (7.4)	13 (5.1)
		2002	252	130 (51.6)	72 (28.6)	16 (6.3)	1 (0.4)	26 (10)	7 (2.8)
		2003	250	123 (49.2)	60 (24)	21 (8.4)	7 (2.8)	32 (13)	7 (2.8)
36	MPC (Junior College) Baripada +2 (Commerce)	1999	143	101 (70.6)	21 14.7)	6 (4.2)	0 (0.0)	14 (9.8)	1 (0.7)
		2000	151	93 (61.6)	31 (20.5)	11 (7.3)	3 (2.0)	11 (7.3)	2 (1.3)
		2001	143	89 (62.2)	21 (14.7)	7 (4.9)	0 (0.0)	21 (15)	6 (4.2)
		2002	152	72 (47.4)	37 (24.3)	10 (6.6)	1 (0.7)	30 (20)	2 (1.3)
		2003	129	98 (76)	9 (7)	1 (0.8)	1 (0.8)	19 (15)	1 (0.8)

Fig. IV-E

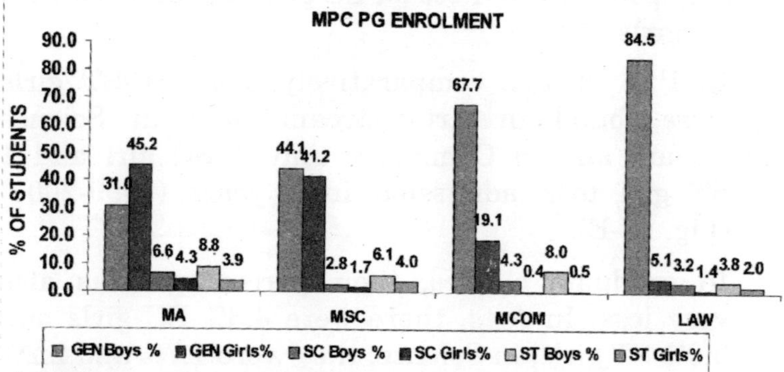

Analysis:

4.12 Enrolment of SC/ST Girls in Institutions of General Education in Mayurbhanj District Tribal District

Since Mayurbhanj District has the highest tribal population in the State, it was expected that enrolment of tribal girls would be quite considerable. But in this

Fig.IV-F

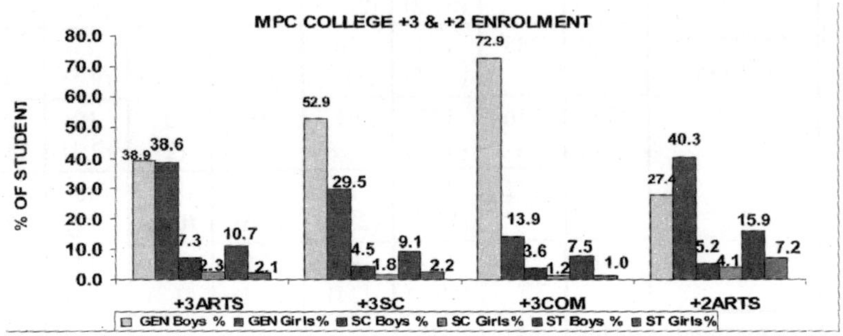

district also, enrolment in co-education and technical colleges was found extremely low. Seven general colleges, one Engineering College and one University (North Orissa University) under our research project have been studied and the enrolments for five years have been shown in the report (Table – 4.4).

4.12.1 M.P.C. (Autonomous) College

1. The enrolment in Post Graduate classes was found very poor. It was 4.3% for SC girls and only 3.9% for ST girls.
2. In P.G. classes comparatively more SC/ST girls were found in Arts stream than in Science stream and in Commerce only 1 SC girl and 1 ST girl took admission in 5 years (1999-2003) (Fig. IV-E).
3. In graduate classes, their percentage was also very less. In Arts, there were 4.3% SC girls and 3.9% ST girls; in Science, they were 1.7% and 2.2% respectively. In Commerce, either one or two or no SC/ST girl took admission.
4. Due to Autonomous status, a large number of seats were lying vacant, since the minimum cut off mark for admission was 40%.

4.12.2 M.P.C. Junior College (Higher Secondary) –

1. In Higher Secondary Stage, a slightly higher enrolment rate of SC/ST girls was noted. Looking into the record of enrolment, it was found that for 5 years average, percentage of SC girls and ST girls in Arts stream was 4.0% and 7.2% respectively; in Science they were 1.5% and 3.4% and in Commerce, 0.7% and 1.6% respectively (Fig.IV-F).

2. Intake of SC/ST students (both boys and girls together) was more than 8% and 12% i.e. seats reserved for them. However, for tribal girls, the percentage remained stagnant throughout the last five years, while a steady increase in tribal boys' enrolment was noticed. (Table 4.13:Enrolment in Other Institutions of Mayurbhanj District.)

4.12.3 Government Women's College

1. This college offers Under-Graduate programmes for girls in Arts stream only. Surprisingly, the percentage of tribal girls opting for this college is relatively higher than other colleges offering such courses.

2. Being a government institution requiring nominal fees is the primary reason for such preference. Besides, being exclusively for girls, this college is a natural preference of SC/ST parents.

3. Offering only pass course, an easier option, it is natural for SC/ST girls to prefer this college to M.P.C. (Autonomous) College, where Honours stream is compulsory and therefore tougher. The average percentage of SC girls is 6.56 and that of ST girls 17.8.

Table: 4.13 – Enrolment in Other Institutions of Mayurbhanj District

Sl. No.	Name of the Institution	Year	Total	General		SC		ST	
				Boys %	Girls %	Boys %	Girls %	Boys %	Girls %
37	Govt. Women's College (+3 Arts) Baripada	1999	128	- -	93 (72.7)	- -	7 (5.5)	- -	28 (21.9)
		2000	128	- -	99 (77.3)	- -	10 (7.8)	- -	19 (14.8)
		2001	128	- -	101 (78.9)	- -	6 (4.7)	- -	21 (16.4)
		2002	128	- -	97 (75.8)	- -	9 (7.0)	- -	22 (17.2)
		2003	18	- -	94 (73.4)	- -	10 (7.8)	- -	24 (18.8)
38	Sree Maa Mahila Vidyalaya (+3 Arts) Baripada	1999	42	- -	40 (95.2)	- -	0 (0.0)	- -	2 (4.8)
		2000	87	- -	77 (88.5)	- -	0 (0.0)	- -	10 (11.5)
		2001	58	- -	50 (86.2)	- -	1 (1.7)	- -	7 (12.1)
		2002	114	- -	94 (82.5)	- -	7 (6.1)	- -	13 (11.4)
		2003	55	- -	44 (80)	- -	2 (3.6)	- -	9 (16.4)
39	Sree Maa Mahila Vidyalaya (+2 Arts) Baripada	1999	119	- -	93 (78.2)	- -	3 (2.5)	- -	23 (19.3)
		2000	119	- -	102 (85.7)	- -	3 (2.5)	- -	14 (11.8)
		2001	65	- -	48 (73.8)	- -	4 (6.2)	- -	13 (20)
		2002	81	- -	66 (81.5)	- -	2 (2.5)	- -	13 (16)
		2003	94	- -	72 (76.6)	- -	5 (5.3)	- -	17 (18.1)

Fig. IV-G

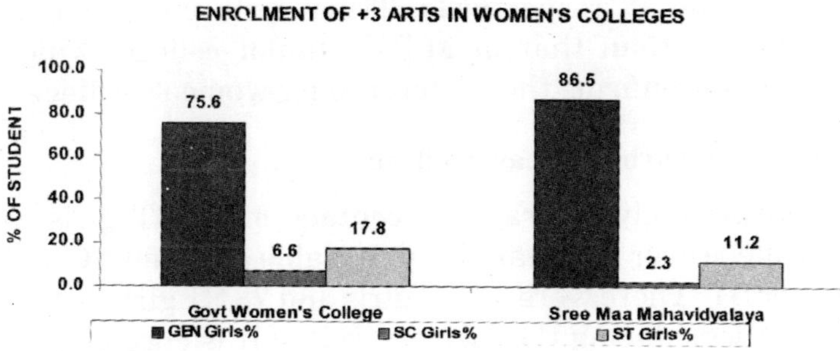

Analysis

4.12.4 Sree Ma Mahavidyalaya

1. This college offers Under-Graduate and Higher Secondary programmes only in Arts stream.
2. The intake in +3 classes in this college is higher than M.P.C. (Autonomous) College, but lower than Government Women's College. SC/ST girls show preference for women's college. But lack of infrastructure in this private college may account for the differential between this and the Government Women's College (Fig. IV-G).

Table: 4.14 – Enrolment in Mayurbhanj Law College

Sl. No.	Name of the Institution	Year	Total	General		SC		ST	
				Boys %	Girls %	Boys %	Girls %	Boys %	Girls %
40	Mayurbhanj Law College, Baripada	1999	796	649 (81.5)	52 (6.5)	32 (4)	12 (1.5)	34 (4.3)	17 (2.1)
		2000	793	660 (83.2)	49 (6.2)	28 (3.5)	10 (1.3)	30 (3.8)	16 (2)
		2001	789	700 (88.7)	23 (2.9)	20 (2.5)	7 (0.9)	20 (2.5)	19 (2.4)
		2002	705	607 (86.1)	34 (4.8)	12 (1.7)	7 (1)	30 (4.3)	15 (2.1)
		2003	746	620 (83.1)	39 (5.2)	30 (4)	16 (2.1)	30 (4)	11 (1.5)

3. The percentages of SC/ST girls in +2 classes are 3.8 and 17 respectively. Tribal girls' enrolment is higher than that in M.P.C. Junior college, which again confirms the preference for women's college.

Analysis

4.12.5 Mayurbhanj Law College

Surprisingly, average percentage of SC/ST girls in this college over five years is appreciable at 1.4 for SC and 2.03 for ST. There were 52 SC girls and 78 ST girls in this Law College during the last five years. It is encouraging to see so many ST girls taking up Law course.

Table: 4.15 – Enrolment in North Orissa University

Sl No	Subject with Sanctioned Strength	Year	Students Admitted	No. of Students Enrolled					
				General		SC		ST	
				Boys	Girls	Boys	Girls	Boys	Girls
1	M.Sc. in Wild Life Conservation (20)	2002	5	4	0	1	0	0	0
		2003	6	4	2	0	0	0	0
		2004	4	4	0	0	0	0	0
2	M.Sc. in Bio-Technology (20/30)	2002	20	8	12	0	0	0	0
		2003	30	11	18	1	0	0	0
		2004	30	14	14	1	1	0	0
3	M.Sc. in Environmental Science (20)	2002	9	6	3	0	0	0	0
		2003	5	3	2	0	0	0	0
		2004	Closed						
4	M.A. in Library Science (20)	2002	10	4	4	1	0	0	1
		2003	17	3	9	2	1	0	2
		2004	11	2	9	0	0	0	0
5	M.A. in Tribal Studies (30)	2002	4	3	1	0	0	0	0
		2003	6	2	2	0	0	1	1
		2004	4	0	3	0	0	0	1
6	Master in Business Management (30)	2002	-	-	-	-	-	-	-
		2003	19	13	6	0	0	0	0
		2004	30	19	9	0	0	2	0

7	Master of Law (LLM)(24)	2002	22	18	2	1	0	1	0
		2003	24	19	4	1	0	0	0
		2004	20	13	2	4	0	1	0
8	M.A. in Education (Distance Education) (30)	2002	23	3	19	2	1	0	0
		2003	20	5	14	1	0	0	0
		2004	32	13	17	0	1	1	0

Table: 4.16 – Enrolment in North Orissa University (Subjects Started from 2004)

Sl. No.	Subject with Sanctioned Strength	Total no. of Students Admitted	No. of Students Enrolled					
			General		SC		ST	
			Boys	Girls	Boys	Girls	Boys	Girls
1	Botany (16)	16	6	7	0	1	0	2
2	Chemistry (20)	20	11	5	2	1	1	0
3	Physics (20)	16	8	6	0	1	1	0
4	Zoology (16)	16	5	9	0	0	1	1
5	Economics (32)	28	6	16	2	1	1	2
6	B.Sc. in Bio-Informatics (48)	10	6	4	0	0	0	0
7	P.G. in Remote Sensing and GIS (16)	6	4	2	0	0	0	0

Analysis

4.12.6 North Orissa University, Baripada

1. This University was established in 1998 mostly for the educational needs of tribal students of Mayurbhanj and Keonjhar districts, but only 5 tribal girls and 4 SC girls took admission during last three years (2002-2004).
2. Since most of the subjects were unconventional and self financing, most SC/ST girls could not avail the opportunity of studying in this new University.
3. After Post-Graduate classes in conventional subjects

like Economics and Science, subjects were shifted from M.P.C. Autonomous College to the University in 2004, 4 SC and 5 ST girls took admission in these courses. Thus, SC/ST girls prefer to pursue easier and conventional subjects in higher education.

Table 4.17: Enrolment of SC/ST Students in Technical Institution in Tribal District, Mayurbhanj

Sl. No.	Name of the Institution	Year	Total	General		SC		ST	
				Boys %	Girls %	Boys %	Girls %	Boys %	Girls %
41	Seemanta Engineering College, Mayurbhanj	1999	191	131 (68.6)	36 (18.8)	9 (4.7)	4 (2.1)	8 (4.2)	3 (1.6)
		2000	314	247 (78.7)	45 (14.3)	15 (4.8)	3 (1.0)	3 (1)	1 (0.3)
		2001	324	243 (75.0)	64 (19.8)	8 (2.5)	5 (1.5)	3 (0.9)	1 (0.3)
		2002	389	295 (75.8)	70 (18.0)	8 (2.1)	6 (1.5)	6 (1.5)	1 (0.3)
		2003	280	216 (77.1)	36 (12.9)	16 (5.7)	1 (0.4)	10 (3.6)	1 (0.4)

Analysis

4.12.7 Seemanta Engineering College

1 Although it is the only Engineering College in Mayurbhanj district intended to draw tribal students to technical education, the intake of tribal students is not encouraging. During last 5 years (1999-2003), 19 SC girls and 7 ST girls took admission in this college, compared to 56 SC boys and 30 ST boys. Thus, SC/ST girls in this technical college were very few in number.

2 Their percentage in different years is 0.4 to 2.1 for SC girls and 0.3 to 1.6 for ST girls. Average intake of SC/ST girls over 5 years is mere 1.3% and 0.56% respectively. Proper counselling and special

coaching is very much needed for these students at +2 level.

4.13 Conclusion

On the whole, it was observed that participation of SC/ST girls in technical education is much less than in general education. At higher level of education, in traditional subjects requiring low fees and in comparatively easier subjects, enrolment of SC/ST girls is better but never at par with general students. Moreover, these girls' enrolment in women's colleges is comparatively higher. Obviously, parents prefer women's colleges for their daughters.

With SC/ST Students in College

In Class Room

In Hostel

5

OUR STUDENT RESPONDENTS: PERSONAL DATA AND SOCIO-ECONOMIC BACKGROUND

5.1 List of Institutions/Colleges

Student respondents were selected from different educational institutions from Orissa and from different streams of general education, technical education and also professional courses. Institutions were mainly chosen from State Capital, Bhubaneswar, where students from different districts come for higher education and from Mayurbhanj district with highest tribal population. Some women's colleges and some co-educational colleges were chosen to bring out a comparison. Assuming that there were 12% ST students and 8% SC students in a class (government reservation rule), efforts have been made to interview 10% of such students in a class. However, although at higher secondary level, their number was almost proportional to affiliated strengths in respective classes at higher levels of education, this was not the case, particularly in post graduate and technical courses, where sufficient numbers of students were not available. Care was taken to choose students from different social strata and from different economic backgrounds. Many students, staying in college/university hostels, were interviewed to asses their views on special hostel facilities provided for them.

The interview schedule contained several separate sections to find out views on different aspects. The first part (Part A), contained 17 questions which described respondents' socio-economic background, school background and performance in the last examination they appeared.

Table: 5.1 – List of Institutions/Colleges

Sl No.	Name of the College	SC Students		ST Students	
		No. of Students	%	No. of Students	%
1.	Utkal University, Bhubaneswar	23	20.3	20	12.7
2.	Rama Devi Women's College, (Autonomous), Bhubaneswar	10	8.8	17	10.8
3.	Rama Devi Junior College, Bhubaneswar	13	11.5	15	9.5
4.	B.J.B. College, Bhubaneswar	28	24.8	18	11.5
5.	College of Engineering and Technology, Bhubaneswar	05	4.4	05	3.2
6.	Institution of Technical Education and Research, Bhubaneswar	05	4.4	05	3.2
7.	Kalinga Institute of Industrial Technology, Bhubaneswar	05	4.4	05	3.2

8.	Kaustuv Institute of Self Domain, Bhubaneswar	04	3.5	04	2.5
9.	North Orissa University, Baripada	01	0.9	04	2.5
10.	M.P.C. (Autonomous) College, Baripada	02	1.8	17	10.8
11.	M.P.C. Junior College, Baripada	04	3.5	15	9.5
12.	Government Women's College, Baripada	04	3.5	16	10.2
13.	Shree Ma Mahavidyalaya, Baripada	02	1.8	04	2.3
14.	Mayurbhanj Law Collge, Baripada	02	1.8	05	3.2
15.	Seemanta Engineering College, Baripada	03	2.7	01	0.6
16.	S.C.B. Medical College, Cuttack	02	1.8	06	3.8
	Total	113	100	157	100

Thus, 113 SC girls and 157 ST girls from 16 different institutions pursuing different courses were interviewed.

5.2 Personal Details of Respondents

Part A of the questionnaire also dealt with personal details involving name, class, institutions age, caste/tribe, religion, marital status, etc which were noted down at the beginning of interview.

The student respondents were 270 in number (157 ST girls and 113 SC girls). Care has been taken to cover all the 16 institutions under study along with different courses, their number being proportional to number of

Table: 5.2 – Personal Details of Respondents

Sl. No.	Personal Information	Variables	SC		ST	
			No. of Students	Percen tage	No. of Students	Percen tage
1.	Class	+2 Science	08	7.1	13	8.3
		+2 Arts	23	20.4	22	14.0
		+2 Commerce	01	0.8	02	1.3
		+3 Science	08	7.1	17	10.8
		+3 Arts	14	12.4	41	26.1
		+3 Commerce	02	1.7	02	1.3
		M.A.	16	14.3	21	13.3
		M.Sc.	07	6.3	05	3.2
		M.Com.	02	1.7	03	1.9
		M.B.A.	03	2.6	04	2.5
		Law	03	2.6	05	3.2
		Engineering	24	21.2	16	10.2
		Medical	02	1.7	06	3.8
		Total	113	100	157	100
2.	Age	14-16	05	4.4	13	8.3
		17-19	42	37.2	57	36.3
		20-22	53	46.9	68	43.3
		23-25	13	11.5	16	10.2
		Above 25	0	0	03	1.9
		Total	113	100	157	100
3.	Marital Status	Married	02	1.8	03	1.9
		Unmarried	111	98.2	154	98.1
		Total	113	100	157	100
4.	Religion	Hindu	113	100	119	75.8
		Muslim	0	0	00	0
		Christian	0	0	13	8.3
		Sikh	0	0	00	0
		Sarnanism	0	0	25	15.9
		Total	113	100	157	100

SC/ST students expected to be in a class according to government reservation rule. The courses are +2, +3, P.G. (Arts, Science, Commerce), Engineering, Medical, M.B.A. and Law courses.

(i) **Class** – Effort has been made to select 10% of ST and SC girls supposed to be present in a class as respondents. It has been found that the percentage of SC/ST students is maximum in Arts in all classes (+2, +3 and P.G.) and in Commerce, their number is minimum. In technical education, their number is comparatively more in engineering than in other branches. Reservation of 30% seats for girls in engineering courses in Orissa is perhaps the reason for this.

(ii) **Age** – Age lies between 14-25 years; in P.G. classes the age of SC/ST girls seems to be slightly higher than general girls. This can be ascribed to late enrolment and periodic discontinuance at school level.

(iii) **Marital Status and Religion** – Very few girls (1.9% ST and 1.8% SC) were found to be married, which indicates that they do not continue studies after marriage.

A few tribal students (8.3%) were found to be Christians. However, in case of SCs, all respondents mentioned their religion as 'Hindu'. It is difficult to ascertain whether some were SC Christians since conversion to Christianity also does not entitle a SC student to get benefit of reservation.

5.3 Districts to Which Respondents Belong

The SC respondents were found to have come from 19 districts, the maximum being from Cuttack and Dhenkanal, where as the ST respondents hailed from 12 districts, the largest number being from Mayurbhanj

(61.8%). This is understandable as quite a few institutions have been selected from Mayurbhanj district; also many girls from this district stay in the special women's hostel of the State Capital (included under the study) for higher education.

Table: 5.3 – Districts to which Respondents Belong

Sl. No.	Name of the District	SC		ST	
		No. of Students	Percen tage	No. of Students	Percen tage
1.	Angul	02	1.8	00	00
2.	Balasore	11	9.7	02	1.3
3.	Bargarh	01	0.9	00	0.0
4.	Bhadrak	07	6.2	00	0.0
5.	Cuttack	14	12.4	00	0.0
6.	Dhenkanal	14	12.4	00	0.0
7.	Gajapati	01	0.9	03	1.9
8.	Ganjam	04	3.5	00	0.0
9.	Jagatsinghpur	09	8.0	00	0.0
10.	Jajpur	04	3.5	01	0.6
11.	Kalahandi	00	00	02	1.3
12.	Kandhamal	00	00	15	9.6
13.	Kendrapara	08	7.1	00	0.0
14.	Keonjhar	03	2.7	08	5.1
15.	Khurdha	12	10.6	00	0.0
16.	Koraput	00	00	04	2.5
17.	Malkangiri	00	00	03	1.9
18.	Mayurbhanj	09	8.0	97	61.8
19.	Nabarangpur	01	0.9	00	0.0
20.	Nayagarh	03	2.7	00	0.0
21.	Puri	07	6.2	00	0.0
22.	Raygarh	00	0.0	03	1.9
23.	Sambalpur	02	1.8	08	5.1
24.	Sundargarh	01	0.9	11	7.0
	Total	113	100	157	100

5.4 Tribes/Castes to Which Respondents Belong

The tribal students were found to have come from 16 different tribes whereas SC students were from 12 different castes. A few tribal girls showed their ignorance about the identity of their original tribes, perhaps due to loss of contact with their own community in villages after they continued living in urban localities.

It is found that a large number of ST girls belonged to Santal families. This was expected since literacy and awareness among tribals is comparatively higher in Santal community. In case of SCs, most students were found from Dhoba caste, generally found in large numbers in towns.

Table: 5.4 – Tribes/Castes to which Respondents belong

Sl. No.	SC			ST		
	Name of Caste	Frequency	Percentage	Name of Tribe	Frequency	Percentage
1.	Dewan	05	4.4	Oram	10	6.4
2.	Keuta	08	7.1	Santal	80	31.0
3.	Kaibarta	22	19.5	Khadia	07	4.5
4.	Hadi	17	15.0	Ho	06	3.8
5.	Dhoba	25	22.1	Kisan	06	3.8
6.	Gokha	03	2.7	Allavali	02	1.3
7.	Ganda	11	9.7	Gonda	05	3.2
8.	Pana	09	8.0	Kandha	04	2.5
9.	Bauri	01	0.9	Sabar	01	0.6
10.	Kandara	07	6.2	Soura	01	0.6
11.	Bathudi	01	0.9	Bhuyan	06	3.8
12.	Tanti	04	3.5	Kolho	06	3.8
13.		-	-	Bhumij	11	7.0
14.		-	-	Bathudi	03	1.9
15.		-	-	Saoule	01	0.6
16.		-	-	Don't know	08	5.1
	Total	113	100	Total	157	100

5.5 Language Spoken by SC/ST Stuents

Though many tribal girls speak in their own tribal language among themselves and at home, a large number (21%) speak only in Oriya. In case of SCs, the language used is only Oriya.

Table: 5.5 – Language Spoken by Respondents

Sl. No	Language Spoken	SC		ST	
		Frequency	Percentage	Frequency	Percentage
1.	Oriya	113	100	33	21.0
2.	Kharia	-	-	11	7.0
3.	Santal	-	-	75	47.8
4.	Kuduk	-	-	03	1.9
5.	Ho	-	-	07	4.5
6.	Kisan	-	-	03	1.9
7.	Kui	-	-	01	1.6
8.	Kolho	-		06	3.8
9.	Bathudi	-	-	01	0.6
10.	Don't know	-	-	15	9.6
	Total	113	100	157	100

Since a large number of respondents are from Santal tribe, many of them (47.8%) prefer to use their own language at home. Even 43.9% of students have said that they used their own Olchiki, the language/ script of Santals. However, 30% of tribal girls have said that they only used Oriya language and even 9.6% have said that they did not know whether they had a language of their own. Among SCs, all respondents spoke only Oriya since SCs do not have any specific language as tribal people do.

5.6 Place of Residence of Respondents

Most ST girls were found to be staying in hostels, since they had come from interior villages. But in case of SCs, more girls were found to be staying with parents than in hostels, being largely urban based.

59.2% of ST and 41.6% of SC girls are hosteliers. Tribals mostly live in their communities in villages and their children have to come to towns to stay in hostels for higher education. SC girls seeking higher education mostly live in towns. However, 41.69% of SC respondents also stay in hostels. So hostel is an important requirement for girls' higher education.

Table: 5.6 – Place of Residence of Respondents

Sl. No.	Place of Residence	SC		ST	
1.	With Parents	51	45.1	37	23.6
2.	With Relatives	11	9.7	13	8.3
3.	Students' Hostel	47	41.6	93	59.2
4.	With Friends	04	3.5	14	8.9
	Total	113	100	157	100

5.7 Educational Background of Parents

SC/ST students were found to have come from families with different educational background.

It was observed that in case of SC fathers, 48.7% were graduates and 12.4% were post-graduates whereas in

Table: 5.7 – Educational Background of Parents

Sl.No.	Level of Education	SC Parents		ST Parents	
		Father	Mother	Father	Mother
1.	Illiterate	07(5.3)	22(19.5)	13(8.3)	46(29.3)
2.	Up to class-V	0(0)	16(14.2)	5(3.2)	23(14.6)
3.	Up to class-VII	03(2.7)	22(19.5)	10(6.4)	38(24.2)
4.	Up to Matric	22(19.5)	29(25.7)	36(22.9)	37(23.6)
5.	Up to +2	11(9.7)	17(15.0)	28(17.8)	9(5.7)
6.	Graduate/Degree	55(48.7)	05(4.4)	51(32.5)	4(2.5)
7.	Post Graduate	14(12.4)	02(1.8)	14(8.9)	0(0)
8.	M.Phil/Ph.D.	01(0.9)	0(0)	0(0)	0(0)
	Total	113(100)	113(100)	157(100)	157(100)

(Number in parentheses shows the percentage)

case of ST fathers, 32.5% were graduates and 8.9% were post-graduates. Thus it was found that girls perusing higher education mostly have educated fathers, and SCs fathers had better education than STs.

Regarding mother's education, more ST mothers were illiterate (29.3%), whereas for SCs only 19.5% mothers were illiterate. More of the SC mothers were found to have education beyond matriculation than STs. Thus, it was encouraging to see that even very uneducated mothers have sent their girls for higher education. This clearly indicates a change of mindset among SC/ST women in recent times.

5.8 Occupation of Parents

Most of our respondents were found to have come from families of government servants.

It was found that 61% of SC parents and 56% of ST parents were government employees. Thus, persons having government jobs due to reservations send their children for higher education with the hope of getting the same facilities in the next generation also. 27% of SC parents and 25% of ST parents have jobs in private

Table: 5.8 – Occupation of Parents

Sl. No.		SC		ST	
		Father	Mother	Father	Mother
1.	Government Employee	63(55.8)	06(5.3)	79(50.3)	9(5.7)
2.	Pvt. Employee	21(17.7)	08(7.1)	36(22.9)	7(4.5)
3.	Wage Earner	0(0	01(0.9)	00(0)	00(0)
4.	Agriculture	11(9.7)	04(3.5)	32(20.3)	6(3.8)
5.	Business	17(15)	01(0.9)	9(5.7)	01(0.6)
6.	Politics	1(0.9)	00(0)	1(0.6)	01(0.6)
7.	Home Maker	0(0)	93(82.3)	00(0.0)	133(84.7)
	Total	113(100	113(100)	157(100)	157(100)

(Number in parentheses shows the percentage)

sector. But 82.3% of SC mothers and 84.7% of ST mothers are housewives looking after their families, without any job.

5.9 Annual Income of Parents

Our respondents were found to have come from different economic background.

Very few girls have come from poor families, i.e. with annual income less than Rs.15,000. This is because for such low income group it is difficult to afford higher education. It is only 4.49% and 6.4% in case of SCs and STs respectively. SC students have been found to have come from comparatively more sound economic background then ST students.

Table: 5.9 – Annual Income of Parents

Sl. No.		SC		ST	
		Frequency	Percentage	Frequency	Percentage
1.	<15,000	5	4.4	10	6.4
2.	15,000 – 55,000	49	43.4	91	57.9
3.	> 55,000	50	44.2	46	29.3
4.	Don't know	09	8.0	10	6.4
	Total	113	100	157	100

5.10 School Background of Respondents

A few ST girls have passed matriculation (Class – X) from special schools run by SC/ST Development Department whereas none of the SC respondents were from these schools. This was expected since from the record of SC/ST Development Department it was found that out of 55,063 students in such schools, 65.7% were STs and only 16.9% were SCs. Maximum numbers of students in both categories were from Oriya medium co-education schools and girls' schools depending on availability of schools in their areas. However, 10.5% of ST students and 9% of SC students were found to have come from

English Medium Schools, mostly run by missionaries.

Table: 5.10 – School Background of Respondents

Sl. No.	Schooling	SC		ST	
		No. of Respondents	Percen tage	No. of Respondents	Percen tage
1.	Ashram Co-ed School	0	0	03	1.9
2.	Ashram Girls' School	0	0	21	13.0
3.	Oriya Medium Co-ed School	64	56.6	76	46.9
4.	Oriya Medium Girls' School	39	34.5	45	27.8
5.	English Medium Co-ed School	08	7.1	17	10.5
6.	English Medium Girls' School	02	1.8	00	0.0
	Total	113	100	157	100

5.11 Educational Proficiency

The educational proficiency of SC/ST girls was assessed from their performance in last examination.

It was observed that SC students showed better performance than ST students at all levels of examination. Also, it was observed that their percentage in first

Table: 5.11 – Performance in Last Examination

Sl. No.	Last Examination appeared	SC			ST		
		1st Div	2nd Div	3rd Div	1st Div	2nd Div	3rd Div
1.	H.S.C.	26 (23.0)	09 (8.0)	00 (00)	28 (17.8)	15 (9.6)	3(1.9)
2.	+2 Arts	05 (4.4)	07 (6.2)	02 (1.8)	03 (1.9)	13 (8.3)	26(16.6)

3.	+2 Science	15 13.3)	10 (8.8)	07 (6.2)	05 (3.2)	17 (10.8)	08(5.1)
4.	+2 Commerce	00 (0.0)	01 (0.9)	01 (0.9)	00 (0.0)	00 (0.0)	00(0.0)
5.	+3 Arts	6 (5.3)	14 (12.4)	00 (00)	10 (6.4)	13 (8.3)	05(3.2)
6.	+3 Science	2 (1.8)	06 (5.3)	00 (00)	05 (3.2)	03 (1.9)	01(0.6)
7.	+3 Commerce	1 (0.9)	01 (0.9)	00 (0.0)	00 (0.0)	2 (1.3)	00(0.0)
	Total	55 (48.7)	48 (42.5)	10 (8.9)	51 (32.5)	63 (40.1)	43(27.4)

(The numbers in parenthesis indicate percentage)

division is better at High School Certificate Examination (23.0% for SC and 17.8% for ST). However, it declines at higher levels of examination: 13.3% at +2 Science and 1.8% at +3 Science for SCs and 10.8% and 3.2% for STs respectively.

In all, only 48.7% of SCs and 27.4% of STs were able to secure first class in last examination. Tribal girls, however, have shown better result than SCs at degree level. Probably, only good tribal students, really interested in studies, continue till higher level.

5.12 Conclusion

Our respondents were found to belong to different regions of the State and from varying social backgrounds. A very large number of them stay in hostels to pursue higher education away from their native place. The number of SC/ST students is more in general educational institutions than in technical institutions and among technical courses their number is maximum in Engineering. Most of the respondents were found from educated families (graduate fathers in case of 62% of SC respondents and 41.4% ST respondents) and parents working in government or private sector. Only 12% SC families. **The inevitable conclusion is that girls from educated families and from families with good economic condition, predominate in higher education and educational opportunities in SC/ST communities have not dispersed widely.**

6

FACING ODDS: CONSTRAINTS AS SEEN BY SC/ST GIRLS

Our respondents were found to have come from different socio-economic background. To assess the constraints they encounter while pursuing higher education, they were asked several questions through interview schedule. They were frank in their opinion and were happy to share their feelings.

6.1 Economic Constraints

(1) Annual Income:

Family annual income of respondents was first analyzed to find out if they had to face economic constraints for pursuing higher education. It was observed that 40.7% of SC and 54.2% of ST respondents were found to be from families with annual income less than Rs. 35,000/-. Obviously, they faced economic constraints for incurring expenditure in higher education. However, 39.5% of SC and 24.2% of ST students had family annual income more than 65.000/-, and as such, had comfortable financial status. Economic condition of SCs was clearly better than that of STs.

When we visited the parents of a few tribal students

in their villages, their poor economic status was clearly visible from the thatched roofs and mud walls of their houses.

Two tribal girls, Basantimaye Tudu and Duleri Tudu of village Sanabrahmanamara near Baripada narrated how much labour they had to do to earn some money for their educational expenses. They were studying in Panchayat High School at Kuabuda, which is a residential school for tribals, five kilometers away from their village. Though food was free there, they had to buy their books and stationeries. So during holidays they prepared ropes from a type of long grass, called Bubei grass, which is the main cottage industry in that area. Sometimes even they worked in road construction to earn some money during holidays.

Headman of the village, Ratan Marandi, admitted that it was very difficult for the villagers earning livelihood from daily labour to afford education for children. Many girls had to discontinue education even after Class IX because they could not arrange the required fund.

"I have seven children, three sons and four daughters. My daughters have to work in the field and earn some money, even if they want to study". – says daily labourer Bhaiga Bersa of village Sukhuapoda in Kuliana block of Mayurbhanj. Sending them to high school became very difficult for him (textbooks are not free at high school level), sending them to college was out of question.]

Thus, financial constraint is a major bar for higher education of tribal girls. Only children of families with sound economic background come for higher education.

(2) Financial Support for Education

When students staying in hostels of college and

university were asked about the source of financial support for education, 80.5% of SC and 66.2% of ST respondents said that they received financial support from the monthly earnings of their parents or guardians. Only 19.5% of SC and 31.2% of ST students depended on agricultural income of parents. This shows mostly the children of parents with regular job could afford higher education. None of the SC students had taken any loan for studies whereas 4 ST students had availed of such loan for their education. Clearly, ST students faced greater financial difficulties.

(3) Opinion Regarding Adequacy of Funds

When students were asked whether the money they received from their homes was sufficient for them, only 75.2% SCs and 69.4% STs replied that it was manageable. However, 24.8% SCs and 30.6% of STs felt that they faced difficulties.

(4) Availability of Scholarships

Students were asked several questions regarding availability of Post-Matric Scholarship and adequacy of the amount. 32% of SC respondents and 30% of ST respondents said that they did not receive any scholarship. When asked about the reason for not getting scholarship, out of them, 30.6% of SCs and 38.3% of STs said that the reason was the income limit. Sadly, 33.3% of SCs and 29.8% of STs among them were not aware of this facility. Obviously, there is need for creating awareness about the Post Matric Scholarship Scheme among students as soon as they enter college. Unfortunately, 22.2% SC and 25.5% ST students did not get assistance as they did not know how to apply. Authorities should take care to see that SC/ST students apply for such scholarships in time.

It is really sad that 5.3% of SC and 12.7% of ST respondents complained about not receiving the stipend in time to pay their examination fees and other expenditures.

6.2 Social Constraints

Respondents were asked 15 questions regarding social constraints they faced while pursuing studies and staying in hostels, due to their social backwardness. Their views were assessed through questions on choice of friends, choice of room-mates, attitude of general caste students, etc.

(1) Encouragement for Higher Education

To our question about how they were encouraged to come for higher education, the students offered varied answers.

Table: 6.1 – Encouragement for Higher Education

Sl. No.	Persons Encouraging	SC		ST	
		No. of Respondents	Percentage	No. of Respondents	Percentage
1.	Parents	68	60.2	90	57.3
2.	Brother/ Sister	21	18.6	19	12.1
3.	Family Relations	11	9.7	19	12.1
4.	Teachers	04	3.5	06	3.8
5.	Others	09	8.0	23	14.6
	Total	113	100	157	100

Most students have been encouraged to come for higher education by their parents and family relations. Many of them were encouraged by their elder brothers/ sisters who have received higher education. Thus, when a member in the family is educated, others follow suit. But it is surprising that only 3.5% of SC and 3.8% of ST students have said that they were encouraged by their teachers. Teachers at school level should provide encouragement to SC/ST students for higher education, which they rarely seem to do.

(2) Gender Disparity in Education:

When asked whether any kind of gender disparity exists in their community, more than half of the SC girls said that they have felt discriminated in the family compared to boys. Their brothers were pampered and their education was given priority whereas girls were allowed to pursue higher education with a lot of hesitations. **Many SC girls described painful incidents of gender discrimination in the family.**

But in case of Scheduled Tribe students, only 38.2% have said that they have experienced some gender disparity and these respondents were found to belong to upper middle class staying away from the community. However, the remaining 61.8% of respondents (97 students) **had emphatically said that there was no gender discrimination in the family and they were treated equally with their brothers.**

Thus, generally, no gender discrimination in family for higher education was felt by ST students as in case of SC students. However, a few tribal girls have mentioned that sons are generally sent for technical education, like ITIs, Polytechnics etc., so that they may get jobs easily, whereas girls are sent for general education where expenditure is less.

(3) Social Interaction with Fellow Students

(i) Choice of friends and Roommates – When students were asked as to whether they had friends among general caste students, 19.5% of SC students and 26.1% of ST students admitted that they did not have any friends from general caste girls. Some of the SC/ST girls were found to harbour inferiority complex as higher caste girls seemed to ignore them.

Then students were asked the names of their two best

friends and their castes. Though 56.1% of SC students and 48.3% of ST students had mentioned that their friends were from general as well as SC/ST caste, 15.8% of SC students and 36.7% of ST students had best friends from their own caste only. When they were asked about their choice of room-mates in hostel, 33.3% SC students and 40.2% ST students of those who stayed in hostels, have expressed that they were sharing rooms in hostels with friends of their own caste, because they felt diffident in company of general caste girls.

Thus, it was observed that SC/ST students staying in hostels, other than special hostels meant for SC/ST, also preferred to have roommates from their own caste. However, they were allotted rooms in mixed groups, when they stayed in a common hostel.

(ii) Relationship with Friend's Family – To our question on their relationship with families of general caste friends, only 54% of SCs and 44.6% of STs replied that they had good relation with these family members. However, 11.5% of SC and 11.5% of ST students have said that they had never been invited to houses of general caste girls. Sadly, 6.2% of SC and 5.7% of ST students felt that caste factor might create problems for their friends while 8.8% of SC and 9.6% of ST students felt shy to interact with friends' families.

"The family members of one of my general caste friends treated me as untouchable, when she took me to her home. I felt really bad and felt like crying". Said Sabita Behera, a +2Arts student of Rama Devi Women's College.

This is not the single case. Four SC students and two ST students have revealed that they were treated as untouchables by their friends' family members. Thus, in spite of the fact that families were educated, many have not got over their caste prejudice.

(4) Apathetic Attitude of General Caste Students

Many of the SC/ST student respondents have narrated incidents of offending behaviour of general caste girls towards them. 11.5% of ST girls and 15% of SC girls have reported that general caste students ridiculed them for entering the educational institute through reservation and not due to merit. Sadly, 22.1% of SC girls have expressed that they were treated as untouchables by general caste students, even by girls from educated families. ST girls were often criticized about their life style and also for not doing very well in studies. Thus, SC/ST girls were generally looked down upon by general caste girls for 'getting certain privileges they did not deserve'. **Such attitude of general caste girls in institutions of higher education is really unfortunate and needs to be corrected.**

6.3 Cultural Constraints

Through pointed questionnaire and personal interview, effort has been made to ascertain cultural constraints felt by SC/ST students while seeking/pursuing higher education.

(1) Family/Community Restriction for Leaving Village for Higher Education

To our question as whether their parents objected to their coming out of the village for higher education in towns, 20.4% of SC students and 52.3% of ST students revealed that they had to try hard to convince their parents for permission to go out for higher education. While in case of SCs, the objection was for safety of girls, in case of STs, it was for fear of alienation from community and possible problems for marriage in future.

They were also asked whether they had to take permission from community leaders in this matter. SC girls said that there was no such custom of taking permission from village leaders. Only 5.7% of ST girls said that they had to take permission from their community leaders. However, it was found later that these girls belonged to some remote villages of KBK district where tribals were still very backward. But the rest of the ST girls (94.3%) said that there was no need for such permission from the community.

(2) Decision Making in the Family

Decision making power is very important in this study, since decision regarding daughter's higher education and sending her to a distant place is first taken in the family. 64.6% of SC respondents and 63.19% of ST respondents confirmed patriarchy in the family by replying that their coming for higher education was solely decided by their fathers. This was taken for granted as fathers were the bread earners in the family. However, 27.4% of SC and 24.2% of ST respondents revealed that the decision was a joint decision of both the parents. In these cases the mothers were found to be educated and the families belonged to higher income group.

As to our question regarding respondents taking part in family decision, only 15.7% SC students' 18.5% ST students, have said that their opinion was sought in family matters. But 9.7% of SC students and 8.9% of ST students were allowed to take their own decision regarding career. Students mostly from engineering, MBA and MCA courses were found to have taken their own decision. Thus, SC/ST students have limited role in deciding their career.

(3) Age of Marriage

Researchers tried to assess whether the girls felt that there could be problem in marriage after they finished higher education. Though a few respondents revealed the predicament of girls aged above 20 years regarding marriage, 45.1% of SC girls and 46.5% of ST girls who pursued post graduate and professional courses, said that they wanted to marry after completion of study, the age of 24-26 years being the ideal age for marriage. Though their parents pressurized them for marriage apprehending difficulty is finding a suitable match at a later age, the girls seemed to give preference to career. Thus, once the SC/ST girls entered institutions of higher learning, they wanted to complete their education before getting married.

(4) Dress Pattern

In case of SC students, 74.3% of respondents preferred traditional dresses whereas 11.5% of respondents preferred modern outfits like jeans and shirts. These girls were mostly hosteliers, who had no parental restrictions or were from families of educated mothers.

In case of STs, though most of them have said that they preferred salwar, kemeez or saree which they also used at home, a few respondents coming from typical tribal villages admitted that they were used to traditional dresses worn is village and felt uncomfortable due to change of dress pattern in town. Only 19% of ST students seemed to opt for jeans/shirts. Thus, a change from the traditional dress pattern is clearly discernible due to education.

(5) Customs and Traditions

Some customs and traditions prevailing in SC/ST communities do create definite barrier for the girls to come out for higher education. 33.6% of SC respondents have expressed that customs like preferential treatment for sons and the belief that it is difficult to arrange a match for highly-educated SC girls are obstacles for higher education.

43.9% of ST respondents admitted that customs

and traditions like early marriage of girls, restrictions on leaving their own community and drinking liquor in the family do create hindrance for higher education. The tribals had not been able to get rid of their addiction to liquor. Even if they earned enough money, they spent most of it on drinking and are not able to provide for higher education of their children.

Sanjubala Pradhan, a tribal woman working as a peon in Rama Devi Women's College for the last 20 years narrated her sad story before the researchers. Her husband, Hari Dehuri, a peon in Reserve Bank of India, earns about Rs.19,000/- per month. They have four daughters and one son and only one of the daughters is married. He drinks regularly and spends most of his salary on liquor. So he does not provide any money for family expenses and poor Sanju has to take the entire burden of the family with her meager income. So it was not possible for her to send the girls to college after matriculation. With tears in her eyes, she requested us to take up the matter with bank authorities. On enquiry, it was found that Hari Dehuri was reprimanded several times for being drunk and remaining absent from duty.

Thus, the habit of taking liquor by tribals is one of the main causes of their low economic and hence educational status.

(6) Interest in Recreational/Co-curricular Activities

SC/ST students were asked several questions regarding their interests in recreational and co-curricular activities besides study. The intention was to ascertain whether their cultural background has affected their interest in participating in different extra-curricular activities, an integral part of education.

93.8% of SC students and 85.9% ST students have

Table: 6.2 – Interest in Outward Activities

SC/ ST	Activities	Yes	No Interest	No Time	Not Aware	Parents do not Allow	Total
SC	Watch TV	106 (93.8)	05 (4.4)	02 (1.8)	0(0.0)	0(0.0)	113 (100)
	Movies	82 (72.6)	14 (12.4)	05 (4.4)	0(0.0)	12(10.6)	113 (100)
	NCC/NSS	13 (11.5)	100 (88.5)	0 (0.0)	0(0.0)	0(0.0)	113 (100)
	Sports	39 (34.5)	68 (60.2)	02 (1.8)	04 (3.5)	0(0.0)	113 (100)
	College Election	58 (51.3)	52 (46.0)	03 (2.7)	0 (0.0)	0(0.0)	113 (100)
ST	Watch TV	135 (85.9)	8(5.1)	11 (7.0)	0(0.0)	0(0.0)	157 (100)
	Movies	92 (58.6)	32 (20.4)	11 (7.0)	0(0.0)	22(14.0)	157 (100)
	NCC/NSS	29 (18.4)	128 (81.5)	0 (0.0)	0(0.0)	0(0.0)	157 (100)
	Sports	71 (45.2)	65 (41.4)	4 (2.5)	17 (10.8)	0(0.0)	157 (100)
	College Election	73 (46.5)	84 (53.5)	0 (0.0)	0(0.0)	0(0.0)	157 (100)

(Number in the parentheses indicate percentage)

said that they watched T.V. Surprisingly, 6.2% of SC girls and 12.1% of ST girls have said that they did not watch T.V. either due to lack of interest or lack of time, which in addition to recreation, would also improve general

Fig. VI-A- SC/ST Girls on College Sports

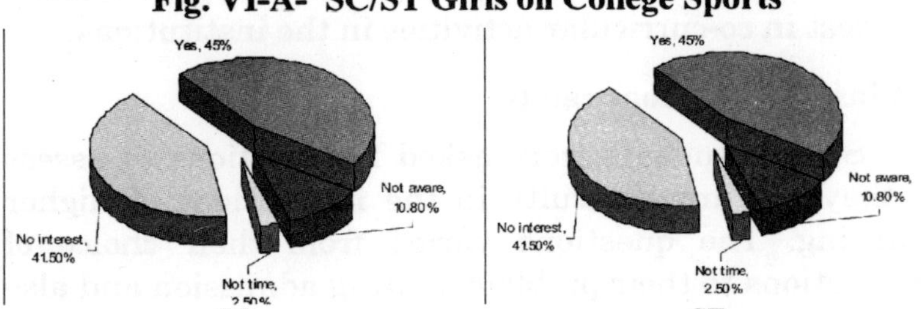

SC ST

knowledge and awareness. Regarding watching movies, 10.6% of SC and 14.0% of ST girls said that they did not watch movies as their parents did not approve of it.

When question was put regarding their participation in NCC/NSS, sadly, 88.5% of SC girls and 81.5% of ST girls replied that they did not join NCC/NSS because they had no interest. **To improve self-confidence and integration with the main stream, SC/ST girls should be enrolled in NCC/NSS with general students and college authorities should encourage them for this.** SC/ST girls, not taking part at least in social activities through NSS, is definitely a matter of considerable concern.

Only 34.5% of SC students and 45.2% of ST students took part in sports whereas 60% SC girls 41.4% ST girls had mentioned that they had no such interest. Though it is believed that tribal girls are good at sports due to their physical built, they did not show interest in it. 3.5% of SC girls and 10.8% of ST girls, specially in the University, even said that they were not aware when sports events were held. Since these girls usually show good performance, authorities should try to involve them in sports activities.

Though 51.3% of SC girls and 46.5% of ST girls have mentioned about participating in college election, very few of them have actually contested in elections. They only participated in casting votes.

Thus, on the whole, SC/ST girls did not show much interest in co-curricular activities in the institutions.

6.4 Institutional Constraints

SC/ST students were asked 25 questions to assess if they felt any difficulty in the institutions of higher learning. The questions varied from their choice of institutions to their problems during admission and also the huddles they faced while pursuing higher studies, which is an important point of investigation.

(1) Choice of Institutions

It was found that maximum number of SC/ST girls had chosen educational institutions nearest to their native place. They were mostly inclined to enter women's colleges, specially colleges with women's hostels. It is interesting to note that many tribal girls from different districts have chosen Utkal University or Rama Devi Women's College in the State Capital for good exposure and career opportunity. Thus, it seems that even tribal girls from educated families have realized the value of good education.

(2) Discontinuation of Studies

When asked whether they had to discontinue their study due to some reason at any point of time, a few of them admitted to have discontinued at certain stage.

5.1% of tribal girls mentioned that they had to discontinue at H.S.C. level for poor result and were subsequently able to make up, whereas none of the SC girls had mentioned about such discontinuation. At +2 stage, quite a few girls have mentioned about discontinuation (12.4% SC and 14.8% ST); but after +3, only 1 SC girls and 2 ST girls had to discontinue. It followed that once the initial hurdles are crossed; the girls become determined and continued their higher studies as per wish.

Table: 6.3 – Discontinuation in Studies

Sl. No.	Discontinuation of Study at Different Level	SC		ST	
		No. of Response	Percentage	No. of Response	Percentage
1.	H.S.C. Level	0	0.0	08	5.1
2.	+2 Level	14	12.4	23	14.8
3.	+3 Level	01	0.8	02	1.3

(3) Difficulty in Admission

Students were asked whether they had to face any difficulty for admission into the institution.

(i) Providing Admission Fees

17.7% SC girls and 46.2% ST girls said that they had difficulty in arranging money to pay the admission fees. This finding calls for support to SC/ST students in this regard. Admission fees may be reduced for SC/ST girls, at least in government institutions.

(ii) Adjusting to New Environment

When students were asked about their feeling after entering the new institution, 9.7% of SC and 20% of ST girls of the University said that it took some time to get over the feeling of discomfort and adjust to the new/ independent environment of University. Clearly, they need help in the initial stages of adjustment.

(4) Problems in the Institution

SC/ST girls were asked whether they faced any problem in understanding lessons in the class.

Table: 6.4 – Problems in the Institution

Sl. No.	Problems in Understanding Lessons	SC		ST	
		No. of Students	Percentage	No. of Students	Percentage
1.	Language Problem	11	9.7	16	10.2
2.	Method of Teaching is not Good	14	12.4	23	14.6
3.	Teachers are not Bothered about Students	02	1.8	01	0.6
4.	No Problem	35	31.0	51	32.5
5.	No Response	51	45.2	40	25.5
	Total	113	100	157	100

As seen from their response, 9.7% of SC and 10.2% of ST girls said that they could not understand lessons because the medium of teaching was English. The problem of language is more acute for ST girls, most of whom had Oriya medium school background. 12.4% of SC and 14.6% of ST girls also complained about method of teaching, which they could not follow. According to them, only lectures were not enough and delivery was too fast to comprehend. Very few students mentioned about teacher's indifference towards their understanding of lessons.

(5) Seeking Teacher's Help

Students were asked whether they sought teacher's advice from time to time. Surprisingly, many of them replied that they have never gone to their teachers beyond class hours.

Fig. VI-B Seeking Teacher's Help

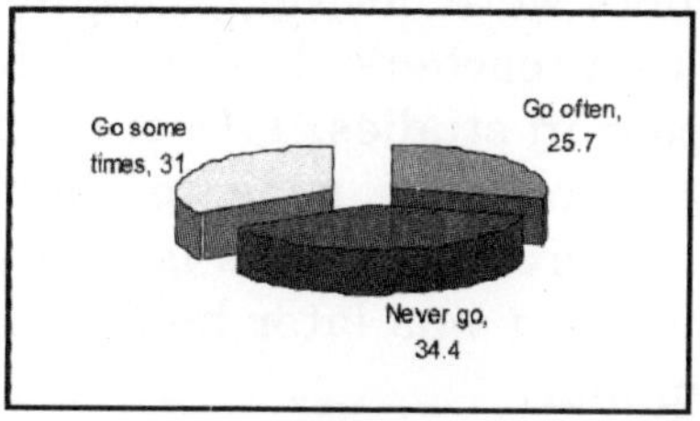

SC

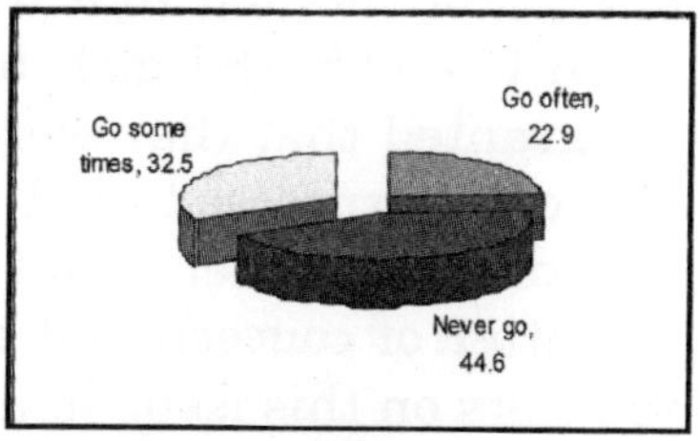

ST

43.4% SC and 44.6% ST girls have said that they had never gone to their teachers to clarify difficulties, most probably due shyness and lack of confidence. Clearly the teachers will have to be more approachable.

(6) Teacher's Attitude

There was an open-ended question regarding teachers' attitudes towards SC/ST girls. The question was: "How do you find your teacher's attitude towards you?" There were varied answers which can be tabulated as follows:

Table: 6.5 – Teachers' Attitude

No. of Obs.	Teacher's Attitude	SC		ST	
		No. of Response	Percentage	No. of Response	Percentage
1.	Co-operative/ Friendly	71	62.8	85	54.1
2.	Encourage to Read More	07	6.2	15	9.6
3.	Not Cooperative	11	9.7	23	14.6
4.	They Think SC/ST Girls are Poor in Studies	04	3.5	15	9.6
5.	Rude	09	8.0	14	8.9
6.	Not worried about Students Problem	11	9.7	05	3.2
	Total	113	100	157	100

Though most students said that teachers were co-operative and friendly, sadly, about 10% of SC and 15% of ST students felt that teachers were not very friendly. Even 13% of SC/ST girls felt that teachers always took it for granted that they were poor in studies. 17% of such students expressed that teachers were rude to them and did not bother about their problems. This is really a matter of concern and discussion was later held with teachers on this issue in a seminar.

(7) Availing Library Facility

To our question on availing library facility, most students (84% of SC and 74% of ST) said that they visited library regularly. But the rest of them, who did not go to library, offered various reasons for this like scarcity of book, too much crowding, lack of time, etc. Surprisingly, one SC student and 12 ST students have expressed that they had no idea about the procedure for availing library facility. It would be useful to explain the library rules to SC/ST students at the very beginning and encourage them to use the facility.

6.5 Conclusion

Primary data regarding review of economic, social, cultural and institutional constraints was collected from student respondents through interview schedules which contained 10 questions on information about economic constraints, 14 about social constraints, 10 about cultural constraints and 26 about educational problems.

Many students (40.7% SC and 54.2% ST) were found to be from families with annual income within Rs.55,000/- which definitely indicated economic constraints for higher education.

From the inter-relation study, it was found that performance of students was related to their economic condition i.e. students from high income group families showed relatively better performance. Their career option and interest in co-curricular activities also depended on family's economic condition.

Regarding social constraints, it was observed that SC/ST girl students felt diffident in company of general caste girls, and preferred roommates and friends from their own caste. They did not like to take food in dining room with others. 19.5% SC and 26.1% ST girls admitted that they had no friends from general caste girls.

As for cultural constraints, they had revealed that all decisions regarding their education were taken by their fathers and they did not mind it that way. Only in case of educated mothers, it was a joint decision. As regards marriage prospects, post graduate students in particular, wanted to complete education before marriage. Most of the students preferred traditional dresses (salwar/ kameez/ sari) whereas a few (11% SC and 19% ST) liked to wear modern dresses like jeans and shirts, which indicated growing influence of modern society. Many tribal girls admitted that they had to convince their parents to allow them to move away from home for higher education, with a lot of difficulty. It is a matter of great concern that 22.1% of SC girls had a feeling of being treated as untouchables by general caste girls. Many SC/ST girls also reported about being ridiculed for getting the so-called "undue privileges".

Regarding problems in educational institutions, the first difficulty faced by SC/ST girls related to arrangement of money for admission. After admission, SC/ST students (9.7% of SC and 20% of ST) found difficulty in adjusting to the new surrounding of the College/University, which was quite different from the schools they were attending. Some students have admitted that they could not understand the lessons because the medium of teaching was English and the method of teaching was different. 43% of SC and 31% of ST students said that they had never gone to their teachers in case of difficulties who, they felt, were not co-operative or sympathetic. They even felt shy to discuss lessons with general caste girls. Some SC/ST girls did not use library facilities. Clearly, the need for orientation/counselling at the commencement of their college life and for greater consideration and empathy on the part of teacher cannot be overemphasized.

7

TOWARDS EQUALITY: IMPACT OF SPECIAL HOSTEL FACILITY ON SC/ST GIRLS

7.1 Introduction

Provision of special hostel facilities for SCs/STs specially SC/ST girls is considered to be a significant policy initiative to further their educational advancement. SC/ST girls hail from a different social milieu; their exposure to higher educational institutions in urban environment is often traumatic; safety and security aspects naturally cause grave anxiety among parents. Documenting and analyzing the relevance of exclusive lodging and boarding facilities for SC/ST girl students should, therefore, be an important constituent of this study.

Accordingly, one of the objectives of our project was to evaluate the impact of special hostel facilities provided to SC/ST girls in pursuit of higher education. State Government is providing hostel facilities both at pre-matric and post-matric level to encourage SC/ST students to come for education. At present, 218 residential High Schools, including 55 for girls are functioning in the State under the ST and SC Development Department. There are 7 Special Adivasi Hostels (for both SCs and STs) at Bhubaneswar, the State Capital (5 hostels for boys and 2 hostels for girls). Besides, there is one such hostel (for girls) at Rourkela. The boarders of these hostels get stipend for 11 months in a year.

Details of Special Adibasi Hostels are as follows:

Table: 7.1 – List of Special Adibasi Hostels

Sl. No.	Name of the Hostel	Location	Category	Seats	Name of the School/College to Which the hostel is Attached
1.	Sahid Laxman Nayak Adibasi Boys' Hostel	Unit-II Bhubenswar	Pre-Matric	100	Government Boys' High School, Unit-I ,Bhubaneswar
2.	Kuntala Kumari Sabat Adivasi Girls' Hostel	Unit-II Bhubaneswar	Pre-Matric	100	Govt. Girls' High School, Unit-II ,Bhubaneswar
3.	Thakkar Bapa Adivasi Boys' Hostel	Unit-III, Bhubaneswar	Pre-Matric	100	Capital Boys' High School, Unit-III, Bhubaneswar
4.	Jagjeven Ram Adibasi Boys' Hostel	Unit-III, Bhubaneswar	Post-Matric	150	B.J.B.College, Rajdhani College and Other Colleges, Bhubaneswar
5.	Dr. B.R.Ambedkar Adivasi Boys' Hostel	B.J.B.College, Bhubaneswar	Post-Matric	150	B.J.B.College, Bhubaneswar
6.	Indira Gandhi Adivasi Womens' Hostel	Unit-IX, Bhubaneswar	Post-Matric	250	R.D.Women's College, Bhubaneswar

7.	Kamal Nehru Adivasi Women's Hostel	Rourkela	Post-Matric	100	Post-Matric Educational Institutions Located at Rourkela
8.	Post Graduate Adibasi hostel (Rented Building)	Acharya Viahr, Bhubaneswar	Post-Matric	48	Post Graduate Students of Vani Vihar

Thus, for girls' pursuing post-matric higher education, there are only two Special Adivasi Hostels, one at Bhubaneswar, attached to Rama Devi Women's College, and the other at Rourkela, where girl students pursuing education in different post-matric educational institutions stay. For girls pursuing post graduate education in Utkal University, there is only one Adivasi Hostel near the campus located in a rented building, catering to only 48 students.

However, inside the campus, there are five ladies hostels for nearly 600 boarders, and in those hostels, special accommodations are provided for SC/ST girls. The lists of these hostels are given below:

Table: 7.2 – List of Women's Hostels in Utkal University

Sl.No.	Hostel	Students Strength
1.	Kuntala Kumari Chhatri Nibas	180
2.	Rama Devi Chhatrinibas	234
3.	Sarala Devi Chhatrinibas	62
4.	Malati Devi Chhatrinibas	100
5.	Ladies Hostel No.V	100

Thus, in Rama Devi Women's College, SC/ST girls are confined to Special Adibasi Hostel, whereas in Utkal University, they are distributed in all the women's hostels. In Mayurbhanj District, there is girls' hostel only in M.P.C. Junior College. Girls in other colleges and North Orissa University have found accommodation in private mess. So the researchers had a chance to interact with SC/ST students in the Special Hostel as well as in general hostels and private mess.

Since the special hostels are under control of SC/ST Development Department and the colleges to which they are attached are under department of Higher Education, the concerned Principals found it difficult to supervise activities of inmates as well as security. Principals are not the appointing authority for the staff of hostel and hence in case of emergency could not employ a watchman or security guard, if required. For small repairs of hostel building also they have to depend on SC/ST Development Department.

Although SC/ST students admitted that they can study better if they stayed in hostels, they had reservations about special hostels. Students, teachers and parents were asked several questions to assess their views on special hostel facility.

7.2 Opinion of Students

Most of the respondents have shown their preference for hostel for better study environment. In Rama Devi Women's College, there is a special hostel for SC/ST girls, where most of the SC/ST girls are accommodated. Utkal University has five women's hostels but a limited numbers of seats are meant specially for SC/ST students. In other colleges there is no special hostel for SC/ST students, who have to compete with general students for hostel accommodation. In general, most of the students (more then 70%) have shown their dislike for special hostel facility for fear of being identified by their caste. They would prefer integration in general hostels. Obviously, reservation of seats for SC/ST girl students in all girls' hostels is necessary.

(1) Study Opportunity

When students were asked whether they thought

opportunity for study was better in hostel than at home, a large proportion of SC girls (47.8%) have shown preference for studying at home, since many of them have their homes in urban areas. Most ST girls on the other hand, come from rural tribal areas with no educational facility. As such, they prefer staying in hostels (47.1%).

Table: 7.3 – Study Opportunity

Better Study atmosphere	SC		ST	
	No. of Students	Percen tage	No. of Students	Percen tage
At Home	54	47.8	64	40.8
At Hostel	42	37.2	74	47.1
No Response	17	15.0	19	12.1
Total	113	100	157	100

(2) Caste of Roommates

Hosteliers were asked about the castes of their room mates. Surprisingly, only 34% of SC girls and 46.2% of ST girls were found to reside with students of their

Table: 7.4 – Caste of Roommates

Caste of Room mates	SC		ST	
	No. of Students	Percen tage	No. of Students	Percen tage
Students of Same Caste	16	34.0	43	46.2
Mixed Groups	31	65.9	46	49.4
No Response	0	0	04	4.3
Total	47	100	93	100

own caste and most of them are boarders of special SC/ ST hostel. But 66% SC and 50% ST had roommates from other castes. Thus, students had no problem in sharing rooms with other caste girls. Obviously, integration of SC/ ST girls with general caste students in women's hostels does not pose much problem and is very desirable.

(3) Security in Special Hostel

Discussion was held with students regarding feeling of insecurity at the place of residence and it was found that 72% SC girls and 68% ST girls sometimes experienced lack of security and most of these girls were hosteliers. Researchers tried to find out the reasons for this feeling of insecurity in special hostel and the girls, who felt insecure, provided varied answers.

Many of them (45%) complained about not having a security guard in the hostel whereas many others (54%) expressed missing parental security which they were used to.

Table: 7.5 – Reason for Insecurity Feeling in Special Hostel

Sl. No.	Reason of Feeling Insecured	SC		ST	
		No. of Girls	Per-centage	No. of Girls	Per-centage
1.	Lack of Parental Security	06	26.1	14	30.4
2.	No Security Guard in Hostel	07	30.5	07	15.2
3.	Not Safe to Go Out in the Evening	04	17.4	10	21.7
4.	Eve-Teasing by Family Members of Hostel Staff	04	17.4	0.3	6.5
5.	No Restriction for Inmates	01	4.3	06	13.0
6.	Living with Other Caste Girls not Safe	01	4.3	06	13.4
	Total	23	100	46	100

When, at the end of research, a Seminar was held with teachers to discuss about difficulties of SC/ST students, this matter was also brought to the notice of the Superintendent of special hostel who explained that absence of security guard might be a temporary phenomenon. She promised to take the required steps to improve the sense of security among inmates. However, the problem of insecurity remains, this hostel not being situated in the college campus.

(4) Library Facility in Hostels

Library facility definitely helps SC/ST students in their pursuit of higher education. Only 84% SC girls and 73% ST girls mentioned about frequent use of college library. The remaining students offered different reasons for not using library facility in college. These included scarcity of books, overcrowding, lack of time, etc. A few students expressed ignorance about the rules regarding use of library facility.

Effort was made to find out about library facility in hostels. It was found that most of the hostels do not have such facility. Only the special hostel in Rama Devi Women's College and women's hostels in a few Engineering Colleges have library facility for inmates.

When questioned about availing the library facility in hostels, only 27% SC and 34% ST girls said to have used

Table: 7.6 – Library Facilities in Hostels

Sl. No.	Facility	SC		ST	
		Students saying 'yes'	Per-centage	Students saying 'yes'	Percentage
1.	Provision of Library in the Hostel	13	27.6	32	34.4
2.	Enough books in the Library	11	23.4	16	17.2
3.	Study Table Provided in the Library	12	25.5	23	24.7
4.	Library Asst. Present to Help	03	6.3	04	4.3

(Students staying in hostel – SC-47, ST-93)

such facility. These students mostly belonged to Adivasi Hostel (special hostel) attached to Rama Devi Women's College. However, only 23% SC girls and 17% of ST girls agreed that there were sufficient books in the library, where as others complained about scarcity of text books in the library. Some students even said that there was no place for study in the library and no library assistant was available to assist them.

Obviously, library facility in the hostels needs to be improved.

7.3 Food Provided in Hostels

As to whether the food provided in hostel was satisfactory, 40.4% of SC girls and 45.1% ST girls gave negative answers.

Table: 7.7 – Opinion about Food Provided in Hostel

Sl. No.	Opinion about Food	SC		ST	
		No. of Students	Percentage	No. of Students	Percentage
1.	Satisfactory	28	59.57	51	54.84
2.	Not Satisfactory	19	40.42	42	45.16
	Total	47	100	93	100

When the superintendent was contacted, she said that a large portion of funds collected for mess was spent on rice only, as per need and preference of students. Therefore it was difficult to provide varieties of items with the amount collected from them. (In the special Adivasi Hostel, only the establishment charge is free but food has to be paid for). Improvement in the quality of food needs to be made.

7.4 Use of Dining Hall

Students were asked whether they took their food in the common dining hall with other students. Surprisingly only 10% of SC and 18% of ST hostel students replied in the affirmative and other students provided different reasons for not using the dining hall. Even in special Adivasi Hostel, the dining hall is not used for taking food, as it is too small to accommodate all inmates even in two batches.

Table: 7.8 – Use of Dining Hall

Sl. No.	Taking Food in Dining Hall	SC		ST	
		No. of Students	Per-centage	No. of Students	Per-centage
1.	Yes, We Use	05	10.6	16	18.3
2.	Sometimes, I Eat There	11	23.4	10	10.7
3.	It is not in Use	13	27.6	41	43.1
4.	Don't Feel Comfortable	04	8.5	07	7.5
5.	It is too Crowded	03	6.4	03	3.2
6.	Prefer to Take Food in My Room with Roommates	11	23.5	16	17.2
	Total	47	100	93	100

This inconvenience was later brought to the notice of Superintendent of special hostel and she was advised to send a proposal for constructions of another dining hall. Other hostel superintendents were requested to encourage SC/ST students to dine with other students and not carry their foods to room, which was otherwise very small.

7.5 Use of Computer

It was found that computer had been provided in the Special Hostel and an instructor was engaged for teaching basics of computers. But when students were asked about their knowledge in computer, 72% of ST and 69% of SC students gave negative answers.

Fig.VII-A-Knowledge of Computer

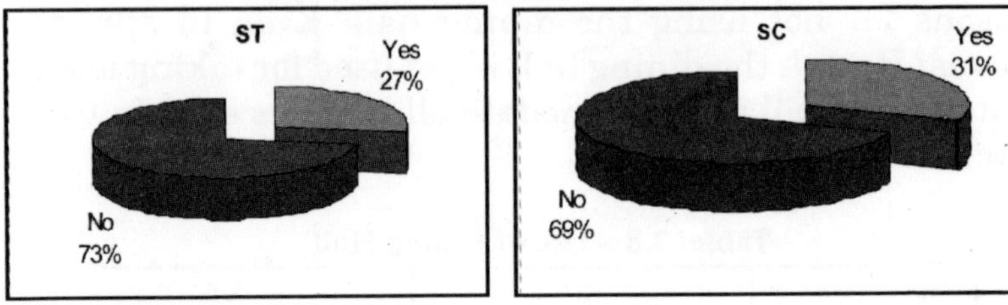

Obviously, students in hostel were not taking advantage of provision of computers for which they should be encouraged by Superintendents and other teachers.

7.6 Opinion about Provision of Special Hostel Facility

Finally, the girls were asked, regarding problems in the hostels which caused hindrance to studies. While various problems were mentioned, most of them were clearly not satisfied with special hostel facility. It was clearly visible that the condition of special hostel was not at all satisfactory compared to other general hostels of the college in matters of building, sanitation, food and security. Better supervision and maintenance by SC/ST Development Department is clearly called for.

When we visited the Special Adivasi Hostel in Rama Devi Women's College, the students freely expressed their discontentment about the existing state of affairs.

7.7 Opinion of Teachers

When teachers were asked about their opinion on special hostel facility for SC/ST girls, only 26.7% said that it was definitely useful for progress of SC/ST education. However, a majority (77.3%) felt that this type of hostel created alienation of SC/ST students from general caste students and brought about inferiority complex in them. It would be better if they are accommodated in general hostels with other girls, they opined.

Students in Special Hostel Adivasi Hostel with Supdt.

Fig.VII-B- Opinion of Teachers about Special Hostel Facility

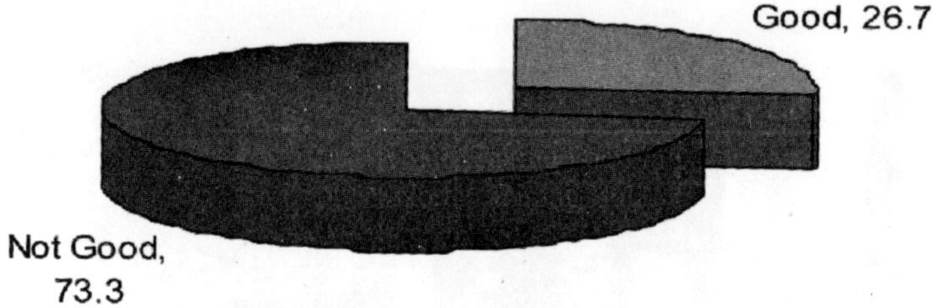

7.8 Opinion of Parents

Mostly SC/ST parents were of the opinion that there should be special hostel for their girls attached to each educational institution, so that more SC/ST girls can be accommodated. They seemed to be reluctant to leave their girls in town, unless there is a secured place like a special hostel. However, most of the educated parents felt that their daughters should be allowed to compete with other girls and stay in general hostel. Caste should not be a criterion for segregation, they felt.

7.9 Conclusion

There are only two government-run Special Women's Hostels for SC/ST students at Post-matric stage, one at Bhubaneswar and the other at Rourkela. The Indira Gandhi Women's Hostel at Bhubaneswar accommodates girl students only from Rama Devi Women's College (total 230 out of which 90% ST and 10% SC), whereas the one at Rourkela accommodates students from different colleges in the city. However, these hostels are run directly by SC/ST Development Department and as such, the concerned Principals found it difficult to control activities of the hostels.

Many (70%) SC/ST students did not like the special hostel facility; 60% did not like the food; 32% complained about improper security and study atmosphere and about 82% SC/ST girls said that they felt alienated from the mainstream because of stay in separate hostel. 77.3% of teachers also felt strongly against this separate hostel arrangement.

Our researchers felt that the SC/ST students, who stayed with general girls in hostels of Utkal University, were quite smart and were free in expressing their views whereas students in Indira Gandhi Women's Hostel of Rama Devi Women's College (Special Adivasi Hostel) seemed rather diffident and were unhappy that they had been put in a separate hostel exclusively meant for SC/ST students. In general, most SC/ST girls do not want special hostel facility in a general college. Actually, on the insistence of tribal girls in 2005, three of them, who came in merit, were allotted seats in Anyatama Hostel of Rama Devi women's College, meant for general students. The matron of the hostel, Suramani Putty, (herself a tribal woman) said that there was never any complaint from any of the boarders in this regard. Therefore, instead of providing special hostel for SC/ST girls, reservation of seats for them in general hostels is a better option. Of course, the stipend provided to SC/ST students should be increased to meet the extra expenditure in general hostels. Such integration would be good for confidence building and better performance.

8

FUTURE PROSPECTS: ATTAINMENT OF SC/ST GIRLS IN HIGEHR EDUCATIONAL INSTITUTIONS

To study the attainment of SC/ST girls with regard to their performance in examination, effort was made to trace their results from different institutions and universities and compare the same with the results of general caste girls and SC/ST boys. However, it was an extremely difficult task, since in the result records, only roll numbers (not names) are mentioned and no mention of caste is made anywhere. Even in the result of Secondary and Higher Secondary Examination of the State, though record is maintained about pass percentage of SC/ST, it is not done separately for boys and girls. So with a great deal of difficulty, the results of SC/ST girls were collected from the Board/Council office. In different institutions, examination roll numbers were matched with their college roll numbers and from the old records of their year of admission, their caste was ascertained. It was a very difficult exercise and in some colleges old admission records were not traceable. However, in almost all colleges, results of at least two consecutive years could be collected and analyzed.

8.1 Result of High School Certificate Examiantion

The percentage of pass of SC/ST students in High School certificate examination, which is conducted by Board of Secondary Education, is always lower than general students. For example, in 2006, the percentage of success among SC/ST candidates was recorded as 42.57% and 37.53% respectively, while the overall percentage of success recorded as 52.49% (including General, SC, ST students). Not only that, a matter of concern is also that among the SC/ST boys and girls, who are able to pass matriculation, most of them get only 3rd division or at best 2nd division. Very few get first division and hence fail to get entry into colleges. Division-wise placement of these passed candidates is given below in percentage.

Table: 8.1 – Percentage of Pass in Different Divisions in H.S.C. Examination

Category	Year	Boys			Girls		
		1st Div.	2nd Div.	3rd Div.	1st Div	2nd Div.	3rd Div.
General	2000	14.35	21.45	21.34	9.33	17.05	16.45
	2001	14.47	20.57	22.26	9.32	16.19	17.19
	2002	14.60	20.36	23.04	9.17	15.61	17.19
	2003	14.19	20.24	21.65	9.77	16.67	17.44
	2004	13.90	19.80	21.81	9.55	16.56	18.05
SC	2000	8.7	23.9	31.6	4.1	13.9	17.7
	2001	9.2	22.0	33.6	3.7	12.2	19.2
	2002	8.5	22.3	33.8	4.1	12.8	18.5
	2003	8.4	22.2	32.1	4.4	13.6	19.2
	2004	8.5	21.8	32.5	3.9	13.1	20.1
ST	2000	7.0	23.9	38.9	2.5	10.7	16.9
	2001	6.7	21.6	38.4	2.8	10.5	20.0
	2002	4.5	22.3	37.9	2.6	11.9	19.9
	2003	6.3	22.6	36.8	2.9	11.9	19.5
	2004	5.7	21.8	36.5	2.8	12.4	20.7

(*Source* : Board of Secondary Education)

Fig. VIII-A- Pass Percentage in H.S.C. in Different Divisions (2004)

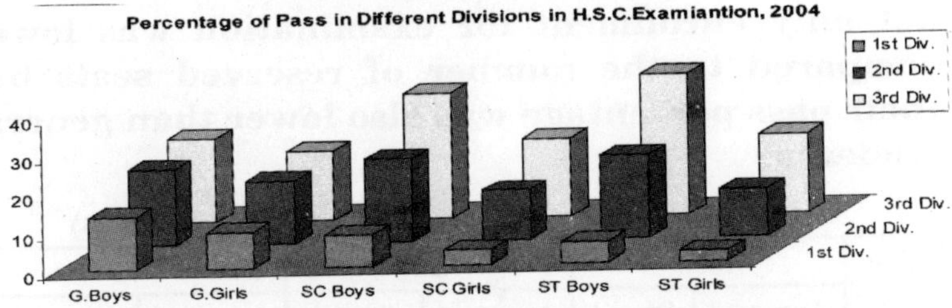

As seen from the result of five consecutive years, the percentage of SC/ST among passed candidates in different divisions hardly varies over the year. The percentage of SC/ST girls in 1st Division remains between 4% and 3%, whereas that of general caste girls is nearly 10%. Result of SC/ST girls is also much lower compared to that of SC/ST boys, which is about 9% and 6% for SCs and STs respectively. Similarly, in second and third division, their percentage is less than general girls. So we conclude that in matriculation (H.S.C.) examination, performance of SC/ST girls is significantly lower than general caste girls and also than SC/ST boys. It would be desirable for the State Board to publish pass percentage of boys and girls separately in case of SC/ST as they do it for the total result. Comparing SC and ST, SC boys and girls show slightly better result than ST boys and girls.

8.2 Result of Higher Secondary Examination

(1) Percentage of SC/ST Students

Higher Secondary Examination (after +2 level, Class XI/XII) in the State is conducted by Council of Higher Secondary Education (CHSE) in three streams (Arts, Science and Commerce) separately and result is declared in different phases. Comparatively, more SC/ST students are found passing out in Arts stream than in Science or Commerce stream. Result of CHSE Examination for six consecutive years (2001-2006) was analysed and tabulated (Table 8.2, 8.3, 8.4). **It was found that not only enrollment for examination was lower compared to the number of reserved seats but their pass percentage was also lower than general students.**

Table: 8.2 – Result of C.H.S.E. Examination (+2 Arts)

Year	Total		SC		ST	
	Appeared	Passed	Appeared	Passed	Appeared	Passed
2000	1,70,344	50,039 (34.65)	17,973	5,244 (29.17)	14,106	4,409 (31.25)
2001	1,47,968	44,053 (29.77)	15,444	3,532 (23.21)	13,581	2,895 (21.31)
2002	1,24,205	66,043 (53.17)	12,737	5,960 (46.79)	11,912	5,256 (44.12)
2003	96,683	65,577 (57.48)	9,586	4,932 (51.45)	9,310	4,445 (47.74)
2004	1,00,090	79,393 (79.39)	10,157	7,441 (73.25)	9,758	7,070 (72.45)
2005	1,03,320	72,988 (70.64)	10,245	6,722 (64.47)	10,714	6,631 (61.89)
2006	1,05,600	64,280 (60.87)	11,345	6,487 (57.17)	12,006	6,211 (51.73)

(Numbers in the parentheses indicate percentage)

In 2006, in +2 Arts, though percentage of pass for general category is 60.57%, it is 57.17% for SC and 51.73% for ST category.

Table: 8.3 – Result of C.H.S.E. Examination (+2 Science)

Year	Total		SC		ST	
	Appeared	Passed	Appeared	Passed	Appeared	Passed
2000	50,434	24,632 (52.75)	3,331	1,217 (40.13)	2,595	790 (32.91)
2001	52,136	20,013 (38.36)	3,490	983 (28.16)	2,916	601 (30.60)
2002	52,565	27,106 (51.57)	3,323	1,299 (39.09)	2,820	849 (30.10)

2003	45,389	27,036 (59.57)	2,800	1,339 (46.44)	2,535	974 (38.42)
2004	43,388	33,189 (76.49)	2,883	1,913 (66.35)	2,592	1,643 (63.38)
2005	42,322	30,119 (71.17)	2,705	1,590 (58.78)	2,515	1,318 (52.40)
2006	45,561	31,389 (70.37)	2,880	1,698 (60.31)	2,806	1,377 (50.75)

(Numbers in the parentheses indicate percentage)

In Science, percentage of pass in general, SC and ST categories are 70.37%, 60.31% and 50.75% respectively.

Table: 8.4 – Result of C.H.S.E. Examination (+2 Commerce)

Year	Total		SC		ST	
	Appeared	Passed	Appeared	Passed	Appeared	Passed
2000	15,720	7,172 (45.62)	946	291 (30.70)	908	233 (25.66)
2001	14,412	6,469 (44.88)	879	245 (27.87)	825	223 (27.03)
2002	13,134	7,771 (59.17)	811	376 (46.36)	730	253 (34.65)
2003	11,655	7,128 (61.16)	647	295 (45.59)	624	241 (38.62)
2004	12,500	9,803 (78.42)	660	435 (65.90)	620	393 (63.38)
2005	12,083	9,055 (74.94)	610	400 (65.57)	612	378 (61.16)
2006	12,102	9,143 (76.65)	619	418 (68.3)	548	287 (54.15)

(***Source*** – Board of Secondary Education, Orissa)

(The numbers in the parentheses indicates percentage)

In Commerce, the percentage of pass for General, SC and ST category are 76.6%, 68.3% and 54.1% respectively.

One encouraging factor to note is that percentage of pass of SC/ST students increased over the years along with percentage of total students.

Fig. VIII-B Percentage of SC/ST Students Passed in CHSE in 2006

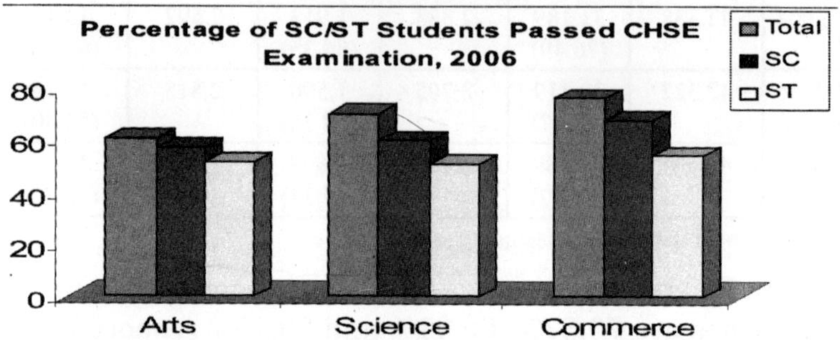

(2) Percentage of SC/ST Girls

Next, we tried to assess the proportion of girl students passed in different streams compared to boy students in same category. It was found that the proportion of girls in SC/ST category appearing for examination is much less compared to their proportion in general category, but their pass percentage seemed to be better than SC/ST boys (except for ST girls in Arts).

It is observed that in all the three streams and both for boys and girls, the pass percentage of SC/ST is always less than that of general students. But surprisingly in all the streams in a particular category (i.e. general/SC/ST) girls showed better result than boys (except for ST in Arts). For example, in +2 Science in 2006 examination, for general category, the percentage of pass for boys and girls is 72.8 and 77.07 respectively. For SCs, this is 65.28 and 68.29 and for STs 50.14 and 57.39 respectively. **Thus, not only for general category, in all the three cast categories, girls seem to be more sincere in studies and show better performance. In Commerce, pass rate for general girls is 90.85% as compared to 76.8% for boys. For SC and ST, it is 81.08% and 59.55% for girls as compared to 68.29 and 54.02 for boys. This is quite remarkable. This shows girls are keen to study in college and SC/ST girls show better in**

Table : 8.5 – Pass Percentage of SC/ST Girls in C.H.S.E. Examination Result of 2006

STREAM		General		SC		ST	
		Appeared	Passed	Appeared	Passed	Appeared	Passed
ARTS	Boys	33,096	19,650 (59.37)	5,541	3,222 (58.14)	5,695	3,073 (53.95)
	Girls	37,854	25,536 (67.45)	3,900	2,289 (58.69)	4,128	2,087 (50.55)
SCIENCE	Boys	22,894	16,689 (72.89)	1,541	952 (61.77)	1,418	711 (50.14)
	Girls	10,840	8,355 (77.07)	625	408 (65.28)	676	388 (57.39)
COMMERCE	Boys	7,783	5,978 (76.80)	429	293 (68.29)	335	181 (54.02)
	Girls	1,741	1,573 (90.35)	74	60 (81.08)	89	53 (59.55)

(The number in the parentheses indicates percentage)
(Source – Council of Higher Secondary Education)

particular performance when come to college and hence deserve more encouragement. This trend has been there for quite sometime.

(3)Placement of SC/ST Students in Different Divisions

Next, we proceeded to find out the distribution of these SC/ST students who passed in different division according to marks secured by them and to compare the same with general caste students passing out in that division.

Table - 8.6 - Students Passed in Different Divisions in+2 Arts

Category	Year	Total No. of Students Passed	1st Div.	2nd Div.	3rd Div.	Compart-ment
Total Students	2001	44,053	1,302 (2.95)	6,242 (14.19)	31,673 (71.89)	4,836 (10.97)
	2002	66,043	2,298 (3.47)	11,178 (16.92)	47,805 (72.38)	4,761 (7.20)
	2003	55,577	2,189 (3.93)	11,720 (21.08)	38,385 (69.06)	3,282 (5.90)
	2004	77,393	5,130 (6.46)	22,696 (28.58)	49,085 (61.82)	2,482 (3.12)
	2005	72,988	3,921 (5.37)	17,896 (24.51)	50,272 (68.87)	899 (1.23)
	2006	64,280	3,844 (5.98)	15,020 (23.36)	44,309 (68.93)	1,106 (1.72)
SC Students	2001	3,532	30 (0.84)	362 (10.24)	2,779 (70.86)	361 (10.13)
	2002	5,960	104 (1.74)	890 (14.93)	4,630 (77.68)	336 (5.63)
	2003	4,932	101 (2.04)	917 (18.59)	3,647 (73.94)	267 (5.41)
	2004	7,441	345 (4.63)	1,929 (25.92)	4,967 (66.75)	200 (2.68)
	2005	6,722	208 (3.09)	1,512 (22.49)	4,908 (73.01)	94 (1.39)
	2006	6,487	249 (3.83)	1,398 (21.55)	4,773 (73.57)	67 (1.03)

ST Students	2001	2,895	21 (0.72)	288 (9.94)	2,360 (81.51)	226 (7.80)
	2002	5,256	76 (1.44)	722 (13.73)	4,210 (80.09)	248 (4.71)
	2003	4,445	54 (1.21)	664 (14.93)	3,491 (78.53)	236 (5.30)
	2004	7,070	214 (3.02)	1,651 (23.35)	5,060 (71.57)	145 (2.05)
	2005	6,631	141 (2.12)	1,249 (18.83)	5,202 (78.44)	39 (0.58)
	2006	6,211	142 (2.28)	1,092 (17.58)	4,916 (79.14)	61 (0.98)

(The number in the parentheses indicates percentage)
(*Source* – Council of Higher Secondary Education)

Table-8.7- Students Passed in Different Divisions in +2 Science

Category	Year	Total No. of Students Passed	1st Div.	2nd Div.	3rd Div.	Compart-ment
Total Students	2001	20,213	2,812 (14.05)	4,291 (21.44)	12,011 (50.01)	862 (4.30)
	2002	27,106	4,749 (17.52)	6,270 (23.31)	14,517 (52.81)	1,160 (4.27)
	2003	27,036	4,763 (17.61)	6,953 (25.71)	14,250 (52.70)	1,010 (3.73)
	2004	33,189	7,910 (23.83)	10,993 (38.12)	13,512 (40.71)	715 (2.15)
	2005	30,119	6,966 (23.12)	9,876 (32.78)	13,128 (43.17)	197 (0.65)
	2006	31,389	8,320 (26.50)	10,380 (33.06)	12,128 (38.63)	408 (1.24)
SC Students	2001	983	74 (7.52)	162 (16.48)	701 (7131)	43 (4.37)
	2002	1,299	127 (9.77)	270 (20.78)	851 (65.51)	45 (3.46)
	2003	1,339	133 (9.93)	297 (22.18)	868 (64.82)	39 (2.91)

	2004	1,913	275 (14.37)	614 (32.09)	978 (51.12)	41 (2.14)
	2005	1,590	222 (13.96)	460 (28.93)	895 (56.28)	7 (0.44)
	2006	1,698	260 (15.31)	544 (32.03)	856 (50.41)	27 (1.59)
ST Students	2001	601	24 (3.99)	89 (14.80)	463 (77.03)	25 (4.15)
	2002	849	45 (5.30)	154 (18.13)	611 (71.96)	35 (4.12)
	2003	974	60 (6.16)	179 (18.37)	696 (71.45)	38 (3.90)
	2004	1,643	145 (8.82)	500 (30.43)	965 (58.73)	27 (1.64)
	2005	1,318	104 (7.89)	331 (25.11)	872 (66.16)	11 (0.83)
	2006	1,377	143 (10.38)	419 (30.42)	803 (58.31)	9 (0.65)

(The number in the parentheses indicates percentage)
(*Source* – Council of Higher Secondary Education)

Table: 8.8 – Students Passed in Different Divisions in +2 Commerce

Category	Year	Total No. of Students passed	1st Div.	2nd Div.	3rd Div.	Compart-mental
Total Students	2001	6,469	594 (9.18)	1,071 (16.55)	4,672 (72.22)	132 (2.04)
	2002	7,771	1,217 (15.66)	1,553 (19.98)	4,769 (61.36)	232 (2.98)
	2003	7,128	932 (13.07)	1,626 (22.81)	4,451 (62.44)	119 (1.66)
	2004	9,803	1,679 (17.12)	2,671 (27.24)	5,263 (53.68)	190 (1.93)
	2005	9,055	1,615 (17.83)	2,354 (25.99)	5,048 (55.68)	38 (0.41)
	2006	9,143	2,090 (22.8)	2,146 (23.47)	4,835 (52.88)	72 (0.78)

SC Students	2001	245	4 (1.63)	25 (10.20)	211 (86.12)	5 (2.04)
	2002	376	15 (3.98)	50 (13.29)	302 (80.31)	9 (2.39)
	2003	300	14 (4.66)	69 (23.0)	212 (70.66)	5 (1.66)
	2004	435	36 (8.27)	91 (20.91)	299 (68.73)	9 (2.06)
	2005	400	44 (11.0)	99 (24.75)	256 (64.0)	1 (0.25)
	2006	418	59 (14.11)	96 (22.96)	262 (62.67)	1 (0.23)
ST Students	2001	223	5 (2.24)	45 (20.17)	172 (77.13)	1 (0.44)
	2002	253	17 (6.71)	36 (14.22)	199 (78.65)	1 (0.39)
	2003	254	12 (4.72)	34 (13.38)	195 (76.77)	13 (5.11)
	2004	393	19 (4.83)	87 (22.13)	284 (72.26)	3 (0.76)
	2005	378	31 (8.20)	77 (20.37)	268 (70.89)	2 (0.52)
	2006	287	25 (8.71)	46 (16.02)	216 (75.26)	0 (0.0)

(The number in the parentheses indicates percentage)
(*Source* – Council of Higher Secondary Education)

Analysis of Result -

From the six-year record of result of C.H.S.E. (Arts, Science and Commerce) it was observed that:

(i) In all the three streams, percentage of students of all categories is maximum in Third Division and the least in First Division. But the difference between the two is much more in case of SC/ST. The performance of SC/ST students in H.S.C. Examination is comparatively weaker in all the streams, Arts, Science and Commerce. Obviously, significant gap between educational attainments of general caste students compared to SC/ST students persists;

(ii) Percentage of students passing in 1st Division is more in Science, than in Commerce and least in Arts. Even SC/ST students' performance is better in Science and Commerce than in Arts. For example, for SCs average pass percentage in 1st Division, in Arts is 1.79 whereas it is 11.81 in Science and 7.33 in Commerce. Probably better SC/ST students opt for Science and Commerce for good job prospects. Students of marginal merit opt for Arts because of limited competition and easier curriculum;

(iii) In all the categories, the percentage of pass in 1st Division was found to be increasing over the years and percentage in 3rd Division decreasing. Thus, SC/ST students' performance seems to be gradually getting better over the years, obviously due to greater awareness and hard work;

(iv) Percentage of girl students in different divisions was not available separately in the Council office, but as seen in individual colleges, girls always performed better than boys, even in case of SCs and STs.

8.3 Result of Utkal University

It was a difficult task to get the results from Utkal University, since the results had to be collected from all the 27 Departments separately. As the result of different departments are published at different times and then sent to Central Office, no centralized data was available. Moreover, nowhere in the result, mention of caste of students was made and so matching of their Roll Numbers in Admission Register and separating the SC/ST students from the list was to be done before recording the results.

8.3.1 Result of Utkal University in Different Streams

After collecting data from 27 departments [enclosed

at Annexure – VII(A)] they were grouped in five categories i.e. Arts, Science, Commerce, Professional Course and Law for analysis. This has also been done for study of

Table: 8.9 – Result of Utkal University, 2003

Year	Subject	Total Strength	Category (SC/ST)	Sex (Boys/ Girls)	Result				
					Total	I	II	III	Fail
2003	Arts	734	SC	Boys	35	6	13	3	5
				Girls	36	13	13	4	0
			ST	Boys	31	7	12	4	3
				Girls	21	2	10	3	2
	Science	211	SC	Boys	8	0	2	0	0
				Girls	4	1	0	0	1
			ST	Boys	7	4	1	0	0
				Girls	6	4	1	0	0
	Commerce	48	SC	Boys	2	0	1	0	1
				Girls	3	1	0	0	0
			ST	Boys	3	1	0	0	0
				Girls	2	0	0	0	0
	Professional Courses	126	SC	Boys	5	2	1	0	0
				Girls	6	5	1	0	0
			ST	Boys	9	5	3	0	1
				Girls	5	3	0	0	1
	Law	25	SC	Boys	3	2	1	0	0
				Girls	1	0	0	0	0
			ST	Boys	0	0	0	0	0
				Girls	1	0	0	0	0

Table: 8.10 – Result of Utkal University, 2004

Year	Subject	Total Strength	Category (SC/ST)	Sex (Boys/ Girls)	Result				
					Total	I	II	III	Fail
2004	Arts	748	SC	Boys	32	8	17	4	1
				Girls	42	17	19	2	0
			ST	Boys	35	15	13	3	0
				Girls	21	5	4	2	1

	Science	223	SC	Boys	10	6	1	1	0
				Girls	7	7	1	0	0
			ST	Boys	14	7	2	0	0
				Girls	6	5	0	0	0
	Commerce	45	SC	Boys	3	1	2	0	0
				Girls	2	2	0	0	0
			ST	Boys	6	1	1	0	0
				Girls	0	0	0	0	0
	Professional Courses	137	SC	Boys	6	5	0	0	0
				Girls	4	2	1	0	0
			ST	Boys	6	1	3	0	0
				Girls	9	7	1	0	0
	Law	25	SC	Boys	2	0	1	0	0
				Girls	1	0	1	0	0
			ST	Boys	2	0	1	0	0
				Girls	0	0	0	0	0

Fig.VIII-C- Utkal University Results, 2004 (Arts)

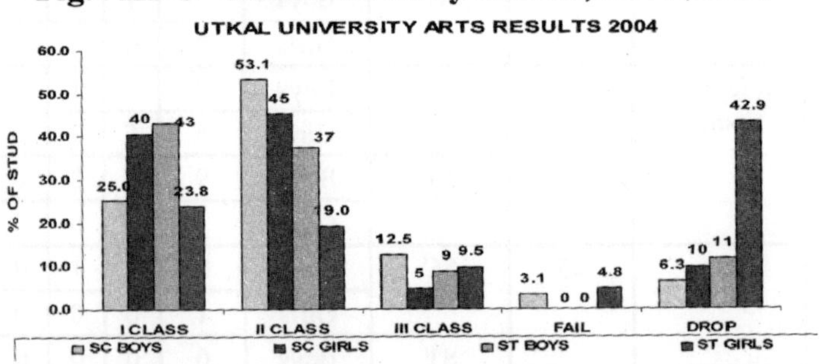

Fig.VIII-D- Utkal University Results, 2004 (Science)

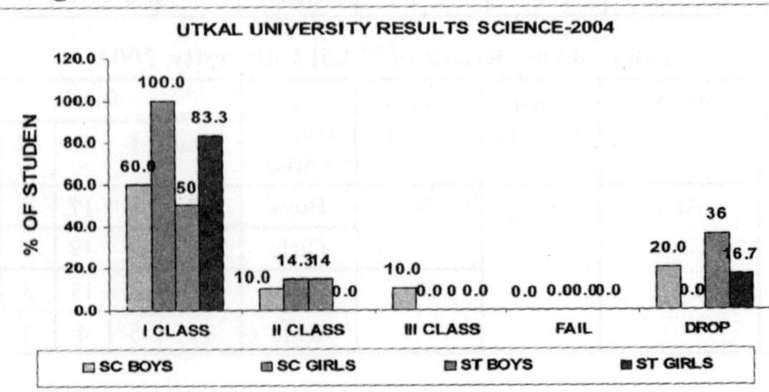

Fig.VIII-E-UtkalUniversityResults, 2004 (Commerce)

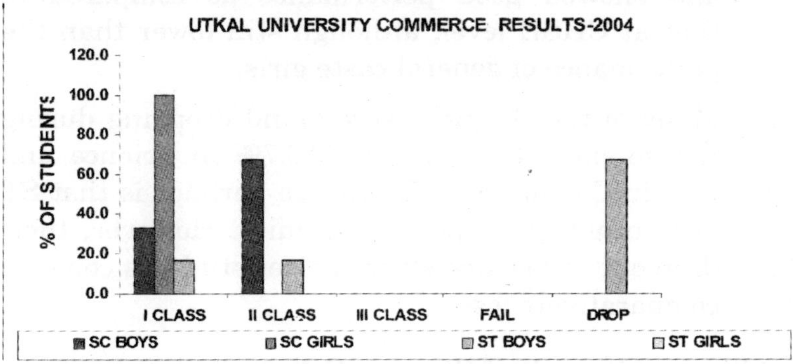

enrolment.

The difference between the total number of students in the class and number of students whose result was published (including, 1st, 2nd, 3rd and Fail category), indicated the number of students dropping out.

8.3.2 Analysis of Result

(i) From the record of result it was observed that in different departments not only the number of SC/ST students is less, but their performance is lower than that of general students, e.g. percentage of pass of general candidates in 1st Division is much higher than the percentage of SC/ST candidates;

(ii) However, when result of SC/ST girls was compared with that of SC/ST boys, it was found that SC/ST girls did much better than boys in all the branches, particularly in Science. For example, in 2004, in Science, out of 10 SC boys 6 got first class whereas in case of girls, all the 7 girls got first class. Similarly, for ST, out of the 14 boys 7 got first class whereas out of 6 ST girls 5 got first class. Most of the SC/ST girls got first class in Science. Thus, girls at Post Graduate level seemed to be sincere in studies and showed good performance as compared to that at CHSE level, although still lower than the performance of general caste girls;

(iii) Many of the ST girls were found dropping during the session (42% in Arts, 16.7% in Science and 65% in Commerce). The reason perhaps is that ST girls could not cope with studies. However, their drop out in Science where better students come, is comparatively less.

8.4 Result of Rama Devi Women's College

The results at +2, +3 and P.G. level were collected from college office and Controller's office (Autonomous Section) for three consecutive years (2003, 2004, 2005) and analysed.

8.4.1 Post Graduate Level

In P.G. classes, there were very few SC/ST students and they secured first division or second division like other girls. But the number securing first division is less than general caste girls.

8.4.2 Degree Level

At Graduate level, the result was recorded for each Honours subject separately, i.e. 12 subjects in Arts, 6 subjects in Science and 2 subjects in Commerce, and then grouped under three categories. It was observed that, at Graduate level, students mostly got 1st class or 2nd class in different Honours subjects [Result enclosed–Annexure –VII (B)], and very few passed without Honours (GPWH). The percentage of girls graduating in 1st division is maximum in Science (more than 95%), followed by Commerce (more than 80%) and then in Arts (about 65%). For SCs and STs also, the same pattern follows. However, performance of ST girls was lower than SC and general

Table: 8.11 – Percentage SC/ST Girls in Different Divisions at +3 Level in Rama Devi Women's College

Stream	Year	Category	Total	I Div.	II Div.	G.P.W.H.
Arts	2003	General	334	215 (64.3)	114 (34.1)	5 (1.5)
		SC	13	8 (61.5)	5(38.5)	0 (0)
		ST	5	3 (60)	2 (40)	0 (0)
	2004	General	314	213 (67.8)	99 (31.5)	2 (0.6)
		SC	20	12(60)	7 (35)	1 (5)
		ST	20	9 (45)	11 (55)	0 (0)
	2005	General	369	244 (66.1)	111 (30)	11 (2.9)
		SC	21	7 (33.3)	14 (66.7)	0 (0)
		ST	16	5 (31.3)	7 (44)	1 (6.3)
Science	2003	General	64	63 (98.4)	1 (1.5)	0 (0)
		SC	2	2 (100)	0 (0)	0 (0)
		ST	4	3 (75)	0 (0)	1 (25)
	2004	General	77	76 (98.7	1 (1.3)	0 (0)
		SC	4	4 (100)	0 (0)	0 (0)
		ST	5	2 (40)	2 (40)	1 (20)
	2005	General	60	57 (95)	3 (5)	0 (0)
		SC	12	11 (91.7)	1 (8.3)	0 (0)
		ST	10	6 (60)	4 (40)	0 (0)
Commerce	2003	General	58	57 (98.3)	0 (0)	1 (1.7)
		SC	1	1 (100)	0 (0)	0 (0)
		ST	0	0 (0)	0 (0)	0 (0)
	2004	General	73	62 (84.9)	10 (13.7)	1 (1.4)
		SC	3	3 (100)	0 (0)	0 (0)
		ST	2	2 (100)	0 (0)	0 (0)
	2005	General	72	58 (80.6)	12 (16.6)	2 (2.8)
		SC	5	4 (80)	0 (0)	1 (20)
		ST	3	3 (100)	0 (0)	0 (0)

(Numbers in Parentheses indicate percentage)

(Source – Office of Rama Devi Junior College)

girl students. The percentage of pass of SC/ST girls in the three streams is given in the following table.

Thus, there were very few SC/ST girls in +3 courses and they seem to be doing well like general students.

Fig.VIII-F-, +3 Level Results of Rama Devi Women's College, 2003, 2004 and 2005

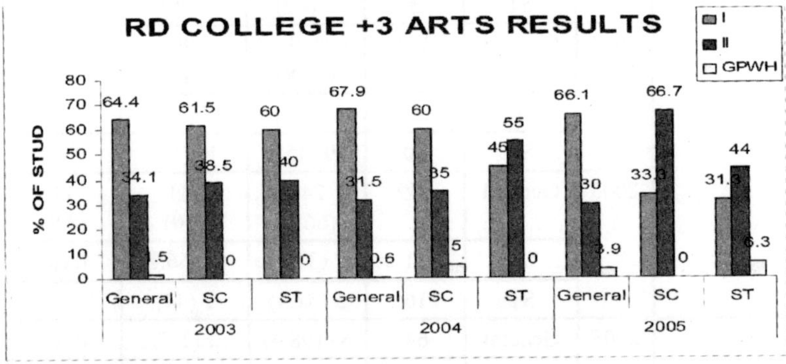

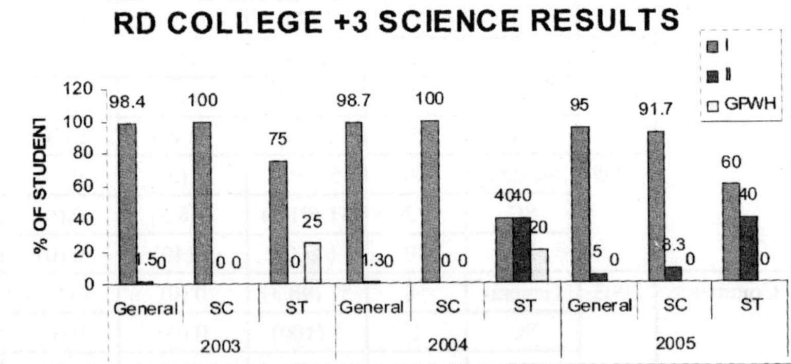

However, performance of SC girls was found better than tribal girls, particularly in Science.

8.4.3 +2 Level (Rama Devi Junior College)

In +2 classes, the percentage of SC students passing in 1st/2nd/3rd division is less than general students but that of STs is much less than both categories. Percentage of students failing in examination is just in the reverse

Table: 8.12 – Results of Rama Devi College (Junior) for +2 Classes

Stream	Year	Category	Total Students	I Div.	II Div.	III Div.	Fail
Arts	2003	General	411	63 (15.3)	82 (19.9)	205 (49.9)	61 (14.8)
		SC	56	0 (0)	6 (10.7)	29 (51.8)	21 (37.5)
		ST	50	1 (2.0)	1 (2.0)	19 (38)	29 (58)
	2004	General	395	52 (13.2)	76 (19.2)	193 (48.8)	74 (18.7)
		SC	41	1 (2.4)	8 (19.5)	19 (46.2)	13 (31.7)
		ST	73	2 (2.7)	1 (1.4)	28 (38.4)	42 (57.5)
	2005	General	410	80 (19.5)	62 (15.1)	247 (60.2)	21 (5.1)
		SC	62	3 (4.8)	11 (17.7)	35 (56.4)	13 (21)
		ST	70	2 (2.8)	5 (7.1)	35 (50)	28 (40)
Science	2003	General	227	117 (51.5)	62 (27.3)	35 (15.4)	13 (5.7)
		SC	19	2 (10.5)	4 (21)	7 (36.8)	6 (31.6)
		ST	29	2 (6.9)	4 (13.8)	9 (31)	14 (48.2)
	2004	General	219	137 (62.5)	46 (21)	17 (17.7)	19 (18.7)
		SC	26	6 (23.1)	9 (34.6)	6 (23.1)	5 (19.2)
		ST	32	5 (15.6)	3 (9.4)	12 (37.5)	12 (37.5)
	2005	General	215	146 (67.9)	41 (19.1)	18 (8.4)	10 (4.6)
		SC	22	6 (27.2)	7 (31.8)	3 (13.6)	6 (27.3)
		ST	33	3 (9.1)	5 (15.1)	14 (42.4)	11 (33.3)

Commerce	2003	General	118	41 (34.7)	28 (23.7)	30 (25.4)	19 (16.1)
		SC	2	0 (0)	0 (0)	1 (50)	1 (50)
		ST	4	1 (25)	1 (25)	2 (50)	0 (0)
	2004	General	124	55 (44.3)	42 (33.8)	12 (9.7)	15 (12.1)
		SC	3	0 (0)	0 (0)	1 (33.3)	2 (66.6)
		ST	6	1 (16.7)	0 (0)	1 (16.7)	4 (66.6)
	2005	General	119	61 (51.3)	19 (15.9)	15 (12.6)	24 (20.2)
		SC	9	0 (0)	2 (22.2)	3 (33.3)	4 (44.4)
		ST	4	0 (0)	1 (25)	1 (25)	2 (50)

(Numbers in Parentheses indicate percentage)
(Source – Office of Rama Devi Junior College)

order. With much difficulty, the result of SC/ST students could be recorded by first locating their names and caste in admission register, then their examination roll number from Council papers and finally their performance from the published result. The results for three years can be assessed from the following table.

As seen clearly from the table, percentage of pass in all the divisions for SC/ST students is less than general students while the percentage in fail category is maximum for ST students (e.g.57% in Arts, 37% in Science and 66%

Fig.VIII-G +2 Level Results of Rama Devi Women's College, 2004

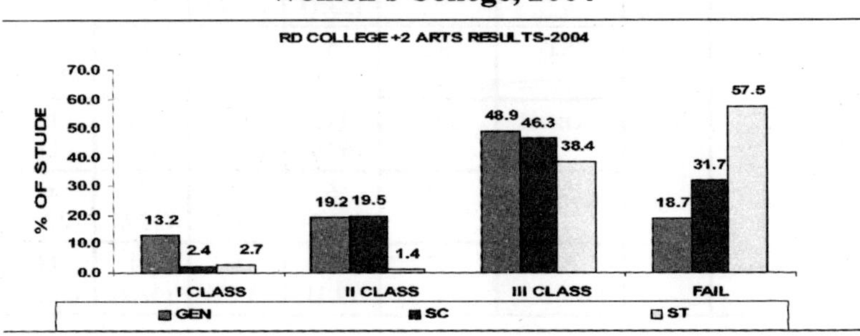

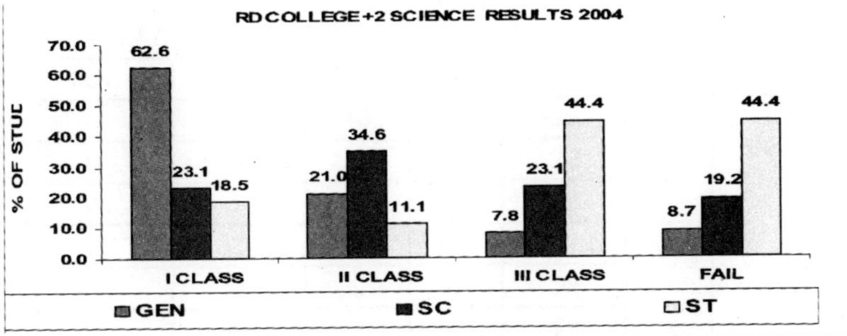

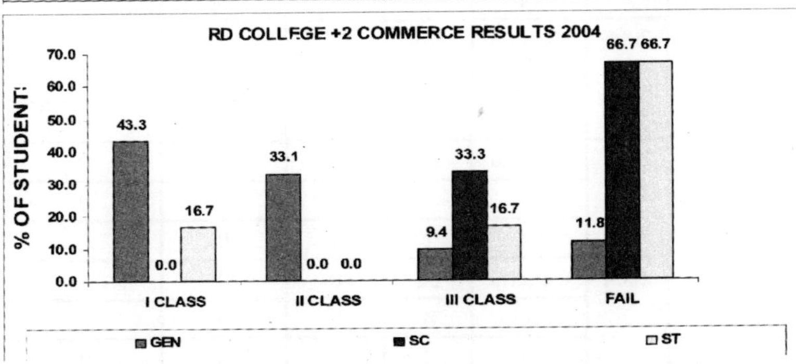

in Commerce in 2004). Obviously, SC/ST girls at higher secondary stage need extra care regarding studies.

8.5 Result of B.J.B. College

In B.J.B. College (Autonomous) meant for graduate students, honours is offered in 14 Arts subjects, 7 Science subjects and 2 Commerce subjects. There is no post graduate course in this college.

8.5.1 Degree Level (+3 level)

As seen from enrolment records (Chapter-III), in +3 classes the number of SC/ST students is very less and that of girls is negligible. These girls seemed to do very well in Science (almost 100% first class). In Arts and Commerce; more got first class than second class. Result for three years was collected for each honours subject separately and then collated into three groups, Arts, Science and Commerce. The combined result for SC/ST

Table: 8.13 – Result of Girls in B.J.B. College at +3 Level

Stream	Year	Category	I	II	GPWH	Fail
Arts	2003	General	178	61	6	0
		SC	5	3	0	0
		ST	1	1	0	0
	2004	General	151	46	2	1
		SC	7	2	0	0
		ST	3	2	0	0
	2005	General	169	75	7	0
		SC	8	0	2	0
		ST	0	0	0	0
Science	2003	General	29	5	0	0
		SC	3	1	0	0
		ST	2	1	0	0
	2004	General	32	0	0	1
		SC	4	0	0	0
		ST	2	0	0	0
	2005	General	32	5	0	0
		SC	1	1	0	0
		ST	2	0	0	0
Commerce	2003	General	50	7	0	0
		SC	1	1	1	0
		ST	1	1	1	0
	2004	General	53	7	0	0
		SC	1	1	0	0
		ST	3	2	0	0
	2005	General	49	18	0	0
		SC	0	1	1	0
		ST	0	0	0	0

girls has been given in the following table. The result of General/SC/ST students, both for boys and girls, is enclosed at Annexure–VII(C).

As seen from the table, although few in number, most SC/ST girls have performed well; none of them has failed and very few missed honours.

8.5.2 +2 level (Higher Secondary Level)

Table: 8.14 – Result of Girls in B.J.B. College at +2 Level

Stream	Year	Category	I	II	GPWH	Fail
Arts	2003	General	54	59	80	29
		SC	1	6	12	10
		ST	0	1	2	4
	2004	General	29	43	89	50
		SC	0	2	1	4
		ST	0	0	2	3
	2005	General	77	68	80	42
		SC	2	5	20	21
		ST	0	1	3	4
Science	2003	General	92	15	8	15
		SC	1	3	0	1
		ST	4	1	1	1
	2004	General	97	19	10	14
		SC	4	2	0	0
		ST	1	1	1	1
	2005	General	99	25	46	15
		SC	2	0	2	3
		ST	1	2	1	3
Commerce	2003	General	16	10	2	4
		SC	0	0	0	0
		ST	0	0	0	0
	2004	General	22	3	3	3
		SC	0	1	1	0
		ST	0	0	0	1
	2005	General	29	2	8	6
		SC	2	1	3	2
		ST	0	0	1	1

In B.J.B. Junior College (for +2 classes), performance of SC/ST girls was found very poor as compared to general girls. Particularly in Arts, very few SC girls secured first class and no ST girls did so.

As seen from the table, very few SC/ST girls got first class. In Arts, it is within 5% for SC and 0% for ST while about 25% of general girls got first class. Similarly in Science, 40% of SC and 30% of ST girls got first class whereas it was about 70% in case of general girls. In Commerce, in 2003, there were no SC/ST girls. In 2004, only 2 SC girls and 1 ST girl were there out of which 1 SC girl got third class and 1 ST girl failed. In 2005 out of 8

Fig. VIII-H – Results of B.J.B. College at +2 level (2004)

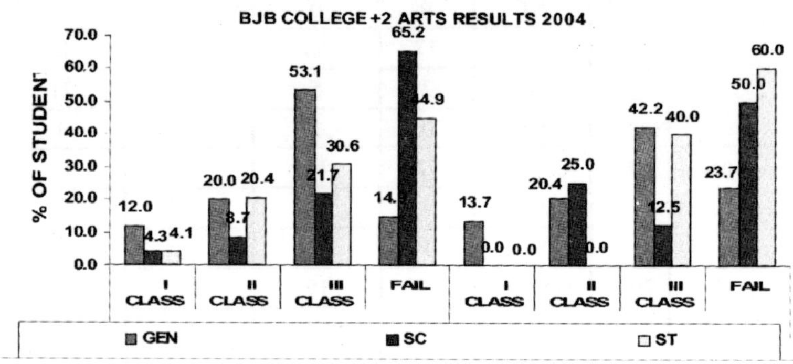

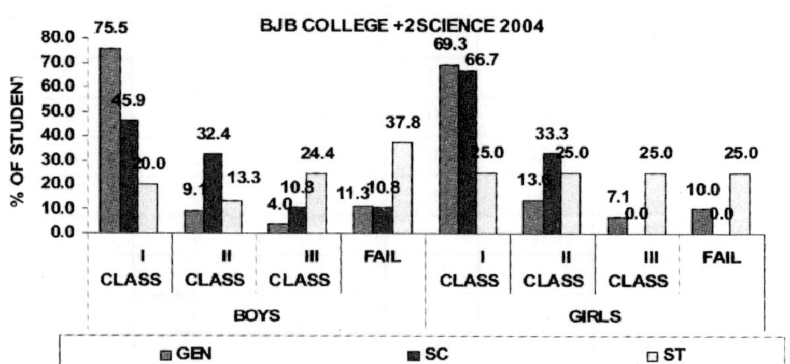

Fig. VIII-I Results of M.P.C. College (+3)

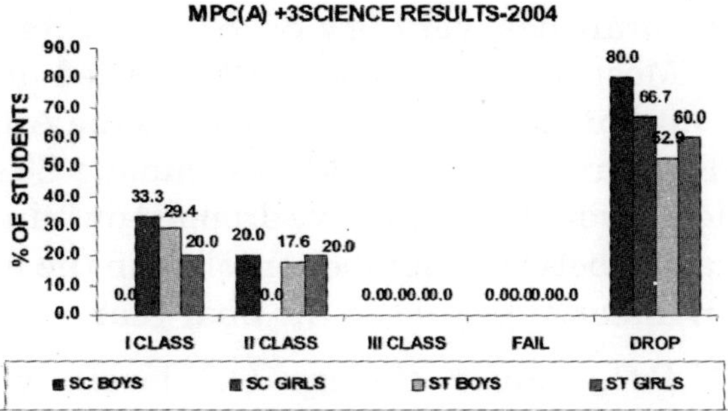

SC girls 2 failed and out of 2 ST girls one failed. During three years of observation, only 2 SC girls, got first class and none of the ST girls did so. But result of general girls was found very good.

Thus, contrary to +3 level, SC/ST girls could not show good result as compared to general girls at +2 level; rather their performance was better in women's college.

8.6 Result of College in Tribal District of Mayurbhanj

(i) In M.P.C. (Autonomous) College, Baripada, in P.G. Classes, very few SC/ST students were found. However, performance of SC/ST girls was lower than SC/ST boys in all the branches, Arts, Science, Commerce [Result enclosed at the Annexure-VII(D)].

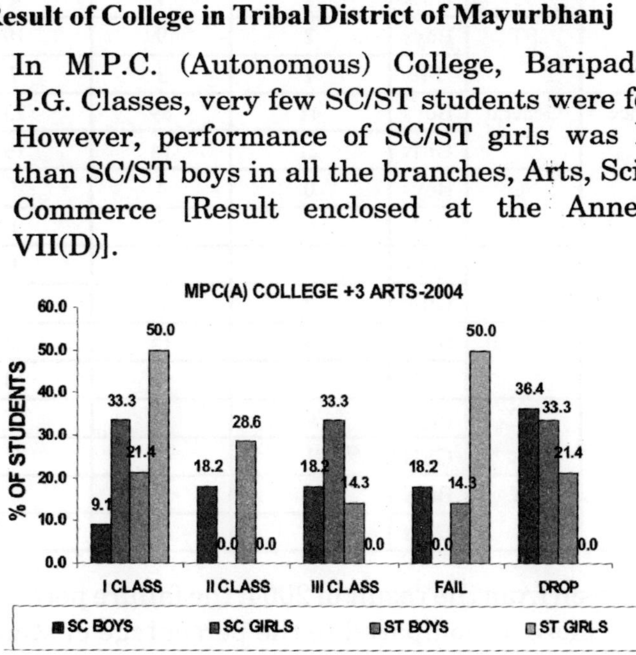

(ii) In +3 classes also, the same pattern followed, i.e. in all the branches, very few SC/ST students got first class. Most of the students either failed or passed without honours [Result enclosed at the Annexure-VII(E)]. Particularly in Science, among STs, many students were found to have dropped out since there was a gap between number enrolled in the first year and number appeared in the final year.

(iii) In M.P.C. Junior College (+2 level), very few students got first class in Arts and Commerce.

Table: 8.15 – Result of 2004 SC/ST Girls in M.P.C. Junior College (in Percentage)

Stream	Category	Sex	I	II	III
Arts	General	Boys	7	9	12
		Girls	4	8	16
	SC	Boys	0	2	1
		Girls	1	1	4
	ST	Boys	2	9	19
		Girls	1	3	7
Science	General	Boys	41	39	23
		Girls	21	14	19
	SC	Boys	0	4	3
		Girls	0	3	1
	ST	Boys	2	3	1
		Girls	2	2	1
Commerce	General	Boys	8	15	35
		Girls	11	18	13
	SC	Boys	0	0	3
		Girls	1	0	0
	ST	Boys	0	2	6
		Girls	2	0	0

As seen from the result of 2004, the failure percentage is much more as compared to the percentage of students who passed in this college. Only 1 SC girl (out of 21) in Arts and 1 SC girl (out of 2) in Commerce got first class, whereas none (out of 1 SC 7 ST girls) from Science got first class. However, in Science, ST girls showed comparatively better result than ST boys. This College is in the predominantly tribal area and is the only Government college for +2 Science at Baripada (naturally all good tribal girl students were found in this college).

(iv) In Sree Ma, Mahavidyalaya, a woman's college where most of the average students go, the result was not at all good. At +3 level, there were very few SC/ST girls and despite being a pass course, many of them failed. At +2 level, most of the girls either failed or passed in third division and none of them got first division though the course offered was only Arts.

(v) In Government Women's College, where there is only +3 Arts, most of the general students got first class, but not SC/ST students, who mostly passed in third division or failed.

Thus, in women's colleges, performance of girl students was not good compared to co-education colleges in the tribal district of Mayurbhanj.

Fig. VIII-J-Results of M.P.C. College (+2)

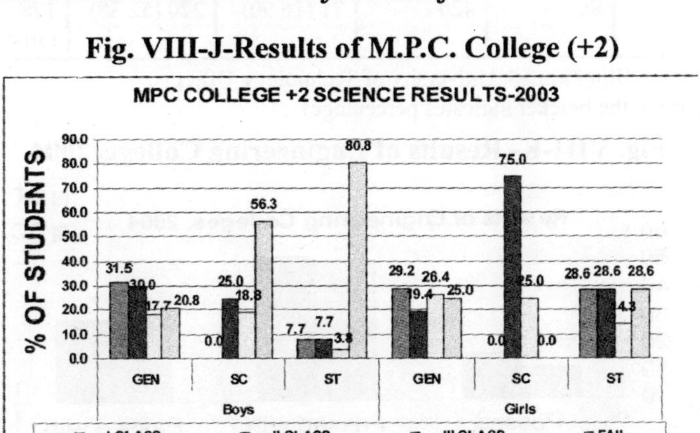

8.7 Result of Technical College

(i) In technical colleges, many of the SC/ST girls got first class and very few got second class, just like general students. Obviously, in technical colleges, there is hardly any difference in performance between general and SC/ST students.

(ii) However, after **Biju Pattnaik University of Technology (BPUT)** was established in 2003, it was found from the result of 2004 that only 16% of SC and 11.3% of ST students cleared the examination, whereas 52.3% SC and 50.9% ST passed having a back paper and 30.4% SC and 40.5% ST were asked to appear again in next year (year back). Thus, many students could not cope with the new syllabus of Technical University.

Table: 8.16 – Result of BPUT (2004) (23 Engineering Colleges Included)

Year	Category	Total Students	Passed(P)	Passed with Back Paper(XP)	Passed with Year Back(X)
2004	ST	212	24	108 (50.94)	86 (40.56)
	SC	420	71 (16.90)	220 (52.38)	128 (30.47)

(*Source* – Biju Pattnaik University of Technology Office)
(Figure in the bracket indicates percentage)

Fig. VIII-K- Results of Engineering College, 2004

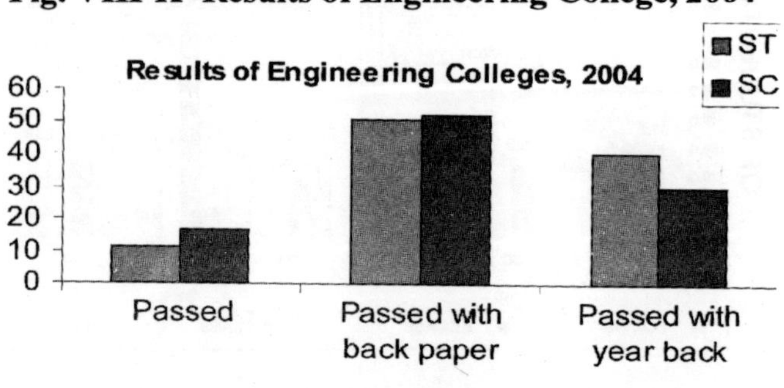

(iv) **Seemanta Engineering College**, situated near the border of Orissa, also caters to engineering education of three other highly-populated tribal states West Bengal, Jharkhand and Bihar. Following the Orissa Government reservation rule of 30% of reservation of seats for girls, it was expected that many tribal students particularly girls, would pass out from this college. Sadly, from the result of 2001 and 2002 of this college, it was found that in 2001, there were only 1 ST boy and 1 SC girl and in 2002, 3 SC boys and 1 SC girl.

Table: 8.17 – Result of Seemanta Engineering College

Year	Sex	Category	Result			
			Total	I	II	III
2001	Boys	General	149	133	08	00
		SC	00	00	00	00
		ST	1	00	00	00
	Girls	General	29	27	01	00
		SC	01	01	00	00
		ST	00	00	00	00
2002	Boys	General	148	116	02	00
		SC	03	03	00	00
		ST	01	00	00	00
	Girls	General	30	27	00	00
		SC	01	01	00	00
		ST	00	00	00	00

Thus SC/ST girls in this tribal district have not been able to take advantage of Technical Education.

8.8 Final Indication

As the result of different colleges were analysed and compared with that of general girls, there was clear indication that the performance of SC/ST girls was much below the general caste students.

8.9 Factors Influencing Performance

Efforts have been made to determine different factors in their lives which influenced their educational attainment. For this purpose interrelations between different data collected have been used. For ascertaining achievement of SC/ST students, the performance in last examination has been taken as indicator. Performance was found to be influenced by different factors related to family background.

(1) Father's Education

It is evident from the above table that, 81 out of 113 of SC respondents and 93 out of 157 ST respondents have come from educated families, i.e. father educated up to graduate level. The table shows that performance positively depends on father's education. A maximum of 52.5% of SC and 37.6% of ST girls have got first class and they are from families with educated fathers. So extra attention from students from illiterate and poorly-educated families is very much required to improve their performance.

Table: 8.18 – Father's Education Influencing Performance

Father's Education	Performance in Last Examination							
	SC				ST			
	1st Div.	2nd Div.	3rd Div.	Total	1st Div.	2nd Div.	3rd Div.	Total
Illiterate	02 (33.3)	03 (50)	01 (16.7)	06	02 (15.4)	04 (30.8)	07 (53.8)	13
Up to Matric	11 (42.3)	13 (50)	02 (77)	26	14 (27.5)	20 (39.2)	17 (33.3)	51
Up to Graduate or above	43 (52.5)	32 (40)	06 (7.5)	81	35 (37.6)	39 (42)	19 (20.4)	93

(2) Father's Occupation

It is seen from the above table that students with

father either a government or private employee show good performance. Thus, students from government or private employees' family having good exposure to urban culture give importance to education and fare well in examination. So girls from rural areas with agriculture as family occupation should be given more attention.

Table: 8.19 – Father's Occupation Influencing Performance

Father's Occupation	Performance in Last Examination							
	SC				ST			
	1st Div.	2nd Div.	3rd Div.	Total	1st Div.	2nd Div.	3rd Div.	Total
Employment in Govt. and Pvt. Sector	42 (49.4)	35 (41.1)	07 (8.2)	85	40 (34.7)	48 (41.7)	27 (23.4)	115
Agriculture	03 (27.3)	07 (63.6)	01 (9.0)	11	05 (15.6)	12 (37.5)	15 (46.8)	32
Others (Business, Politics etc.)	09 (52.9)	06 (35.3)	02 (11.8)	17	03 (30)	05 (50)	02 (20)	40

(3) Mother's Education

Very few respondents have well-educated mothers (only 13 out of 157 ST and 24 out of 113 SC). There is, however, a clear indication of positive relationship

Table: 8.20 – Mother's Education Influencing Performance

Mother's Education	Performance in Last Examination							
	SC				ST			
	1st Div.	2nd Div.	3rd Div.	Total	1st Div.	2nd Div.	3rd Div.	Total
Illiterate	10 (45.5)	10 (45.5)	02 (9.0)	22	10 (21.8)	18 (39.1)	18 (39.1)	46
Up to Matric	32 (47.8)	28 (41.8)	07 (10.4)	67	35 (35.7)	41 (41.9)	22 (22.4)	98
Up to Graduate or above	13 (54.2)	10 (41.6)	01 (4.2)	24	06 (46.2)	04 (30.8)	03 (23)	13

between mother's education and performance. 54.2% of SC respondents and 46.2% of ST respondents of these who have secured first class have well educated mothers. So girls having uneducated mother were found to have low performance and hence they need more encouragement and guidance.

(4)Mother's Occupation

As seen from the above table, respondents with mothers working in government or private sectors fare much better than others, particularly in case of STs.

Table: 8.21 – Mother's Occupation Influencing Performance

Mother's Occupation	Performance in last Examination							
	SC	ST						
	1st Div.	2nd Div.	3rd Div.	Total	1st Div.	2nd Div.	3rd Div.	Total
Employment in Govt. and Pvt. Sector	07 (50.0)	07 (50.0)	0 (0.0)	14	08 (50.0)	06 (37.5)	02 (12.5)	16
Agriculture	02 (50.0)	02 (50.0)	0 (0.0)	04	0 (0.0)	04 (57.1)	03 (42.9)	07
Home maker	46 (48.4)	39 (41.0)	10 (10.52)	95	42 (31.8)	54 (40.0)	38 (28.1)	134

Fig. VIII-L- Performance of Students Having Working Mothers.

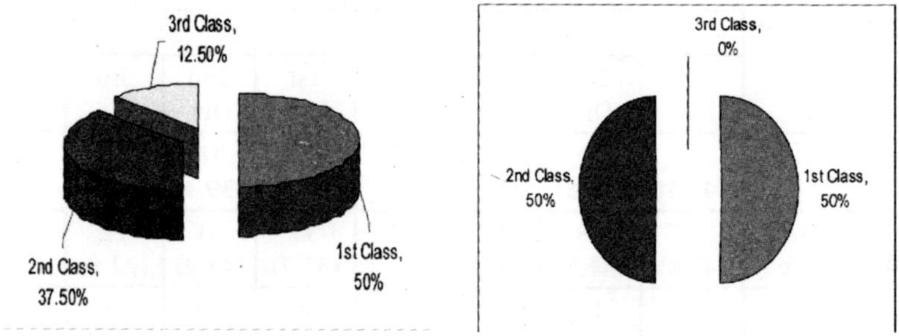

ST SC

(5) Annual Family Income

It has been observed that students with sound financial background show better performance in examination.

Table: 8.22 – Family Income Influencing Performance

Annual Family Income	Performance in Last Examination							
	SC				ST			
	1st Div.	2nd Div.	3rd Div.	Total	1st Div.	2nd Div.	3rd Div.	Total
<15,000	04 (80.0)	01 (20.0)	0 (0.0)	05	0 (0.0)	04 (40.0)	06 (60.0)	10
From 15,000 to 55,000	22 (44.9)	21 (42.9)	06 (12.2)	49	30 (32.9)	37 (40.7)	24 (26.3)	91
> 55,000	29 (49.15)	26 (44.06)	04 (6.77)	59	21 (37.5)	22 (39.2)	13 (23.2)	56

Only a few students i.e. 5 out of 113 in SC and 10 out of 157 in ST have family income less than 15,000 per annum. 60% of these ST girls got 3rd Division. So performance of higher and middle income group is distinctly better than those from lower income group. (Only 4 SC students have shown good performance in spite of low family income). In other words, family income is clearly related to academic performance.

Thus specific factors were responsible for low performance of SC/ST girls.

8.10 Conclusion

To study the attainment of SC/ST girls, a thorough analysis of their performance in the examination was conducted and compared with that of general caste students. It was indeed a very difficult task, since no where in the records of results either names or castes of candidates are recorded. Even the examination roll number is never the same as the college roll number and so it was very difficult to find out caste from admission records and match with results. However, due to the co-operation of Secretary, Board of Secondary Education; Chairman, Council of Higher Secondary Examination; Chairman of P.G. Council, Utkal University and Principals of different colleges, all possible efforts could be made and results collected using old records.

It was observed that, at High School level, performance of SC/ST girls is lower than general girls and also SC/ST boys. Between SCs and STs, the performance of SCs seems to be slightly better than that of STs in both the categories, boys and girls. However, for both SC and ST, performance seems to be getting better over the years.

At Higher Secondary level also, it was found that percentage of pass of SC/ST boys and girls is always less than that of general caste girls in all the streams, Arts, Science and Commerce. But surprisingly in all the streams except Arts, General/SC/ST, girls showed better results than boys. This shows that girls are keen to study in college and show better performance in college than in school. The percentage of students passing in 1st division is higher in Science, followed by Commerce and then Arts. The same pattern follows for SC/ST students also. But performance of SC/ST students, though not at par with general students, shows the same trend in showing improvement over the years. Unfortunately, percentage of SC/ST girl students in first division could not be available separately from the Council, and had to be studied in different colleges individually.

After collecting data from 27 departments separately and then compiling into six groups, Arts, Science, Commerce, Professional Courses, Law and Commerce, the result in Utkal University was analysed. It was observed that the percentage of students of general caste passing in first division is much more than percentage of

SC/ST students. However, when results of SC/ST girls was compared with that of SC/ST boys, it was found that girls did much better than boys in all the branches, more so in Science. However, many ST girls were found dropping out. Considering the results of SC/ST students in Rama Devi Women's College, separately for P.G., +3 and +2 classes, it was observed that SC/ST students in P.G. are very few and did not do very well. In +3, they seem to do well like general caste students. Between SCs and STs, the performance of SCs is comparatively better. At +2 level, percentage of pass of SC/ST girls in all the divisions is less than that of general caste girls where as in fail category, the percentage of ST girls is maximum followed by SC.

In B.J.B. College, (largest co-education college in the State), the number of SC/ST students is very less and that of SC/ST girls is negligible. However, at +3 level, their performance was very good but not at +2 level. At +2 level, performance of SC/ST girls is better in the women's college than in co-education college.

When result of SC/ST girls in M.P.C. College, Baripada (Tribal District of Mayurbhanj) was analysed, it was found that performance of SC/ST girls in P.G. and +3 level is lower than that of SC/ST boys in all the branches, Arts, Science and Commerce. Many ST girls were found dropping out. At +2 level, ST girls showed better result than ST boys, indicating entry of good ST girls students into this college.

Looking at the result of ShreeMa Mahavidyalaya a private women's college in Baripada, it is found that result is not at all good either at +3 or +2 level. Even in Government Women's College, most of the SC/ST girls students failed in examination. So, in the tribal district of Mayurbhanj, performance of SC/ST girls in women colleges is not good as compared to co-education college.

Finally, factors, which effected SC/ST girls' performance, were analysed through interrelationships of data collected. It was confirmed that their performance depends on Parents' educational level, parents' financial condition and also their occupation. It was clear that SC/ST girls from poor, uneducated rural families needed extra care.

9

POLICIES FOR EDUCATIONAL DEVELOPMENT OF SC/ST: IMPLEMENTATION AND EFFICACY

9.1 Introduction

At the time of framing of Indian Constitution, the need for special provisions to safeguard the interest of SC/ST, the most disadvantaged section of the society, was felt and sincere effort was made to disperse the fruits of development of free India equally among all sections of the society. Accordingly, special provisions have been included in our Constitution to promote the social, educational and economic interests of these two weakest of the weaker sections of the society and guidelines issued for implementation of these safeguards adequately.

Constitution of India guarantees the following safeguards:

Social

1. Equality before Law (Article-14);
2. The state to make special provisions for the

advancement of any socially and educationally backward classes of citizens or for the Scheduled Castes and Scheduled Tribes (Article 15[4]);

3. Equality of opportunity for all citizens in matters relating to employment or appointment to any office under the State (Article 46);

4. The state to make provisions for reservation in appointments or posts in favour of any backward class citizens which, in the opinion of the State, is not adequately represented in the services under the State (Article 16 [4]).

5. Appointment of a Commission to report on the administration of the Scheduled Areas and the Welfare of the Scheduled Tribes in the States (Article 339).

6. Appointment of a Commission to investigate the conditions of socially-and educationally-backward classes and the difficulties under which they labour and to make recommendations to remove such difficulties to improve their condition (Article 346).

Economic

7. The State to promote with special care the educational and economic interests of the weaker sections of the people and in particular of the Scheduled Castes and Scheduled Tribes and protect them from social injustice and all forms of exploitation (Article 46).

8. Grant-in-aid from the Consolidated Fund of India each year for promoting the welfare of the Scheduled Tribes and administration of Scheduled Areas (Article 275[1]).

Political

9. Reservation of seats for the Scheduled Castes and

Scheduled Tribes in the House of People (Article 330).

10. Reservation of seats for the Scheduled Castes and Scheduled Tribes in the Legislative Assemblies of the States (Article 332).

11. Reservation of seats for the Scheduled Castes and Scheduled Tribes in every Panchayat (Article 243D).

Not only provisions of safeguards in the Constitutions were made and guidelines were issued, but a Commission was also established in 1978, titled "National Commission of Scheduled Castes and Scheduled Tribes" to oversee the implementation of various safeguards provided for Scheduled Castes and Scheduled Tribes.

9.2 Policies of Educational Development of SCs/STs

Prior to 1950, the Government of India had no direct programme for the educational development of Scheduled Tribes and Scheduled Castes. With the adaptation of the Constitution, the promotion of education of Scheduled Tribes and Scheduled Castes has become a special responsibility of the Central as well as the state Government. Keeping the different problems of SCs and STs in views, efforts have been made during different plan periods to provide various facilities for the educational development of Scheduled Castes and Scheduled Tribes. In this regard, particular reference can be made to the tribal sub-plan approach, which came into existence as the main strategy from Vth Five Year Plan and in which top-priority has been accorded to elementary education. The second important development in the policy towards education of SC/ST came with implementation of the National Policy of Education (1986), which specified among other things:

1. Expansion of school provision for SC/ST;

2. Provision of hostel facilities;
3. Subsidizing cost of education by providing incentives like abolition of tuition fees, provision of free books, uniforms, school bags etc;
4. Development of curricula and instruction material in tribal language at initial stage and then switching over to regional language;
5. Recruitment of teachers within the community by relaxing qualification if necessary;
6. Establishment of Ashram Schools on a large scale in tribal areas.;

Thus, NPE (1986), as updated in 1992, envisages emphasis on intervention for correction of social imbalances and empowerment of women and disadvantaged sections.

9.3 Special Provision by Central Government

The Central Government, on its part, supports various initiatives of the State Government in this regard. Some of the initiatives taken by the Central Government envisaging special provision for SCs and STs in the field of higher education are:

1. Reservation of seats for SCs and STs in Central Government institutions including IITs, IIMs, RECs, Central Universities, Kendriya Vidyalayas, Navodyay Vidyalayas, etc. There is also relaxation in the minimum qualifying cut-off stages for universities, colleges and technical institutions, apart from such reservation. U.G.C. has established SC/ST cells in 113 universities to ensure proper implementation of the reservation policy.
2. Remedial and special coaching is provided to SC/ ST students to improve their academic skill and linguistic proficiency.

3. UGC provides relaxation for SC/ST candidate in cut-off marks for Junior Research Fellowship (JRF) and also for appearing in the NET examination required for appointment of Lecturer.

4. Out of 1,43,000 scholarships at Secondary level for talented children from rural areas, 13,000 are reserved for SC/ST and under National Talent Scheme Examination (NTSE) conducted by NCERT, 225 scholarships are exclusively reserved for SC/ST.

9.4 Schemes of State Government for Educational Development of SC/ST

Central and State Governments are jointly responsible for implementing programmes meant for all-round development of SC/ST in Orissa. The Welfare department, which was in charge of welfare of SC/ST and OBC, was renamed as ST and SC Development Department with effect from 22nd February, 1999. Scheduled Tribe and Scheduled Caste Development Department is the nodal department of State Government to carry forward the goals enshrined in Article 46 of the Constitution with financial help from Central Government. Most of the ongoing activities of the Department are sustained by budgetary support from the non-plan budget of the State Government. The development programmes and projects have been implemented with Special Central Assistance for the Tribal Sub-Plan received from Ministry of Tribal Affairs, Special Central Assistance for Special Component Plan (SCP) received from the Ministry of Social Justice and Empowerment, Grants in-aid received under Article 275(1) of the Constitution, funds received under several Central Plan and Centrally Sponsored Plan Scheme from Ministries of Tribal Affairs and Social Justice and Empowerment, allocation under State Plan including

Additional Central assistance under RLTAP for KBK districts, etc.

9.5 Educational Institutions and Hostels

Orissa was the pioneer in setting up special Residential Educational Institutions for educational development of SC's/ST's. The department runs a number of educational institutions exclusively for SC/ST students. There are 218 Residential High Schools including 55 for girls, 112 Ashram Schools (M.E. standard), 37 Kanyashrams (M.E. standard), 143 Residential Sevashrams (Primary School with residential facilities) and 1031 Non-residential Sevashrams. Besides the hostels attached to above 510 residential institutions of this Department, there are 1548 Priamry School hostels (40 seated) in TSP areas. The Department also maintains 7 Special Adivasi hostels including two for women college students, one in the State Capital and the other at Rourkela.

9.5.1 Tribal High Schools

It is agreed by all that the education at High School level be given top most importance so that SC/ST students can do well in matriculation and cope up with college education.

It has been observed that the pass percentage of SC/ST students from Residential Tribal High Schools is always higher when compared to their pass percentage in Annual H.S.C. Examination in all schools, including these run by SC/ST Development Department.

Thus, percentage of success of SC/ST students in Residential Tribal High Schools is higher than the average percentage of success of SC/ST students in Orissa Board of Secondary Education as a whole. So these tribal schools have definitely helped a lot for educational development of SC/ST students.

Table: 9.1 – Result of Annual H.S.C. Examination

Year	In Schools Run by SC/ST Development Department		In All Schools (including Tribal High Schools)		
	SC Students	ST Students	SC Students	ST Students	Percentage of Success including All Students
2003	55.73	58.82	34.55	31.63	44.2
2004	64.39	63.70	37.26	34.81	46.2
2005	66.39	68.30	43.02	40.43	52.3
2006	66.60	65.30	42.57	37.53	52.49

Source – (1) Board of Secondary Education;
(2) Annual Report of SC/ST Development Department, Government of Orissa

Fig. IX-A – Performance of SC/ST Students in H.S.C. Examination

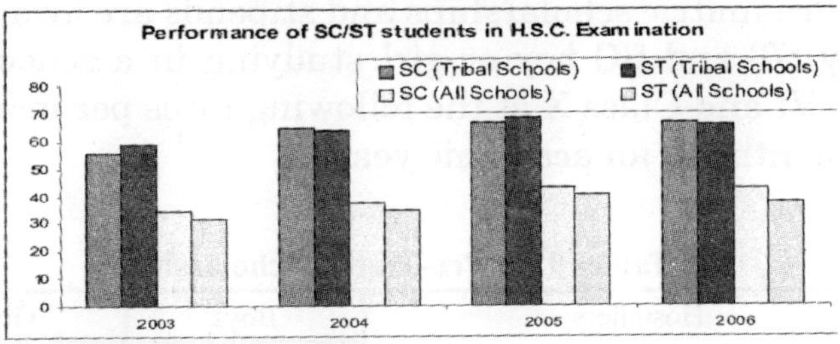

Source – (1) Board of Secondary Education;
(2) Annual Report of SC/ST Development Department

9.5.2 High Schools

There are only 55 Tribal Girls' High Schools in the State and more such schools will definitely help in sending more girls to college.

The number of general high schools is also much less as compared to primary schools in the tribal areas. It was reported that 80% of tribal girls have no scope of going to school after class-V. Since they cannot go to a distant village, more high schools, particularly for girls are needed in tribal areas.

9.5.3 Model Schools

In order to provide quality education to meritorious tribal students it has been proposed to establish 10 model schools in eight districts of the State under the management of Orissa Model Tribal Education Society (OMTES). Each school will have Class VI to Class XII. Already +2 Science has been started in 3 model schools and student stipend increased from Rs.300/- to Rs.500/- for boys and from Rs.325/- to Rs.500/- for girls. During 2005-06, 2,642 students including 1,264 girls enrolled in these model schools. These schools will definitely help to draw tribal girls to higher education.

9.6 Scholarship/Stipend

(i) Pre-matric Scholarships

Pre-matric scholarships and stipends are awarded to every ST and SC boy or girl studying in a school from class VI and Class X at the following rates per month for ten months in an academic year.

Table: 9.2 – Pre-Matric Scholarship

Hostellers		Boys	Girls
		Rs.500/-	Rs.325/-
Day Scholars	Class-VI & VII	Rs.10/-	Rs.15/-
	Class-VIII - X	Rs.15/-	Rs.20/-

(ii) Post-Matric Scholarship (PMS)

Post-Matric scholarship is awarded at different rates for different courses as per Government of India's Scheme. Scholarship to SC/ST students is a thrust area of SC/ST Development Department's activity in the State. The rate of Post- matric Scholarship has been enhanced during Xth Plan (2002-2007) by Government of India

Table: 9.3 – Post-matric Scholarships

Group	Hostellers	Day Scholars
I - Degree Courses in Engineering, Medicine, Agriculture, Veterinary Science, M.B.A.. M.C.A.	Rs.740/- (Earlier Rs.425/-)	Rs.330/- (Earlier Rs.190/-)
II - Professional Courses not Included in Gr.I, i.e. CA/ICWA/CS etc., P.G Diploma Courses in Medicine, Engineering, Post Graduate Courses in Science, Arts and Commerce	Rs.510/- (Earlier Rs.290/-)	Rs.330/- (Earlier Rs.190/-)
III - General Courses up to Graduation Level and Certificate Course	Rs.355/- (Earlier Rs.230/-)	Rs.185/- (Earlier Rs.120/-)
IV - Class-XI, XII in 10+2 System	Rs.235/- (Earlier Rs.150/-)	Rs.140/- (Earlier Rs.90/-)

(Source – SC/ST Development Department, Government of Orissa)

with effect from 01.04.2003 and Government of Orissa has adopted this from 01.08.2005.

The income ceiling has also been revised. Earlier, the ceiling of annual income was Rs.49,000/- for full maintenance and full course fee and Rs.65,290/- for half maintenance and full course fee. However, the income ceiling for receiving full maintenance allowance and full course fee for all courses is now Rs.1,00,000/-. As such, more students will now receive P.M.S. at higher rate.

9.6.1 Awareness of Students about Stipend

(a) Students were asked whether they received government stipend/scholarships. Only 68.1% of SC students and 70% of ST students replied in the affirmative. The remaining 32% of SC and 30% of ST did not get the benefit.

(b) When asked about the reason for not getting stipend, they gave various reasons.

Table: 9.4 – Reasons for not Availing Stipend

Sl. No.	Reasons	SC		ST	
		No. of students	Percen-tage	No. of Students	Percen-tage
1.	Not Applied	08	22.2	12	25.5
2.	Not Aware about This	12	33.3	14	29.8
3.	Parent's Income does not Permit	11	30.6	18	38.3
4.	No Facility	05	13.9	03	6.4
	Total not getting stepped)	36	100	47	100

Out of the students, who did not get stipend, 22.2% SC and 25.5% ST students could not apply in time and 33.3% SC and 29.5% ST beneficiaries were not aware about the facility.

> *"We did not know how to write applications for getting scholarships" – said Shantilata Murmu and Bangimani Tudu of +2, 1st year class of Rama Devi Women's College". When we knew that we had to apply for scholarships, the last date was already over and college office did not take our applications – said Suramani Pingula and Jyoti Larka or +2 1st year class, MPC Junior College, Baripada.*

30.6% SC and 38.3% ST students were not eligible, as their family income did not permit it. 5 SC students and 3 ST students studying in self-financing course in North Orissa University said that the course did not have such provision. **College authorities should take care to**

Fig. IX-B- Adequacy of Stipend.

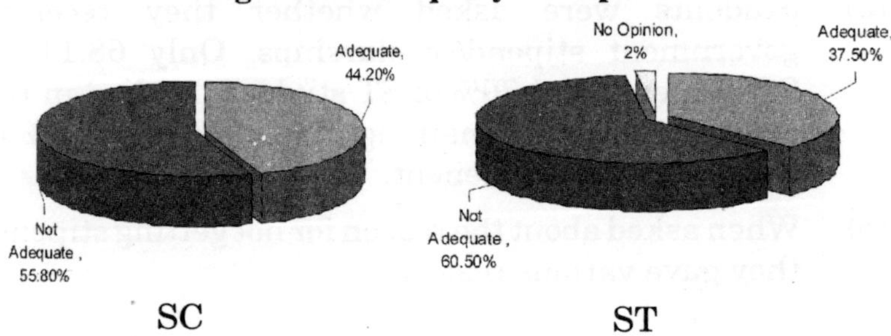

ensure that all eligible SC/ST students are aware and apply in time.

9.6.2 Student Views an Adequacy of Stipend

To our question on adequacy of stipend, 44.2% of SC and 60.5% of ST respondents have said that it was not sufficient.

More ST students found it inadequate because of their low economic status. However, the amount provided at the time of survey has already been enhanced in the Xth Plan, which they had not availed.

9.6.3 Disbursement of Stipend

From the records of disbursement of stipend in different institutions, following difficulties were observed.

(i) Many students failed to apply in time. So they should be properly counselled.

(ii) The amount often reached late, after students left the college and had to be returned to Government.

(iii) Students did not get the money in time to pay their examination fees at the end of the session. So arrangement for timely disbursement is very urgent.

> *"After reminding three times, the funds for scholarships of SC/ST students was released by Welfare Department and by that time students had passed out and already left the college. We had to notify three times in college notice board and also in local dailies, since we could not get their address. Ultimately a major portion of the funds had to be returned to Government" – said Principal, Rama Devi Women's College, Bhubaneswar*

25% of teachers interviewed reported misuse of stipend money by SC/ST students. Sometimes small misappropriations were reported at clerical level.

9.7 Reservation of Seats in Educational Institutions

(i) According to State Government rules, 20% seats (12% ST and 8% SC) are kept reserved for admission into all educational institutions starting from Higher Secondary to Post Graduate level in all courses.

(ii) In case the seats reserved at the existing rate have been filled up and it is found that there are more eligible students in these categories, the Principal of the college has been authorized to admit 10% additional students of these communities (6% of ST and 4% of SC).

(iii) Recently even these reservations were found insufficient, and since 2004, the Principals have been given power to admit 18% more SC/ST students, if many SC/ST students are left cut (10% for ST and 8% for SC).

(iv) There is a proposal by SC/ST Development Commission at U.G.C. to increase reservations to 38% (22%+16%) in the State proportional to their population.

9.7.1 Students' Views on Policy of Reservation of Seats

(i) Surprisingly 29.2% SC students and 14% of ST students said that they were not aware of reservation of seats for them. Even they did not know whether they have availed such reservation for entry into college.

(ii) Those who were aware about reservation were asked whether they thought the reservation provided to SC/ST students was adequate compared to the

Table: 9.5 – Awareness about Reservation in College

Awareness	ST		SC	
	Number	Percentage	Number	Percentage
Yes	135	86	80	70.8
No	22	14	33	29.2
Total	157	100	113	100

number seeking admission. 55.8% of SC students and 47% of ST students said that they needed more reservation so that more of the students from their category could come for higher education.

(iii) Then they were asked whether this policy of reservation of seats in educational institutions had been useful for them, only 31.6% of SC and 34.0% of ST students felt that the policy was useful and the rest had different opinions. Many had the opinion that only reservation in seats would not attract more students to higher education.

9.7.2 Opinion of Heads of Institution/ Teachers about Reservation of Seats

More than 75 teaches and heads of the institutions were contacted and their views on the policy of reservation of seats in educational institutions for SC/ST students

Fig. IX-C Opinion of teachers about Reservation of Seats

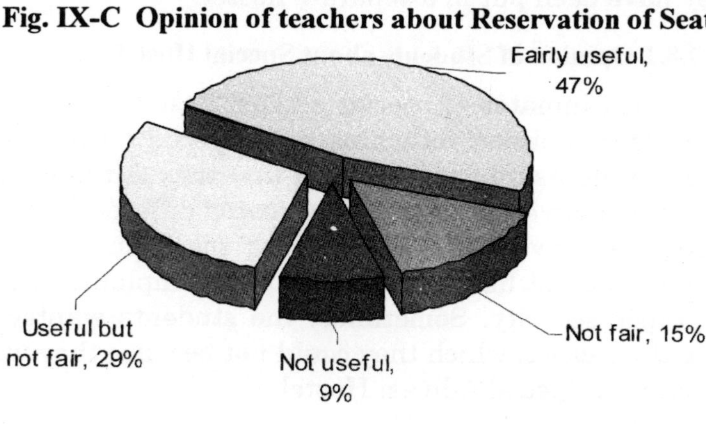

were sought. About reservation policy of government, 46.7% were of the opinion that the policy was useful, whereas 29.3% felt that it was definitely useful but not fair for the student community as a whole. 9.3% felt that it was not useful since SC/ST students could not take proper advantage of it. The remaining 14.7% felt that reservation was not at all fair and should not be there.

9.8 Special Hostel Facility

As already discussed in previous chapter, students staying in Special Adivasi Hostel of Rama Devi Women's College (i.e. Indira Gandhi Women's Hostel) and students of Utkal University staying in all the five general women's hostels of the university were interviewed and their opinion sought about Government policy of provision of special hostels for SC/ST girls. Altogether 47 SC students and 93 ST students in different hostels were interviewed.

SC/ST girl students staying in hostels of Utkal University seemed to be quite free in expressing their views and were as good as general girls in their outlook. But students in Indira Gandhi Women's Hostel of Rama Devi Women's College, which meant exclusively for SC/ST girls, seemed quite diffident and were unhappy that they have been put in a separate hostel.

9.8.1 Opinion of Students about Special Hostel

When inmates of special adivasi hostel were asked about their opinion regarding such special hostel, most of the students (about 82%) said that they felt alienated from the main stream and were treated differently in the college as they have been put in a special hostel. 60% of them did not like the food and 32% complained about improper security. Sometimes, the students wanted to hide their caste, which they could not because they were inmates of Special Adivasi Hostel.

Some students demanded that they should be allotted seats in general hostels and allowed to compete with others on merit. Last year, authorities were bound to allow two tribal students to stay in general hostel with other girls.

9.8.2 Opinion of Teachers about Special Hostel

When teachers were asked about their opinion on special hostel for SC/ST girls, only 26.7% said that it was definitely useful for progress of education among SC/ST girls. However, 73.3% felt that separate hostel facility creates alienation from general caste students and all students should stay together for better integration.

9.8.3 Opinion of Parents about Special Hostel

Many parents said that Special Adivasi Hostels have helped SC/ST girls to come for Higher Education; such hostels should be attached to each Government College. Thus, parents' views were different from their daughters staying in such hostels.

9.9 Special Coaching Facility for Engineering and Medical Entrance (Upgradation of Merit Scheme)

Upgradation of merit scheme is available in three colleges under our study, though it is implemented in 13 colleges for SCs and 5 colleges for STs for 244 SC and 136 ST students in Orissa. These three colleges are: B.J.B. Junior College, Bhubaneswar, Rama Devi Women's Junior College, Bhubaneswar and M.P.C. Junior College, Baripada. The scheme is aimed at imparting special coaching to the more meritorious ST/SC students to secure admission in Medical and Engineering courses. Government of India provides 100% central assistance for the purpose and at the rate of Rs.15,000/- per student per year towards (boarding and lodging charges at the rate of Rs.500/- per month, pocket money at the rate of Rs.100/- per month and books and stationary worth Rs.2000/-. It also provides Rs.7000/- per year per student towards the cost of special coaching to be arranged by the institution).

(i) The scheme is definitely a very useful for SC/ ST students to help their entry into professional courses. However, as seen from the records, girls have not been able to take advantage of it like boys. Most of the girls are not aware of this facility provided in the college.

(ii) In the report of the Principal of B.J.B. Junior College to Government regarding performance of students availing upgradation of merit scheme in the session 2003-04, it was mentioned that attendance in the coaching classes was encouraging at the beginning of the session but declined subsequently. However, it was observed that most of the students attending such classes regularly qualified for JEE 2004. But, in the list, 11 ST students (there was no provision of SC students) who qualified in OJEE, only one girl named Sonali Khera was there. In 2005, out of 35 ST students availing coaching, 19 students qualified for OJEE, 6 students qualified for AIJEE and 5 students qualified for IIT. However, among them, only 4 were girls who qualified for OJEE only. Among SCs, out of 20 students availing coaching, 15 qualified for OJEE, 6 for AIJEE and 2 for IIT. Among them only two girl students were there who qualified for OJEE.

(iii) Sri Bharat Chandra Nath, senior clerk of the college, who was in charge of SC/ST upgradation scheme, mentioned that students attending coaching classes, try to avoid the tests held during the classes. Students are paid 2/3rd of the amount only if they have minimum 60% attendance and full amount if they have more than 75% attendance.

About girls, he said that since coaching classes are held in the evening and there is no proper security, girls hesitate to come to college after evening and hence cannot avail the opportunity. Very few girls were there in such classes.

(iv) In Rama Devi Junior College, though there is provision for coaching for 25 ST and 20 SC girls, their attendance is very low after the course is started. Since classes are held just after regular classes are over (i.e. at 2 p.m.), students who have to come to college at 7 a.m. hesitate to stay on for the classes. Therefore, coaching classes should be held according to the convenience of the girls, not of the teachers, it was felt.

(v) Sri Ratikanta Mohanty, Senior Clerk in-charge of SC/ST upgradation schemes was contacted to find out the efficacy of such coaching classes. He mentioned that attendance was low after the books were distributed. Students even complained about coaching not being entrance examination oriented and being taken by the same teachers who taught in general classes.

He suggested orientation classes for SC/ST students as well as their parents for effectiveness of such scheme. But there was no record of their entry to professional colleges.

(vi) In M.P.C. Junior College also more number of boys than girls joined coaching classes. Classes could not be held regularly because attendance was very low after distribution of books.

(vii) It is very sad that sometimes girls were found avoiding such coaching classes just because they would be identified as SC/ST students, which they do not want. This is an important reason why quite a few students prefer outside coaching classes instead of availing in-house free coaching.

9.10 Coaching Classes for Civil Services

As found out from Annual Report of SC/ST Development Department, funds were sanctioned to Utkal University by Ministry of Tribal Affairs and Ministry of Social Justice and Empowerment for coaching of ST and SC students respectively. Also a matching grant from State Government was given to Utkal University, Orissa Study Circle and Coaching-cum-Guidance Centre, Bhubaneswar.

SC/ST students staying in girls' hostels of Utkal University seemed to be unaware of such programmes. When the officer-in-charge of the concerned centre was contacted, it was found out that in 2003 only 7 SC girls and 9 ST girls, and in 2004 only and 12 SC girls and 9 ST girls were imparted coaching. The authorities said this was advertised openly in local newspapers and the beneficiaries were expected to know. Moreover, sometimes delay in sending U.C. by University authority caused delay in receiving further grants for continuations of scheme.

So, it was felt that the scheme should be notified properly in girls hostels and some seats should be kept reserved for girls. Success record should be maintained to attract more girls. A SC/ST officer-in-charge should be specially entrusted with the responsibility of running the scheme.

9.11 Factors influencing Awareness of Students about Different Government Polices

It has been found that although government provides several incentives to SC/ST students for higher education, they are not able to take proper advantage of these due to lack of awareness. An attempt was made to ascertain the factors responsible for such lack of awareness.

9.11.1 Annual Income

It seems, their awareness about reservation in seats in colleges is greater when annual income is more i.e. more than 15,000. But in all the income groups the awareness about free coaching is less and it is minimum in high income groups, since they do not bother about free coaching as they are able to afford private coaching. Awareness about reservation in government jobs is not

Table: 9.6 – Impact of Annual Income on Awareness of Government Policies

Annual Income	SC/ ST	Awareness about Facility				
		Total No.	Reservation of Seats in Colleges	Reservation in Government Jobs	Reservation in Politics	Free Coaching
<15,000	SC	5	5 (100.0)	4 (80.0)	1 (20.0)	2 (40.0)
	ST	10	6 (60.0)	5 (50.0)	4 (40.0)	3 (30.0)
15,000 – 55,000	SC	49	36 (73.5)	15 (30.6)	12 (24.5)	11 (22.4)
	ST	91	80 (87.9)	37 (40.7)	21 (23.1)	17 (18.7)
>55,000	SC	59	39 (67.8)	19 (23.7)	18 (22.0)	17 (20.3)
	ST	56	49 (87.5)	27 (45.7)	13 (23.2)	16.36 (21.4)

(The number in the parentheses indicates percentage)

adequate in most income groups. This shows that SC/ST students are not aware about their rights and privileges.

9.11.2 Father's Education

As seen from the table, definitely father's education has influenced the awareness of SC/ST students about different policies of Government. Though awareness is more when father is more educated, awareness of reservation in politics and about free coaching seems to be marginal.

9.11.3 Place of Residence

As is evident from the above table, the students

Table: 9.7 – Influence of Father's Education on Awareness about Government Policies

Father's Education	SC/ ST	Total No.	Awareness about Facility			
			Reservation of Seats in Colleges	Reservation in Government Jobs	Reservation in Politics	Free Coaching
Illiterate	SC	6	4 (66.6)	2 (33.3)	1 (16.7)	1 (16.7)
	ST	13	11 (84.6)	5 (38.5)	2 (15.3)	2 (15.3)
Up to Matric	SC	25	17 (68.0)	9 (36.0)	5 (20.0)	5 (20.0)
	ST	51	45 (88.2)	25 (49.0)	10 (19.6)	13 (25.5)
Upto Graduate or More	SC	81	58 (71.6)	54 (66.7)	24 (29.6)	24 (29.6)
	ST	93	79 (84.9)	39 (41.9)	24 (25.8)	21 (22.6)

(Number in the parentheses indicate percentage)

staying with parents or relatives were more aware of different reservation policies probably due to discussion among family members. Most of the SC/ST students were not aware about reservation in political representation. Strangely, only 27% SCs and 17% STs from among hosteliers know about provision of free coaching. Hence

Table: 9.8 – Influence of Place of Residence on Awareness about Government Facility

Place of Residence	SC/ ST	Total No.	Awareness about Facility			
			Reservation of Seats in Colleges	Reservation in Govt Jobs	Reservation in Politics	Free Coaching
With Parents or Relatives	SC	62	46 (74.1)	23 (37.14)	21 (33.9)	21 (33.9)
	ST	50	45 (90.0)	24 (48.0)	14 (28.0)	27 (54.0)
In Hostel or Mess	SC	51	34 (66.7)	15 (29.4)	10 (19.6)	17 (27.5)
	ST	107	81 (75.7)	45 (42.1)	24 (22.4)	19 (17.8)

(Number in the parentheses indicate percentage)

awareness about different programmes should be generated at school level and in particular, in hostels.

9.12 Conclusion

It was found that many SC/ST students did not know about reservation facility provided to them for admission in colleges. But those, who were aware, felt that 20% reservation (12%+8%) for them was not adequate. However, the opinion of college teachers in this regard was different, many of whom felt the system unfair. About the provisions of stipend, the only difficulty noticed was that sometimes funds reached colleges by the time students had already left the college and the amount could not be disbursed. Care need to be taken to see that the stipend is disbursed in time, in any case before forms for final examination are filled up. Students should also be persuaded and guided to apply in time.

The special hostel facility for SC/ST students is neither sited by the students nor by the teaches, since it is felt that it widens the gap between SC/ST and general students. SC/ST girls seem to develop inferiority complex because of and demands scouts in general hostels as per merit. This is a very important factor to note for policy makers.

Although free coaching is provided to +2 students under up-gradation of merit scheme in some junior colleges for entry into Engineering and Medical Colleges, most students were found unaware of such facility. Students should be properly intimated about the scheme in their respective institutions at the time of admission.

During discussion, many post graduate SC/ST girls, staying in hostels revealed that they did not know how to prepare for State or Central Civil Services Examination and they definitely needed guidance. Special counselling for SC/ST girls is an urgent need, particularly about how to enter into employment after graduation/post graduation. Students have reported that they have not been able to take advantage of free coaching centres meant for SC/ST students which run courses only occasionally because of irregularity in receiving funds. They were also not able to afford high fees in private coaching centres in the town. On the whole, along with educational opportunities, coaching and career counselling need to be made available to all SC/ST students in institutions of higher learning.

10

RECIPE FOR CHANGE: SUGGESTIONS FROM STAKE HOLDERS

No doubt, policies formulated and implemented by both Central and the State Government aim at all round development of SCs and STs including educational development of these communities. In reality, there is a considerable gap between policy goals and outcome. Policies for welfare of SCs/STs are mostly formulated by the Central Government (Ministry of Social Justice and Empowerment for SCs and Ministry of Tribal Affairs for STs) while most tasks of implementation are left to the State Government (both the Department of Education and the Department for Development of SCs and STs).

Before arriving at conclusions as to what can be done to attract more SC/ST girls to higher education and enhance their performance/ professional skills, efforts were made to obtain opinions/suggestions from different sections. These include SC/ST students themselves who are already in institutions of higher education, their parents, teachers, Heads of Institutions and Hostel Superintendents/Wardens. We have been able to interview a few prominent personalities including policy makers and administrators, who have been involved in formulation and implementation of programmes for SC/ST. Some of these personalities belonging to SC/ST have had high educational attainments and success.

10.1 Suggestions from Students

Emphasis has been placed on opinions of persons who have to encounter the constraints themselves i.e. SC/ST girl students, in the educational institutions. The interview schedule [enclosed at Annexure X(A)] used for them, also mentioned – "Write in a few words your opinion about any policy changes or remedial measures which should be introduced to increase access of SC/ST girls to higher education". Researchers talked to them freely prior to taking their views. Also, at the end of the interview schedule (Section-B), meant for assessment of educational constraints, it was mentioned "Are you finding any problem in getting education institutionally? If yes, suggest some remedial measures (for both college and hostel)". As such, students had a chance of expressing their difficulties and also offering suggestions for overcoming them.

As stated earlier, 157 ST girls and 113 SC girls from 16 different institutions of higher education were interviewed. Students were from +2 to P.G. level and there were a few Engineering and Medical students. Naturally, they had varied views and offered different suggestions.

10.1.1 Institutional Problems

(i) The common problem faced by both SC and ST students was in understanding lessons. Coming mostly from rural background, they found it difficult to follow lessons taught in English and cope with the mode of teaching mostly confined to delivering lectures.

They indicated that they would be happy if the teachers cared to explain some difficult portions in Oriya language.

(ii) They also felt that they were invariably taken for granted as dull students and were generally left out by teachers while questions were asked in the class. They were eager to try to reply according to their capability if asked questions in the class and due encouragement was offered.

(iii) +2 students in particular felt inferior to the other general caste students coming from English medium schools, who were familiar with a substantial portion of the course and were paid greater attention by teachers.

In this regard, their suggestion was to arrange some extra doubt-clearing classes for them in small groups by caring and sympathetic teachers.

10.1.2 Problems in Hostels

As mentioned earlier, SC/ST students never wanted to stay in a separate hostel being segregated from others. They were sometimes ridiculed by teachers as well as fellow students for belonging to SC/ST hostels. Moreover, facilities in these hostels including food quality was found inferior as compared to general hostels.

So their suggestion was to put them in general hostels according to merit and sanction some extra financial help to make payment for hostel establishment charges (it is free in Special SC/ST hostel).

10.1.3 Other Suggestions by Students

1. Reservation of seat should be provided not only for SC/ST students, but a portion of it should be kept reserved for SC/ST girls. In case of non-availability of such students, the seats can be allotted to SC/ST boys.

2. Students should be given option to study either in English or Regional Language.

3. Proctorial system should be introduced in colleges with one proctor (teacher) in charge of 20 SC/ST students, who would provide counselling as well as look into their difficulties personally.

4. Doubt, clearing classes should be arranged for SC/ST girls, where teachers would clear their doubts, if needed in regional language.

5. Special hostels for SC/ST students creates more alienation and girls feel embarrassed to be marked as belonging to lower castes. A better option would be to reserve seats for them in general hostels and providing subsidy for lodging/boarding charges.

6. A few SC/ST students have suggested that Government should give increment to parents working in lower level jobs who send their children, specially girls, for education beyond graduation.

7. SC/ST cell should operate in each college just like in Utkal University to look into various problems faced by SC/ST students.

10.1.4 Suggestion of Students regarding Tribal Community

Tribal girls offered some suggestions particularly relevant to their community. These are:

(i) Opening of more professional institutions near the tribal localities.

(ii) Provision of some incentives to parents living in rural areas to motivate them to send their girls for higher education.

(iii) Opening of career counseling centres for tribal students in tribal areas to provide information regarding different courses after matriculation.

(iv) Generating awareness among tribal communities about the value and utility of education with the help of non-government volunteers, health workers etc. whom they trust.

(v) Taking help of educated persons from the tribal community in spreading education among tribals.

(vi) Sensitizing Pradhans or heads of tribal communities about the importance of education for girls.

10.2 Opinion of Parents

Parents of SC/ST students were chosen from different social strata with different economic background and different profession. Our researchers visited the parents at home/office for a free and frank discussion.

As seen from table 10.1, out of 30 ST and 20 SC parents, 19 STs were from State Capital and 11 from tribal district of Mayurbhanj. But out of 20 SC parents, 17 belonged to the capital city of Bhubaneswar and only 3 belonged to Mayurbhanj. Their occupation varied from government service to shop keeping and wage earning. They had varied educational qualifications. Some were illiterate. A few ST respondents belonged to interior tribal villages in the district of Mayurbhanj with absolutely no facility for education. Their opinion about different matters relating to girls, education was sought and they were very happy to express their views [Interview Schedule enclosed – Annexure- I(B)].

Table: 10.1 – List of Respondents (Parents)

Sl. No.	Personal Information	Variable	No. of Respondents	
			SC	ST
1.	Sex	Male	14	19
		Female	6	12
2.	Place of Residence	Tribal District of Mayurbhanj	3	12
		State Capital, Bhubaneswar	17	18

3.	Occupation	Government Employee		12	13
		Private Employee		03	02
		Shop Keeper		02	03
		Agriculture		02	01
		Business		00	01
		Retired Government Employee		00	01
		Shop Keeper		00	03
		Wage Earner		00	02
		No Work		01	04
		Housewife		00	01
4.	Age	30-35		02	01
		36-40		03	06
		41-45		09	16
		46-55		05	05
		>56		01	02
5.	Educational Qualification	Illiterate		01	04
		M.E.		02	02
		High School		08	11
		Intermediate/Diploma		04	07
		Graduate		03	04
		Post Graduate		02	02
6.	Tribe/ Caste to which Belong	Caste	No.	Tribe	No.
		Dhoba	10	Santal	18
		Pana	4	Bhumij	04
		Tanti	2	Oram	01
		Bhuyan	1	Bhuyan	02
		Bathudi	2	Munda	01
		Deewar	1	Kandha	04

Clearly, our parent respondents belonged to different communities/castes and had varied educational qualifications. Naturally, they had different views on girls' education.

10.2.1 About Girls' Education

About 75% of ST parents seemed to have realized

the importance of girls' education and agreed that in the present age, it was not only a basic necessity but also gave ample scope for better future. However, a few of them (25%) in the interior villages thought that there was no need for higher education for girls. Rather, they should stay at home to learn cooking and take care of domestic chores. One lady even said that she had not missed anything in life because she was illiterate.

Among SCs, almost all of them have encouraged their daughters for higher education. A mother, Saraswati Sethi, herself educated up to middle school level with an illiterate husband said that job for girls was not a priority but education would help them to get good life partners and lead a happy life. Surprisingly, one lady herself a matriculate and working as library assistant, said that if girls were educated, they would be able to protect themselves from domestic and other forms of violence. She has sent all her daughters for higher education. One has joined ICICI bank after graduation and the other is studying Business Law. It is interesting to know that one Diploma Engineer parent has opined that girls need education more than boys, since the children are more influenced by mother. Thus, educated SC persons have realized the vâlue of education and are keen to educate their daughters depending on availability of opportunity.

10.2.2 About Sending Girls to Hostels

Regarding our question on allowing daughters to stay in hostel for higher studies, sadly 50% of tribal parents said that girls should not be allowed to stay in hostel, as it was not safe for them. A few tribal women also said that girls should get educated only up to the level to which education facilities are available in the locality. Even a few were apprehensive of their daughters getting alienated from their community while staying in hostel and of the risk of inter-caste marriage. But 50% of tribal parents, who were more educated, wanted their daughters to avail the best of education and exposure staying in a good hostel.

In case of SCs, most of the parents (more than 70%) have said that girls should stay at home as long as possible. If no such educational institutions are available in the locality (like Medical or Engineering), the girls can be permitted to stay in hostels away from home. One Manoj Kaibarta, a diploma holder in Mechanical Engineering working in a private industry and guardian of a SC girl wanted his sister to go out for higher education and stay in a hostel for better exposure to outside world.

10.2.3 About Girls Taking up Jobs

To our question whether they wanted their daughters to take up jobs after completing education, most of SC/ ST parents answered in the affirmative. They preferred secured government jobs for their girls and among all the government jobs, preference was for teaching. A few of them, who had negative opinion about girls taking up jobs, said that woman's career depended on the will of husband and in-laws. Their view was, "Unless in-laws permit, girls, despite educational qualification, should not take up any job".

10.2.4 About Progress in Employment of Girls

When asked whether SC/ST girls were taking up employment more and more, all SC/ST parents agreed. The reason, according them, was changing views of girls, who wanted independent income and decent life. The reservation policy of government helped them to some extent. However, a few of the ST parents revealed that there was no educated girl in their community; as such the question of employment of educated girls did not arise.

10.2.5 About the High Dropout Rate

When it was pointed out that the dropout rate among SC/ST was much more than general students, almost 80% of SC parents and 60% of ST parents attributed the reason to poverty. About 60% of SC/ST parents also felt that inability to cope with the curriculum and apathy of uneducated parents were also important reasons. About 20% SC and 40% of ST parents felt that it would be difficult to find out a suitable match if girls are more educated and as such, took away their girls from school.

It is a matter of concern that most of the tribal girls (about 80%) have to end their education with matriculation because of unavailability of colleges near or around their locality. This deficiency is more acute in backward tribal districts than coastal districts of the State.

10.2.6 Awareness about Incentives

Parents were asked whether they were aware of various facilities provided to students of SC/ST communities by government. Almost all parents, who stay at Bhubaneswar, said that they knew about some of the facilities provided by government, i.e. reservation of seats in colleges, stipend and job reservation. However, some poor tribal parents of villages around Baripada (Mayurbhanj district) seemed unaware of such facilities. Awareness among women was still less. Clearly, greater awareness regarding government programmes for disadvantaged sections in interior areas is called for.

10.3 Suggestions from Parents

Most of the parents interviewed were found to be happy that they could offer their views on girls' education. After obtaining their views on different issues including their apprehension about change of girls' attitudes after higher education, they were requested to offer suggestions

Discussion in Village

With Students

With Parents

for bringing more SC/ST girls to the educational fold.

The Suggestions Offered Were

1. Girls' hostel should be attached to each women's college to accommodate SC/ST girls.
2. More women colleges should be established near tribal localities.
3. Financial help should be substantial so that they would not need any money from home.
4. Security arrangements in women hostels should be strict.
5. The girls should be taught about their own culture in college so that they do not get alienated from their community.

10.4 In their words...

"My daughter is the only girl in the village who has appeared in +2 examination. I want her to study more and get a job in future" –**Pitambar Tudu of Village Sana Brahmanamara near Baripada** says very proudly. A retired Army man (very rare in their community), who has settled in the small interior village after retirement, has realized the importance of education. He even teaches the children of the community free of cost in his house. He admitted that people in the village never realized the fruit of education and he was lucky that he went away in search of job, got into defence services, stayed out for many years and hence acquired the changed outlook. "We prefer to have daughter than sons since they bring us bride price, some times even two cows and some money"– says **Ratan Marandi, the head man of a small tribal village, Sana Bramhanamara near Baripada.** He admits that it was difficult for the villagers, earning livelihood from daily labour, to afford education for children. A few girls who were sent to stay in a tribal school hostel (at Panchayat High School, Kuabuda, 5 kms from their village) had to discontinue for this reason. Even during holidays, the girls coming home made ropes from bubei grass to earn some money to buy their books. Only food was free in tribal hostels, they complained.

"I have seven children, 3 sons and 4 daughters. My daughters have to work in the field and earn some money, even if they want to study" – says daily labourer **Bhaiga Bersa of village Sukhuapada in Kuliana block of Mayurbhanj**. Sending them to High School became very difficult for him (text books are not free at High School level). Sending them to colleges was out of question.

"Education for girl is more important than for boys, because they have to educate their children also" – says **Manoj Kaibarta of Babusahi, Baripada**. He belongs to Deewar Community (SC) and staying with parents, tries to educate his sisters to the extent possible from out of his meager income as a mechanic.

"I want my daughter to be educated so that she will get an educated life partner" – says **Saraswati Sethi of Bhubaneswar,** herself illiterate with a matriculate husband. They have sent their daughters for post-graduation study in the University despite financial constraints.

"I think reservation of posts for SC/ST is no longer required, since our children are also educated and can face competition" – says **Minanayana Dei, a Library Attendant in Rama Devi Women's College**. One of her two daughters is already working in ICICI bank and the other is pursuing Law. Both the girls were very good students throughout and never had to avail the reserved quota.

"I want my daughter to complete post graduation, take up a teaching job and then only get married, though her mother does not like her getting higher education" –

says **Manas Majhi**, who belongs to SC community and works in a private job being educated up to High School only.

Thus, it was obvious that parents are mostly interested in education of their daughters and appropriate opportunity needs to be made available to them.

10.5 Opinion of Heads of Institutions/College Teachers

To ascertain the opinion of Heads of the Institutions/ College Teachers regarding performance of SC/ST girls in their institutions, 75 teaches were interviewed in different colleges and universities besides 10 Principals/ Vice Principals (list enclosed in Table – 10.2). Their views were sought on different aspects involving SC/ST girls in their institution (interview schedule enclosed – Annexure – 10.3). The teachers extended full cooperation not only in filling up the interview schedules but also in discussing about various issues in the seminars held for them.

Table: 10.2 – List of Respondents (Heads of the Institutions/ College Teachers)

Sl. No.	Personal Information	Variables	No. of Respondents
1.	Name of the Institution	Utkal University	15
		Rama Devi Women's College (Autonomous)	21
		Rama Devi Junior College	15
		B.J.B. College (Autonomous)	12
		M.P.C. (Autonomous) College	5
		M.P.C. Junior College	5
		Government Women's College, Baripada	2
		Sree Maa Mahavidyalaya, Baripada	2
		Mayurbhanj Law College	2
		Seemanta Engineering College	2
		Kalinga Institute of Industrial Technology, Bhubaneswar	2

		S.C.B. Medical College, Cuttack	2
		Total	85
2.	Sex	Male	47
		Female	38
		Total	85
3.	Caste	General	78
		SC	3
		ST	4
		Total	85
4.	Educational Qualification	M.Tech., Ph.D.	1
		M.D., Ph.D.	1
		M.D.	1
		M.Sc., Ph.D.	17
		M.A., Ph.D.	22
		M.A./M.Sc./M.Phil	43
		Total	85
5.	Designation	Vice-Chancellor	1
		Professor	7
		Principal	9
		Vice-Principal	3
		Heads of the Department	15
		Senior Lecturer	29
		Lecturer	22
		Total	85

Thus, as far as possible, efforts have been made to interact with teachers from different colleges, since they came in contact with different kinds of students who came to their institutions. For example, girl students in Medical/Engineering Colleges might show different attitudes compared to SC/ST girls in the small women's college at Baripada.

10.5.1 About SC/ST Students

With the help of carefully designed interview

schedule [a copy attached Annexure – I(C)], their opinion on different aspects has been analyzed. The interview schedules of 75 teachers have been analyzed (Vice Chancellor and Principals mentioned separately).

Table: 10.3 – Opinion of College Teachers

Sl. No.	Opinion on the Topic	Yes		No		Sometime		Total	
		No.	%	No.	%	No.	%	No.	%
1.	Whether they Interact with Parents of SC/ST Girls	62	82.7	13	17.3	-	-	75	100
2.	Whether Noticed Parents' Concern about Girls Staying outside	20	38.7	42	56	04	5.3	75	100
3.	Whether SC/ST Students Seek Teacher's Help	25	33.3	43	57.3	07	9.4	75	100
4.	Whether SC/ ST Students Participate in College Election	64	85.3	11	14.7	-	-	75	100
5.	Whether SC/ST Students Find Difficulty in Adjustment to New Surroundings	66	88	09	12	-	-	75	100

82.7% of teachers had interaction with the parents of SC/ST students. Others have mentioned that they had no scope, since they were not in charge of admission in the institution. 38.7% teachers have mentioned that parents were very much concerned when they left their girls in hostel. Only 33.3% teachers have said that SC/ST girls freely discussed their doubts like other students, 9.4% felt they came only occasionally but 57.3% said they never approached for such discussion. So teachers should encourage the SC/ST students to come to them for guidance without any hesitation. Only 14.7% of teachers have noticed SC/ST girls not taking part in college election.

10.5.2 About Special Hostel Facility

Teachers were asked an important question regarding their opinion on special hostel for SC/ST girls. 73.7% of the teachers opined against separate hostels as they felt that segregation created a sense of alienation. Only 26.7% thought this arrangement to be beneficial to some extent.

Fig. No. X-A- Opinion about Special Hostel facility

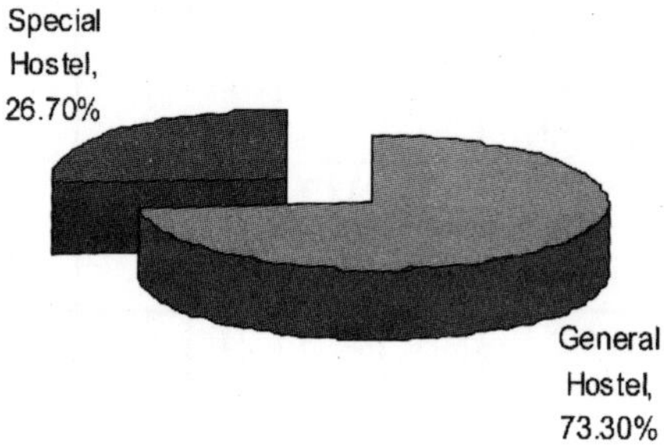

10.5.3 About Performance of SC/ST Girls

Opinions of teachers were sought regarding performance of SC/ST girls in their institutions. 62% of teachers felt that their performance was poor and only 20% thought that the performance was as good as others. Rest 18% thought the performance to be very poor.

Fig. X-B - Opinion about Performance of SC/ST Students

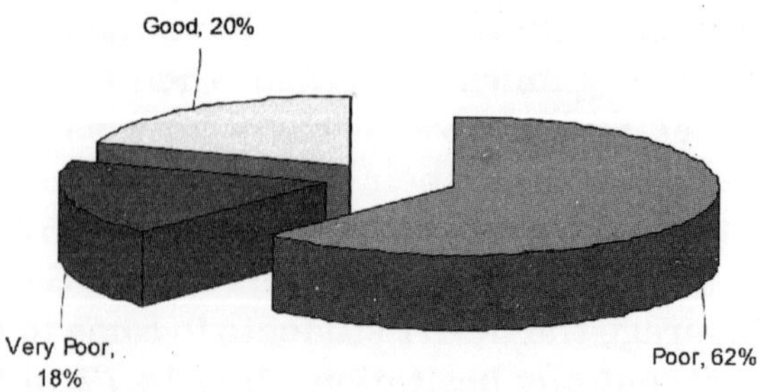

Table: 10.4 – Reason for Poor Performance

Sl. No.	Reasons	No. of Teachers	Percentage
1.	Basically poor in intelligence	09	10.6
2.	Comprehension is poor	17	20.0
3.	Experience at home/schools has not equipped them properly	41	48.3
4.	Poverty	10	11.7
5.	No views	08	9.4

They were also asked about the reason for such low performance.

Thus, about 78% of teachers felt that home and village school condition has led to low comprehension ability.

10.5.4 About Participation in Outward Activities

Teachers were asked about their assessment regarding participation of SC/ST girls in extra-curricular activities in their institutions. 85.3% of teachers said that such students took part in college election and 54.6% felt that only a few of them took part in cultural programmes. Only 45.4% of teachers felt that SC/ST girls took part in college sports. Thus, participation in extra-curricular activities was not up to the mark so far as SC/ST students were concerned.

10.5.5 About Reservation Policy

Teachers were asked whether the existing reservation policy of Government for SC/ST students in admission

Table: 10.5 – Opinion about Reservation Policy

Sl. No.	Opinion About Reservation Policy	No.	Percentage
1.	It is fair and useful for progress of SC/ST students	35	46.7
2.	It is useful but not fair	22	29.3
3.	It is not necessary	07	9.3
4.	It is not fair	11	14.7
	Total	75	100

was fair and useful. Many thought it to be useful but some thought that it was not fair for the general category students.

Thus over 50% of teachers felt that reservations were unfair/unnecessary.

10.5.6 About Scholarship Schemes

Teachers were asked whether the scholarships for SC/ST students were beneficial and properly utilized. Teachers gave varied answers.

Table: 10.6 – Opinion about Scholarship Schemes

Sl. No.	Opinion	Number	Percentage
1.	Yes, they are beneficial and properly utilized	42	56
2.	They are beneficial, but too liberal and not utilized properly by students	16	25.3
3.	Scholarship money does not reach in time	17	18.7
	Total	75	100

Thus, 18.7% of teachers complained about scholarship money not reaching in time.

10.6 Suggestions from College Teachers/ Heads of the Institutions

To get suggestions from teachers, three seminars were held at Rama Devi Women's College, B.J.B. College and Department of Women's Studies, Utkal University. In the seminars, personal views of students collected earlier were explained by the Principal Investigator. Our researchers also met principals and heads of institutions to seek their views on what could be done to improve academic standards of SC/ST girls. Most of them agreed that counselling should be done at school level, prior to entering college, since teaching in collage is quite different from that at school. Among the suggestions received, the important ones are:

1. Counselling for SC/ST girls at the beginning of academic session should be given importance.
2. Parents of SC/ST girls should also be invited to attend the orientation programme held for students.
3. Special provision for hostel accommodation for SC/ST girls should be made.
4. Spoken English classes should be held for SC/ST students at the beginning of session to compensate for their deficiency in English language.
5. Wherever possible, option should be provided for studying in regional language.
6. If required, SC/ST students may be put in a separate section to provide extra academic assistance.
7. Teachers taking special classes for SC/ST girls should be trained for that.
8. Special cultural programmes should be arranged for SC/ST girls to show their talents.
9. Girls should be provided the opportunity of availing "earning while learning" scheme in the college.
10. Proper motivation for them should be created by using audio-visuals from time to time.

10.7 Suggestions from Important Personalities/Bureaucrats/ Educationists

Efforts were made to elicit views of some leading personalities of the State whose opinion counted a great deal in policy making/ implementation.

10.7.1 Hon'ble Member of Parliament, Dr. Giridhar Gamango, Ex-Chief Minister of Orissa

This great tribal leader of Koraput, who has been a prominent champion of tribal interest, felt that Education Policy should be different for tribal areas. Education for

SCs/STs should be linked with employment; otherwise there is no purpose in educating them. According to him "Ashram schools are no longer relevant in the present time; rather SC/ST students need integration with general students". He feels that there should be special hostels in each sub-division head quarter and district and state headquarters, where bright SC/ST students from different schools may be admitted and intensive coaching provided.

10.7.2 Hon'ble Minister, SC/ST Development Department, Orissa, Sri Chaitynya Prasad Majhi

Being the Cabinet Minister in-charge of Development of SC/ST and having been Minister of Higher education earlier, this eminent tribal leader had definite views on higher education of SC/ST. He deplored the social stigma attached to SC/ST students in many educational institutions. Belonging to the tribal district of Mayurbhanj, he reminisced how the successive Kings of Mayurbhanj had promoted education in this ex-Princely State with the help of foreign missionaries and outside experts

He expressed disappointment regarding available reservation for SC/ST not being proportionate to their population in the State, which should be the case according to U.G.C. norms. He has been making efforts to increase the present percentage of 20% to 38%, the SC/ST proportion in State population. He expressed satisfaction that college education has been giving increasing confidence to SC/ST girls. The dress code recently introduced has helped greater integration of SC/ST girls with others.

10.7.3 Dr. Tara Dutt, Principal Secretary SC/ST Development Department, Orissa

Dr. Dutt, as an Indian Administrative Service Officer, was posted in different parts of the State in different capacities. While posted as Director, Tribal Welfare; he took keen interest in history and culture of tribals, and wrote the book "Tribal Development in India (Orissa)", in two parts. Presently, being posted at the highest position of State Government in "Scheduled Caste and Scheduled Tribe Development Department", not only is he trying his best to promote their educational development but also has been successful in raising their educational standard to some extent. His idea was, "It is important to provide them enough facilities for elementary education first, since they have been long neglected by British Government deliberately in this regard". He was unhappy that the number of primary schools in tribal areas is very inadequate as compared to coastal areas and there is considerable deficiency in primary school teachers in tribal areas.

However, because of his sincere effort, coaching classes were provided in Ashram Schools and the result was much better compared to previous years. Last year, 6 tribal schools had nil result in Class X and this year all of them have 100% result, he mentioned. He was happy that XI and XII classes have been opened in all Ekalabya Schools and arrangements have been made for pre-examination coaching for entry into engineering and medical courses. "Government schemes should be for all students not only for bright students" – he remarked emphatically.

10.7.4 Sri Ganeswar Behera – Ex-Minister, Higher Education Department, Orissa

Sri Das, a reputed political leader belonging to SC community, has tried his best for educational development of SC/ST during his tenure as Minister, Higher Education. In his opinion, hostel seat should be assured for each SC/ST students, so that he/she can pursue higher education. He laid emphasis on special coaching classes in colleges for Engineering and Medical, since it is too expensive for SC/ST students to take outside coaching. He has admitted that with a lot of difficulty, he had to arrange Rs.56,000/- for his daughter to admit her into coaching classes in 'TIMES EDUCATION'. He also felt that some seats in professional colleges should be reserved for SC/ST girls.

10.7.5 Smt. Pramila Mullick, Minister, Women and Child Development Department, Orissa

A prominent SC leader, she felt that importance should be given to primary education since literacy is less in SC/ST community. "First the dropout rate in school stage should be checked, then only we can think of higher education" she said. She was not in favour of special hostels for SC/ST girls. She felt very strongly that other things like food, drinking water and basic education are more important for SC/ST than higher education. Even now, there are some tribal communities in forest areas who have to walk 14 kms to collect their ration. So first they have to be made aware about government programmes facilities. Besides, all-out efforts should be made to get SC/ST children to primary schools and retain them there. This work should be entrusted to local N.G.O's.

10.7.6 Smt. Saraswati Hembram, Ex-Minister, Women and Child Development

A prominent tribal leader, she started her political career as a Sarpanch and ultimately became a Minister of the State. From her own experience, she says, "Tribal girls are backward due to lack of awareness and proper guidance. There is always financial problem in the tribal family for which they hesitate to spend money for daughter's education". Her suggestion was that adequate monthly stipend should be provided so that girls would not depend on others for their studies.

Discussion with Leaders

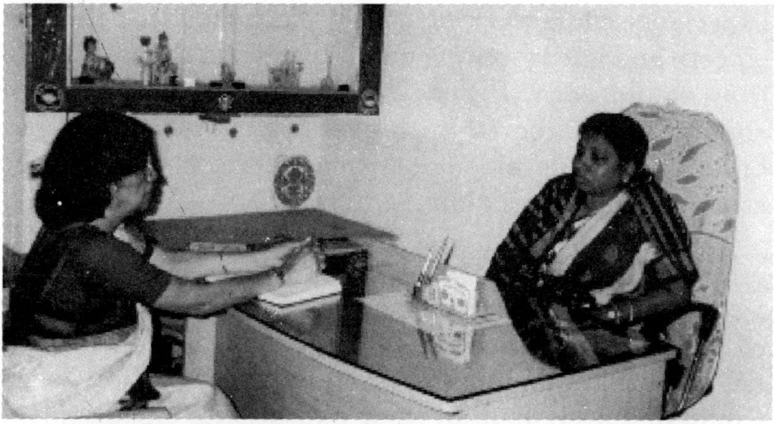

With Ms. Pramila Mullick. (Minister, W & CD)

With Ms. Saraswati Hembrum (Ex-Minister, W & CD)

10.7.7 Prof. Radha Mohan, Information Commissioner, Orissa

A reputed environmentalist and social worker and winner of many international and national awards for his work, he felt that tribal youngsters should be trained differently from a very young age. From his own experience while working with them, he felt that they are sincere and hard working and if trained in different skills they would earn a good livelihood. So their education should be different from university education and job-oriented skill development should form a part of their school/college curriculum.

10.7.8 Sri S.B.Mishra, Former Chief Secretary, Orissa

From his own experience of working for development of the State, he said that more schools and colleges need to be established near tribal communities, which would definitely help in their educational advancement. Besides, girl's schools in tribal areas preferably with good and secure residential facility would definitely attract the girls to schools. "Vocational training should be provided to tribal students in class IX and X" he said. Even if they do not come for higher education, they should be able to secure employment after schooling, he felt.

10.7.9 Dr. Sudarshan Nanda, Vice-Chancellor, North Orissa University

From his own experience at I.I.T., Kharagpur for many years, he felt disappointed that very few tribal students qualified for I.I.T. in spite of 15% reservation and less qualifying mark for entry as compared to general students. He felt that tribal children should be given pre-school training (3-6 years) before entering formal schools, so that they would have interest in study from the very beginning. He suggested special coaching classes for girl students since their number is very less in I.I.Ts. "Tutorial classes at +2 stage is a must even if they are suspended now due to lack of teachers in colleges. If required, some fees can be charged, but these classes would definitely raise their standard" was his opinion.

10.7.10 Dr. P.K. Mishra, Ex-Vice-Chancellor, North Orissa University, Baripada

An eminent educationist of the State and writer of many books on Tribal Culture of Mayurbhanj, has tried his best to attract tribal students to the University and encourage research on tribals during his tenure as Vice-Chancellor.

In his opinion, facilities for SC/ST students should be different for boys and girls according to their requirement. To bring them to standard level of attainment, special coaching should be provided in all subjects. Proctorial system should be followed for SC/ST students. "Teacher-student relationship is very important for socially backward students",–he observes from his long experience as Principal and Vice-Chancellor. In his opinion, such students need constant counselling to raise their level of aspiration.

10.8 Conclusion

Efforts have been made to collect views and suggestions regarding educational development of SC/ST girls, specially in higher education, from different sections of the society, i.e. SC/ST girl students, their parents, college teachers/principals, community leaders, administrators, educationists and important personalities.

They were requested to offer their suggestion, which could be analyzed for policy changes and other remedial measures for increasing access of tribal girls to higher education and their proficiency in education.

One of the most important suggestions from students as well as teacher was about opening SC/ST cells in educational institution to take care of their problems. Other suggestions included awareness generation among students, provision of spoken English class and vocational training.

Opinion of parents varied depending on their social and economic status. But all of them were anxious about SC/ST girls getting employment after completing education. Definitely, a change in attitude was noticed among tribals regarding girls' education which is but natural with passage of time. Emphatic suggestions were made for more women's colleges in tribal localities along with girls' hostels.

Most of the teachers agreed that performance of SCs/STs in institutions was comparatively poor and they needed special attention. Their suggestions included provision of special classes and special counselling and also more programmes aiming at social integration.

Important personalities were contacted for their views. They included Ministers in the present Cabinet, Principal Secretary of the Department, Ex-Chief Minister, Ex-Chief Secretary, M.Ps, M.L.As, Ex-Minister, Vice-Chancellor, etc. They provided us with many suggestions and most important among them were special institutions, special hostels and special coaching. Almost all of them agreed that SC/ST girl students not only needed financial help but also emotional support. Strengthening primary education, reducing dropout rate, providing community and teacher motivation at home and school are other important aspects of improving higher education prospects among SCs/STs.

11

SUMMARY OF FINDINGS AND CONCLUSION

This research project on Higher Education of SC/ST girls of Orissa was commissioned in Rama Devi Women's College (Autonomous), Bhubaneswar, (2004–2006) associating researchers from different fields like Sociology, Political Science, Women's Studies, etc.

Main objectives of the project were to analyse the enrolment pattern of SC/ST girls of Orissa in institutions of higher education including technical education; to investigate the reason for their low participation through a review of economic, social, cultural and institutional constraints; to determine the impact of special hostel facility for SC/ST girls; to study their attainment in regard to their performance and finally, to examine current government policies for promotion of their educational development and recommend remedial measures to improve their access to and achievement in higher education.

The proceeding ten chapters have presented the analysis of secondary and primary data collected by the researchers from different records of educational institutions, examining bodies and State Government records and primary data through interview of students, teachers, parents, people's representatives, policy makers and eminent SC/ST personalities. Their suggestions regarding educational development of SC/ST girls have been recorded and analyzed separately.

Many seminars were held in different educational institutions at the beginning of the project, prior to preparation of interview schedule and also at the end of the project to elicit views of educationists of the State.

(1) Seminar in Utkal University

A seminar was organized in the School of Women's Studies on 23.2.2004 with Prof. Asha Hans, Director School of Women's Studies in chair. This was attended by many eminent academicians and research scholars who have worked on SC/ST issues and government officials associated with SC/ST development programmes. The objective of the seminar was to collect a wide range of suggestions for research design and preparation of questionnaire/interview schedules. Out of many suggestions that came up during discussion, two were very important. One was about assessing whether SC/ST girls took full advantage of existing government facilities. It was suggested that the researchers should investigate whether such benefits were enjoyed only by high-income groups among SC/ST communities. The second important suggestion was regarding special hostel facility for SC/ST girls. Participants suggested investigation regarding the possibility of such facility inhibiting integration of SC/ST girls with the main stream. Views and suggestions that emerged were noted down and relevant points incorporated in the interview schedules.

(2) Seminar in Rama Devi Women's College (Autonomous)

A seminar on "Higher Education of SC/ST Girls" was organized in Rama Devi Women's College (Autonomous) on 22.02.2005 with Smt. K. Chhotray, Principal in chair. By that time scrutiny of interview schedules for students was already over and the director of the research project Prof. Bijoya Mishra with the help of power point presentation explained the low enrolment rate, poor performance and views on academic life in the institution. She sought suggestions from teachers' remedial measures.

Since almost all the teachers of Rama Devi Women's College (Autonomous) and Rama Devi Junior College attended the seminar, many innovative ideas came up and were noted. Among the suggestions important ones were regarding arrangement of special coaching/tutorial classes for SC/ST girls and more programmes for social integration.

(3) Seminar in B.J.B. College (Autonomous)

A seminar on "Participation and Performance of SC/ST students in Educational Institutions" was held in B.J.B College (Autonomous) on 5.3.2005 with Prof. R.P. Rath, Prinicpal in chair. Discussion was held mainly about their performance. Many teachers expressed concern that SC/ST students did not take advantage of institutional coaching classes under upgradation of Merit Scheme but took resort to outside coaching. However, regular tests held in such classes were really helpful, since many students attending such classes were able to secure seats in medical and engineering colleges through J.E.E.

Summary of Findings

From our extensive research covering all aspects of the objectives of the study, the following broad conclusions emerged.

11.1 Enrolment Pattern

Enrolment figures of 16 educational institutions

under the study were collected by researchers for five consecutive years (1999-2003) and enrolment figures of SC/ST girls as compared with those of general girls and SC/ST boys. When the results of 27 departments of Utkal University were analyzed, it was found that though the total number of general caste girls was much more than boys, the reverse was the case in case of SC/STs. Enrolment of SC/ST girls in different higher educational institutions was very low as compared to general caste girls and SC/ST boys.

Enrolment of SC/ST girls in technical education is negligible as compared to general education. As regards the latter, it was found that more SC/ST girls studied Arts subject than Science, Commerce, Professional Course and Law.

The quota of reservation (12% for ST and 8% for SC) has never been filled up in universities and technical colleges. In Rama Devi Women's College which is situated in the State capital and has a special hostel for SC/ST girls, seats for SC/ST needed to be increased at Principal's discretion, since applicants were more. The percentages of SC/ST girls in co-education colleges were much less in women's college and still lower in technical colleges.

However, the enrolment of SC/ST girls was found to be increasing over the years.

11.2 Economic, Institutional, Social and Cultural Constraints as Seen by SC/ST Girls

(i) Economic Constraints

The study of economic constraints revealed that many of them, particularly ST girl students, had financial problems. Although they received stipend from government, it was not sufficient. Not only the amount was inadequate but irregularity in disbursement due to funds not reaching the institutions in time created hardships. Fortunately, the amount has been revised recently, but the entire amount could not be released and there was discontent among students in Utkal University in this issue. It is a matter of concern that some SC/ST students are unaware of such facility and did not apply in time to avail this opportunity.

(ii) Institutional Constraints

SC/ST girls seldom approached their teachers in the institutions in case of difficulty. Some of them felt that teachers were not co-operative, even rude, due to low estimation of their abilities. Some students found difficulty in understanding lessons as the medium of teaching was English. Later, in course of discussion with teachers in seminars, they suggested arrangement of extra classes for SC/ST students and frequent interface for doubt clearing.

(iii) Social and Cultural Constraints

Most SC/ST girls expressed unhappiness regarding indifferent/apathetic attitude of general caste friends and their family members. This is a matter of concern and needs to be tackled for better social integration and more conducive environment.

Though tribal girls are good at sports, very few of them were found to take part in such events. Even they were found reluctant to join the different activities like NCC/NSS/ Red Cross, etc. Such reluctance needs to be overcome through proper guidance from college authorities. They seemed to need help from teachers and general caste friends to join the mainstream. Sadly, quite a few SC girls (22%) felt that they were treated as untouchables by general caste students, even by girls from educated families. 15% of SC girls said that they suffered humiliation on account of their caste. Many SC/ST girls complained that general caste girls criticized them for getting certain privileges that they did not deserve.

11.3 Impact of Special Hotel Facility

Most of the SC/ST students (82%) staying in special hostel, felt that they were treated condescendingly by others for staying in special hostel. **70% of SC/ST students did not like to be segregated in separate hostel**. 60% did not like the food and 32% complained about improper security. In general, SC/ST students did not want special hostel facility in a general college. Even 77.3% of teachers did not approve of discouraged special hostel scheme. However, some tribal parents wanted that there should be special hostel attached to each educational institution so that more tribal girls can be accommodated. On the whole, most of the educated SC/ST parents felt that their daughters should be allowed to compete with other girls and stay in general hostel with them if selected on merit.

11.4 Attainment of SC/ST Girls with Regard to Performance

(i) Regarding performance of SC/ST girls, it was found definitely lower in H.S.C. examination (class X), than general students as well as SC/ST boys. But in Higher Secondary Education (+2), SC/ST girls showed better performance than SC/ST boys, particularly in Science. Even at university level, though the over-all performance of SC/ST girls was lower than general students, SC girls in Arts and ST girls in Science showed better result than boys.

(ii) In women's college, SC/ST girls showed better result (as good as general girls) in +3 but not in +2. In co-ed college, girls did poorly at +2.

(iii) In technical colleges, there is hardly any difference in the level of performance. However, quite a number of SC/ST students were found to have back papers in different subjects.

Thus, it was found that despite low participation,

the performance of SC/ST girls seemed better at higher levels of education, i.e. +3, P.G. and technical courses. Once these girls come up to a higher level, they were found more determined to take up the challenge and hence show good result.

11.5 Current Policies for Educational Development and Their Implication

Efforts were made to assess whether SC/ST girls were taking full advantage of the schemes/programmes formulated for them by Central/ State Government and whether these schemes were actually beneficial for higher education. It was found that sadly quite a few SC/ST students were not even aware of such facilities. Of those who were aware, about 50% indicated that the quantum of reservation was not sufficient and should be increased.

As regards stipend, it was noticed that allocations reached the institutions very late, sometimes after a particular batch had already left college. As such, the amount had to be refunded to concerned department. When this was brought to the notice of government authorities, they said that such delay was on account of late requisition by the principals. In any case, timely disbursement of stipend was absolutely essential, every one felt.

The scheme of providing special hostel facility to SC/ST girls was neither liked by students nor teachers. Integration of all boarders in hostels is essential. For this purpose, reservation of seats for SC/ST inmates is desirable along with subsidized boarding and lodging charges.

There are obvious shortcomings in implementation of upgradation of merit scheme of Central Government which is meant for providing special coaching to brilliant

SC/ST students for entry into medical and engineering courses. This is on extremely beneficial scheme for students. However, it was noticed that unlike boys, SC/ST girls did not take full advantage of this scheme. Many SC/ST girls discontinued coaching classes after receiving the books in the beginning of the course. Either the time of coaching was not suitable for them or they did not want to be identified as belonging to SC/ST. To make the scheme really effective, timing for coaching should be fixed more conveniently and the girls motivated/counselled to participate.

Most SC/ST girls in post graduate classes were interested in getting into State/Central government services, but many have not been able to avail special coaching meant for the purpose. So provisions available in this regard should be advertised properly and classes should be held on regular basis for different batches. More such free coaching centres in the locality and proper counselling seemed imperative.

11.6 Suggestions for Improvement

At the final stage of research, seminars were held in different colleges and the teachers were informed about the views of SC/ST students on different issues and also their difficulties in pursuing studies. These were discussed.

Low performance, high dropout rate and lack of confidence were the main impediments. Many suggestions were offered by the teachers. These included special coaching/tutorial classes as well as spoken English classes and vocational courses in all colleges. Arranging more cultural programmes aiming at social integration would definitely help, it was felt.

11.7 Recommendations having Policy Implications

While arriving at the conclusions as to what can be done to attract mere SC/ST girls to higher education, to enhance their performance and to integrate them into the main stream, views of different stakeholders were considered in course of research analysis. Respondents belonged to different segments, students, parents, community leaders, teachers, heads of institutions, eminent educationists, policy makers and many other important personalities. Recommendations that emerged through consultations and analyses are indicated below:

1. To create awareness about different incentives/ facilities for students, a SC/ST cell should be established in each institution of higher learning as already availabe in universities. The cell would not only bring to the notice of SC/ST students, different facilities meant for them but also assist them in availing such facilities in time.

2. Reservation of seats meant for SC/ST students in institutions should be in proportion to their population and a fraction out of this should be reserved for SC/ST girls.

3. Stipend amount should be disbursed monthly or at least quarterly and not at the end of the session. It should be disbursed through cheque and not in cash to avoid bribery at clerical level.

4. Vocational training should be provided to girls in all colleges along with +2/+3 courses.

5. SC/ST students should be given option to study either in English or regional language.

6. Spoken English classes should be arranged in all colleges at the beginning of the session so that students from Oriya medium schools would not have inferiority complex and can freely communicate in the class.

7. In upgradation of merit scheme, coaching is imparted only to a few good SC/ST students for

entry into Engineering and Medical courses. It could be extended for all SC/ST students instead of providing pocket money to these students, as provided in the scheme.

8. Proctorial system should be introduced in colleges with one proctor (teacher) in charge of 20 SC/ST students, who would provide counselling as well as look into their difficulties in the institution personally.

9. Doubt-clearing classes should be arranged for SC/ST girls, where teachers can clear doubts and in regional language, if necessary.

10. Special Hostel system for SC/ST students creates mere alienation and girls feel embarrassed to be marked as belonging to lower caste. Integration in hostel is desirable. For this, establishment fees should be waived off for SC/ST girls and meals provided at subsidized rate.

11. Career counselling centres should be established at district level to provide information regarding different courses available in different colleges in the district/outside.

12. Coaching centres for civil services and to other government/ public sector jobs should be regularly monitored. All interested SC/ST students should be given opportunity for such classes if qualified, and their progress reviewed. One SC/ST teacher of university should be directly incharge of such scheme when classes are conducted in university.

13. Accommodation in the hostels in university should be provided for a limited period after post-graduation on request to passed out SC/ST candidates at the time of civil service examinations.

14. Some SC students have suggested that government

should give increment to SC/ST parents working in low paid jobs, who send their girls for education beyond graduation.

15. Student respondents also suggested for National/ International youth convention for SC/ST students for better exposure.

Almost everyone agreed that SC/ST girls in the institutions needed special care and attention by the teachers, sympathetic and understanding attitude of fellow students and provision for special coaching by expert teachers.

11.8 Limitations of Study

(i) The study was limited to a few important locations namely, (i) the State Capital, Bhubaneswar, where all important educational institutions (both general and technical) are located with hostel facilities for girls and (ii) the district of Mayurbhanj with high SC/ST population and reasonable facility for higher/technical education. The poor southern parts of Orissa comprising KBK districts, where a special development scheme of Government of India (Planning Commission) is in operation, is not within the scope of present study. A similar study in KBK district would be revealing and useful.

(ii) As found from the study, many SC/ST girl students failed to cross the High School Certificate (Class X) barrier and come to college. So their problems at school level and reason for high dropout at school level (about 75%) need indepth study, which could not be done in this project.

(iii) Hostel accommodation for SC/ST girls (including special hostels facility) is an important positive step towards widening educational opportunities for them. A more indepth study regarding establishment, location and management of such facility in the State would be very helpful, but could not be attempted in the study.

(iv) In the study, only a few technical colleges have been included, where the number of SC/ST girls was insignificant. There are thirty-seven Engineering Colleges and twenty-three Management Colleges under Biju Pattnaik University of Technology in the State. Detailed study of these institutions could provide useful information as to how participation and performance of SC/ST girls in technical education can improve.

(vi) Due to constraints of funds/time, more SC/ST parents in remote areas could not be interviewed. Wider investigation could provide additional information regarding social constraints effecting higher education of girls from these communities.

(vii) Performance of SC girls was found to be lower than general girls and that of ST girls was found lower than both general caste girls, SC girls and even ST boys. A more detailed study, given more time/ funds could lead to better understanding of their problems/ solution.

11.9 Scope for Further Research

1. In Orissa, some districts have favourable female:male sex ratio, yet in these districts SC/ST population is quite high and female literacy in very low (minimum range). This apparent paradox can be an interesting study through a specific project.

2. As seen from the High School Certificate Examination result, percentage of SC/ST girls passing matriculation (H.S.C) is very low as compared to general students. In the State, 143

Table – 11.1 SC/ST Population, Sex-Ratio and Female Literacy

Sl. No.	Neme of District	SC population (in%)	ST Population (in %)	Sex Ratio	Female Literacy
1.	Gajapati	7.5	50.8	1031	28.96
2.	Kandhamal	16.89	52	1008	36.19
3.	Nuapada	13.62	34.71	1007	26.01
4.	Kalahandi	17.67	28.65	1001	29.56
5.	Rayagada	13.92	55.76	1028	24.31
6.	Navarangpur	14.1	55.03	991	21.02
7.	Koraput	13.04	49.62	999	24.26
8.	Malkangiri	21.35	57.43	997	21.28

(*Source* – 2001 census report)

schools in 2006 and 83 schools in 2007 reported zero result in H.S.C examination. More than fifty per cent of such schools are located in tribal areas. The reason assigned was lack of infrastructure and lack of trained teachers in these schools. Such low performance at H.S.C level is an important reason for their low participation at higher level of education. As such, factors responsible for such low performance at school level need to be thoroughly investigated.

3. Hostels are main centres in the development of education among SCs and STs. An in-depth study of implication of special tribal hostels for SC/ST girls including a comparison between hosteliers and day-scholars would be useful.

4. Research is necessary to assess the problem of low enrolment (less than 1%) of SC/ST girls in technical institutions inspite of 30% special reservation for girls over and above the usual reservation for SC/ST in Orissa.

5. Looking at the dismal figure of SC/ST students in

Higher Education, Government has decided to open +2 Science Classes in ten Ekalabya Vidyalayas in the State, so that tribal students passing out from the same school in class X would continue study in class XI. Considering girls' education, Government has decided to upgrade 37 Kanyashrams to Girls' High School so that girls could have a chance to continue in class VIII after passing middle school and more girls would get the opportunity to enter college. In this background, proper awareness and motivation for higher education in essential at school level. A study can be conducted to ascertain modalities for creating interest and awareness for high school education.

6. It was found from the study that SC/ST students are not able to befriend other caste girls easily and feel hurt and humiliated by their apathetic attitude. Measures necessary to address this alienation and bring about greater integration need to be studied in-depth.

7. The study indicates that certain communities like Santal among tribals and Dhobas among scheduled castes are going ahead leaving others far behind. In 2004, a girl from Bonda community passed matriculation examinations for the first time whereas the number of educated women in other communities is quite sizeable such wide discrepancy needs further investigation.

8. Discussion with SC/ST girls with the help of interview guides revealed considerable attitudinal changes brought about by exposure to higher education. They were now more confident and independent minded with broader outlook. They even talked about working against unfair social customs like child labour, child marriage, liquor consumption,

etc. A study for assessment of attitudinal changes of SCs and STs due to higher education would be useful and timely.

Annexure-I(A)

INTERVIEW SCHEDULE FOR SC/ST GIRLS

A. Personal Information

A.1 Name:

A.1 (i) Institution Name:

(ii) Class-	+2 Sc	+3 Sc M.Sc
+2 Arts	+3 Arts	M.A.
+2 Commerce	+3 Commerce	M.Com.
Engineering	Medical	M.B.A

A.2 Age:

(i) 14-16 (ii) 17-19 (iii) 20-22 (iv) 23-25 (v) Above 25

A.3. Marital Status:

Married/Unmarried

A.4. Name of your Caste (Sub Caste)/Name of your Tribe

A.5. Religion:

(Whom do you worship at home)

A.6. (i) Language (Spoken at home)

A.6. (ii) Is there a script for that Language? Yes /No

(a) If no, which script you write?

A.7. Where is your native place?

(i) Village/Town name -

(ii) Block name -

(iii) District name -

A.8. Where are you staying now?

(i) With Parents; (ii) With Relatives; (iii) Student's Hostel;

(iv) With Students; (v) Any other place.

A.9. If you stay in hostel who runs the hostel?

(i) The State Govt.; (ii) The College/University;

(iii) Private Management; (iv) Any other.

A.10. From which school you have passed matriculation?

(i) Ashrama School- (Co-ed School/Girls School)

(ii) Oriya Medium School- (Co-ed School/Girls School)

(iii) English Medium School- (Co-ed School/Girls School)

Examination passed	Name of the Institution	Year of passing	Division
H.S.C.			
+2	Arts/Sc/Com.		
+3	Arts/Sc/Com.		

A.11. Educational Background:

A.12. Medium of instruction in college

(i) English/Oriya

Information Regarding Family

A.13. No. of family members and educational back ground

A.14. Occupation of parents:

(i) Father –

(ii) Mother --

Sl No	Name	Age	Sex	Educational Qualification	Marital Status	Relation with respondent
1						
2						
3						
4						
5						

A15. Monthly Income of Parents:

(i) Father-

(ii) Mother-

(iii) Any other income-

A.16. Education of Parents:

(i)Father

(ii)Mother

A.17. Place of Residence of Parents:

(i)Village/Panchayat HQ/Block HQ/District HQ

(ii)Which among the following is available in your village?

(i) School; (ii) College; (iii) Market; (iv) Post office;

(v) Panchayat; (vi) Hospital/medical center;

(vii) Bank/Cooperative society;

(viii) Electricity; (ix) Water supply; (x) Telephone;

B. Educational Information

B.1. Why did you decide to study in this college?

Below are given some reasons .You may say 'Yes' if you agree to reason,

And 'No' if you do not agree to it

(i) It is the only college in this college. Yes/No

(ii) It is the best college in this area. Yes/No

(iii) It offers special facilities for the SC/ST students. Yes/No

(iv) I could not get admission elsewhere. Yes/No

(v) My parents /relatives advised me. Yes/No

(vi) It is nearer to my home. Yes/No

(vii) There is no particular reason. Yes/No

(viii) If there is any other reason, please mention

B.2. Why did you choose the particular course?

Below are given some reasons. You may say yes, if you agree to a reason, and no if you do not agree to it.

(i) This is relatively easy. Yes/No

(ii) It consists of my favourite subjects. Yes/No

(iii) It is the best and it will be of help in getting me a job. Yes/No

(iv) I could not get admission in the subject of my liking Yes/No

(v) If there is any other reason, please mention.

B.3. Did you discontinue your studies after you have passed H.S.C? If yes, please mention the reasons. Yes/No

B.4. Did you discontinue your studies after you have passed +2? If yes, please mention the reasons. Yes/No.

B.5. Did you discontinue your studies after you have passed +3? If Yes, please mention the reasons. Yes/No

B.6. Mention the name of the person who encouraged you most to take education and relation with him/ her.

B.7. Is there any one in your family who does not support your Post–Graduate studies?

Yes/ No

(a) If yes, mention the relation with the person and cause of opposition.

(b) If yes, how did you overcome the objection?

B.8. Did you have any difficulty at the time of admission? Yes/ No If yes which of the following are true?

(i) Difficulty in selecting the institution;

(ii) Difficulty in entrance test/cutoff mark;

(iii) Difficulty in providing admission fees;

(iv) Difficulty in adjusting to the new environment;

(e) Any other.

B.9. Are you able to understand the teachings of your teacher in the class?

(i) Yes (ii) No (iii) Somewhat.

If No, why?

B.10. Do you ever go to your teacher for seeking guidance or advice?

(i) Yes, I go quite often;

(ii) No, I never go;

(iii) I go some times.

B.11. How do you find your teacher's attitude towards you?

B.12. (i) Do you get any coaching or private tuition?

a. Yes/No

b. If No, why?

B.12 (ii) Do you know about provision for free special coaching in your institution? Yes/ No

B.13. How much time do you devote to your studies everyday?

2hr/3hr/4hr/> 4hr

B.14. How much time do you devote for domestic work every day?

About 1hr /About 2hr /About 3hr /About 4hr /> 4hr /Not relevant, since I stay in Hostel.

B.15. Do you think you need to study more than you do at present?

(i) Yes/No (ii) If yes, what the reason?

B.16. Where do you think the opportunity for study is better?

(i) At home/(ii) At hostel/(iii) No preference.

B.17. Do you often discuss about your studies with your friends?

(i) Yes, always with all the friends;

(ii) With friends of my caste/tribe only;

(iii) I am shy to discuss with them.

B.18. What do you think about your performance in studies?

(i) Very good;

(ii) Satisfactory;

(iii) Poor;

(iv) Very poor.

B.19. What is your performance in exams compared to the previous Exam that you have given?

(i) Better;

(ii) Worse.

B.20. Do you have sufficient books for your entire course?

a. Yes/ No.

b. If yes, from where do you get the books?

(i) I purchase them;
(ii) I get old books from friends;
(iii) I get some books from friends;
(iv) I get some books from library;
(v) Books provided by Govt.

B.21. Do you go to the University library regularly for study?

Yes/ No

If No, Why?

B.22. If you are staying in hostel--------

(i) Do you have a library in your hostel? Yes/No

(ii) Are there enough books in you hostel library? Yes/No.

(iii) Do you study in the library room? Yes/No

(iv) Does someone help you in choosing the books? Yes/No

B.23. Do you read News Paper? Yes/No

If yes,

Daily/Yes, occasionally/Very rarely

If No, state the reasons

B.24. Do you use computer in your hostel? Yes/No

B.25. Do you feel that language is the main barrier in getting education?

Yes/ No

B.26. Are you finding any problem in getting education institutionally? If yes, suggest some remedial measures (for both college and hostel).

C. Economic Information

C.1 (i) What is monthly income of your family?

(ii) What is monthly expenditure of your family?

C.2 Does you family support your education financially? Yes/No

(a) If yes, how?

(b) If no, in what way you support your education

(i) Through part time job;

(ii) Through loan.

C.3. How much money do you get from your home?

C.4. Is that sufficient to live on?

Yes/No

C.5. In what way you get the money from your home?

C.6. Do you have a bank account? Yes/No

C.7. Do you save money? Yes/No

C.8. Do you have any economic obligation to your family? Yes/No

C.9. How would you describe your financial position?

Comfortable;

Moderate;

Difficult.

D. Social Information

D.1. Where do you stay?

(i) Home (ii) Hostel (iii) Mess

a. If you stay in hostel/mess with which other students you share the room?

(i) Students of your own caste/tribe (ii) Students of other groups.

D.2. If you stay in hostel, do you take your food in the dinning hall?

(a) Yes/No

(b) If No, Why?

D.3. Do you have any friends/room mates from general caste?

Yes/No

(a) If yes, do you have good relations with their family members?

(b) If No, why don't you have any friends from general caste people?

D.4.1 Are you satisfied with the food served in hostel?

D.4.2. Do you feel secure staying here?

Yes/No

(a) If yes, why?

(b) If no, why?

D.5. Do you think that the fact that you belong to Sc/St affects the behaviour of your classmates towards you?

(i) Yes, to a large extent/(ii) to some extent/(iii) No, not at all

D.6. Do your classmates know that you belong to SC/ST?

(i) Yes, I think most of them know;

(ii) Yes, I think at least some of them know;

(iii) I doubt if they know;

(iv) I can't say.

D.7. Name two of your best friends and say whether they belong to SC/ST or any other caste.

D.8. Does any of members of your family associate himself or herself with any political party? Yes/No

If yes, mention the name of the political party?

D.9. Do all your family members go for vote? Yes/No

(a) If No, mention the reasons.

D.10. Do you take part in your college election?

Yes/No

(a) If No, why?

D.11. Have you ever felt that after getting education you are becoming different from your own community members? Yes/No

(a) If yes, how?

(b) If no, how?

D.12. What kind of career you aspire for?

D.13.1. Who has decided it?

(i) Yourself; (ii) Father; (iii) Mother;

(iv) Guided by teacher or friends.

D.13.2. What is your plan after completion of study?

E. Cultural Information

E.1. Do you watch T.V? Yes/No

(a) If No, why?

E.2. Do you go for movies? Yes/No

(a) If No, why?

E.3.1. Do you participate in sports held in your institutions? Yes/No

If No, why?

E.3.2 Have you joined N.C.C? Yes/No

E.4. Do you participate in pujas /cultural programme celebrated in the hostel and college?

Yes/No

E.5. Do you worship any God or Goddesses at home? Yes/No

(a) If yes, mentioned the name.

E.6. What are the festivals you celebrate?

E.7. Do you approve inter-caste marriage? Yes/No

(a) If yes, why?

(b) If no, why?

E.8. Will you go for inter-caste marriage if situation arises? Yes/No

E.9. When deciding about your marriage to which fact you shall give more importance?

(i) Economic status (ii) Social status (iii) From my own caste (iv) Education (v) His looks (vi) My parents approval (vii) Any other qualities

F. Information Regarding Government Policies

F.1. Do you get any stipend from the Govt?

1.a. Yes/No

1.a. (i) if yes, how much

1.a. (ii) Do you get it regularly?

1.b. (i.) If No, why?

F.2. If you get scholarship, from which source do you get it?

(a) National Government;

(b) State Government;

(c) If some other source, please mention the source.

F.3. Do you get a freeship? Yes/ No

F.4. Have you availed the reservation facility given by the Govt. at the time of admission?

Yes/No

F.5. Are you aware of the facilities given by the Govt. for schedule caste/schedule tribe?

(i) Yes/No

(ii) If Yes, what are these ?

F.6. Do you think that the scholarship scheme is useful?

(i) Useful; (ii) Fairly useful; (iii) Not useful; (iv) I don't know.

F.7. Do you think that the amount of scholarship is adequate?

Yes /No

F.8. Do you think that the scheme for reservation of admission for SC/ST students is useful?

Very useful/Fairly useful/Not useful/Can't say

F.9. Would you say that the reservations provided are adequate in terms of number of SC/ST students seeking admission?

(i) Yes they are adequate/ (ii) They are not adequate/

(iii) I cannot say.

F.10. Do you think that the number of hostels provided for SC/ST is adequate?

Yes/No

F.11. Are the facilities provided in the hostels satisfactory?

(i) Fully satisfactory/(ii).Unsatisfactory/(iii) .Can't say.

F.12. Given the preference what kind of service will you prefer?

(i) Government; (ii) Semi Government; (iii) Private/ N.G.O;

(iv) Self-employment.

F.13. Are you aware of the fact that certain posts in the Government and in Public Sector Enterprises are reserved for the SC/ST? Yes/No

F.14. Do any of our family members/relatives hold any of the Government post reserved for SC/ST? Yes/No

If yes what post?

F.15. Do you think that the policy of reservation has enabled SC/ST persons to obtain jobs?

(i) Yes to a large extent/(ii) No, it hasn't enabled them/

(iii) I can't say

F.18. Do you think that the policy of reservation has fulfilled a useful purpose?

(i) Yes to a large extent/(ii) Yes to some extent /

(iii) No, not at all /

(iv) I can't say (v) I don't know.

F.19. Are you in favour of introducing reservation in Private concerns?

(i) If Yes, why?

(ii) If No, why?

F.20. Do you think that SC/ST students have advanced so much that they don't need reservation anymore?

(i) Yes, they don't need it anymore.

(ii) No, they need it.

F.21. Do you consider that the programs the Government has launched beneficial for SC/ST?

(i) Beneficial (ii) Fairly beneficial (iii) Not beneficial

(iv) I don't know

F.22. Do you think that reservation and the benefits are damaging the self-respect of SC/STs and lowering their status in society?

(i) Yes/(ii) No/(iii) To some extent/(iv) Can't say

F.23. Do you think that the Government programmes for welfare of SC/ST are administered satisfactorily?

(i) Yes/(ii) No/(iii) Somewhat/(iv) Can't say

F.24.1. Do you feel that education helps to enhance the status o women in tribal society?

F. 24.2. Do you feel that education can play a major role in economic advancement of tribal women? Yes/No

If yes, what type of education it should be? (specify)

F.24.3. Do you feel that educated tribal women are contributing more economic support to their family as compared to uneducated women? Yes/No

If yes, how? (specify)

F25. Are you interested to help illiterate SC/ST girls? Yes/No

If yes, how?

Write in few words your opinion about any policy changes or remedial measures, which should be introduced to increase access of SC/ST girls to higher education.

Address for Correspondence

Annexure- I (B)

INTERVIEW SCHEDULE FOR PARENTS

1. Personal Information

1.1 Name-

1.2 (a) Home Address- (b) Present Address:

1.3 Age - (i) 30-35 (ii) 36-40 (iii) 41-45

(iv) 51-55 (v) 56 and above

1.4 Tribe -

1.5 Religion -

1.6 Types of family - (i) Nuclear (ii) Joint

1.7 Educational Qualification:

(i) Illiterate (ii) M.E (iii) High school

(iv) Intermediate (iv) Graduate (v) Post-Graduate

1.8 Occupation:

(i) Govt. Employee; (ii) Private Employee;

(iii) Marginal Farmer; (iv) Share Cropper;

(iv) Wage Earner; (vi) Business; (vii) Any other.

2. Family Information

2.1. Family Members, their age and educational status-

2.2. How many dependant family members do you have?

2.3. How many family members are contributing to family income?

Sl No	Name	Age	Sex	Educational Qualification	Marital Status	Relation with Respondent

Sl. No.	Name of the Child	Relation with You	Class in which Studying

2.4. How many children are continuing education and in which stage are they?

2.5. What are the household assets in your name? Land/ House

3. Economic Information

3.1. What is your monthly/ annual income?

3.2. What is monthly income of the family?

3.3. What is monthly expenditure of the family?

3.4. Do you own land? Yes/No

(i) If yes, mention in acres-

3.5. Have you taken any loan? If yes, from where?

(i) Bank; (ii) Co-operative society;

(iii) Money; (iv) Any other.

4. Views regarding girls education

4.1. Do you think girls' education is as important as boys?

Yes/No

4.2. Do you think education beyond school is necessary for girls?

Yes/No

(i) If 'Yes', why?

(ii) If 'No', why?

4.3. Do you think you should send girls out of your village and stay in hostel for higher study? Yes/No

(i) If 'Yes', why?

(ii) If 'No', why?

4.4. In your opinion, should the girls also work and add to the family income? Yes/No

4.5 What kind of work you would prefer for the girls of your family?

4.6. What do you think are the reasons for high dropout rate of girls in your community?

(i) Lack of funds;

(ii) They are needed at home;

(iii) Get married at early age;

(iv) They participate in work and contribute to family income;

(v) Any other (Please state).

4.7. What do you think are the main reasons for more girls from your community going for higher education now-a-days?

(i) Improve her own future;

(ii) Increase her income;

(iii) Better marriage prospects;

(iv) Any other (Please state).

5. Policy Incentives

5.1. (a) Are you aware of facilities provided to students of SC/ST communities by Govt.? Yes/No

(b) If yes, mention them.

5.2. Are you availing any Govt. facilities for education of your children?

Yes/No/Not aware

5.3. (a) Are you aware that some jobs in Govt. and public sector are reserved for SC/ST ? Yes/No

(b) If Yes, what type of job?

5.4. Are any of your children getting post-matric scholarships?

Yes/No

(i) If 'Yes', how much?

(ii) If 'No', why?

5.5. Do you think the educated tribal women are providing more economic support to their families compared to uneducated girls?

5.6. (a) Do you think reservation policies of seats in education institutions is helpful? Yes/No

(b) If No, why?

5.7. Do you think reservation of posts in Govt. jobs for

SC /ST is no longer required since they are also equally qualified?

Yes/No

5.8. Do you think the reservation policy is creating negative impact in SC/ST communities since their self-respect is hampered?

Yes/No

(i) If yes, how could it be changed?

6. Change in Attitude

6.1 Did the girls from your community go out for higher education earlier i.e. 10 years ago? Yes/No

6.2 (a) Do you think more girls are going out for higher education recently ?

Yes/No

(b) If Yes, which of the reasons are true?

(i) New colleges have come up nearby;

(ii) Better communication available to reach college;

(iii) Attitudes of people of your community have changed;

(iv) Girls themselves insist on higher education;

(v) Financial condition of family has improved;

(vi) More incentives are provided by Govt;

(vii) Any other reason, please mention.

6.3 (a) Are more girls from your community doing job now than earlier?

Yes/No

(b) If yes, which of the reasons are true?

(i) Girls want their own income;

(ii) More jobs are available due to reservation;

(iii) Family opposition is less;

(iv) Better communication to visit places;

(v) Any other reason, please mention.

6.4 Do you think after higher education there is a change in attitude of girls in your community ?

Yes/No

If yes, mention how?

6.5 Do the girls find it difficult to adjust in your community life, after getting higher education ?

Yes/No

If yes, in what way ?

6.6 Do more girls from your community go for intercaste marriage now-a-days ? Yes/No

6.7 Do you want your daughter to marry the person of your choice? Yes/No

6.8 Do you think that she should marry a boy more educated than her?

(i) Yes (ii) Not necessary.

6.9 Do sometimes problems arise for the marriage of girls because more educated boys are not available in your community?

Yes/No

6.10 Will you allow your daughter to take up a job if available in town staying alone?

(i) Yes/No

(ii) If No, why ?

6.11 Write in a few lines your opinion about sending girls from your families for higher education.

Annexure-I (C)

INTERVIEW SCHEDULE FOR PRINCIPALS/TEACHERS

1. Personal Information

1.1 Name:

1.2 Designation:

1.3 Name of the institution:

1.4 Educational qualification:

1.5 Subject:

1.6 Caste: Gen/SC/ST

2. Institutional Information

2.1 Which classes are you taking in your institution?

Arts: +2 / +3 / PG

Science: +2 / +3 / PG

Commerce: +2 / +3 / PG

2.2 Do you interact with their parents doing the time of their admission? Yes/No

2.3 Do you feel they are very concerned because the girls are staying outside the community?

2.4 Do you have special hostel facilities for SC/ST girls? Yes/No

2.5 Do you feel it is more useful if SC/ST girls stay in special hostel or along with other girls ?

3. Attitudinal Information

3.1 Do you feel that the SC/ST students talk freely to their teachers in case of doubt? Yes/No

3.2 Do the SC/ST students contest in the college union election? Yes/No

3.3 Do the SC/ST students take part in cultural programmes in the college?

Many students/very few students/not at all

3.4 (a) Do they adjust to their surroundings away from family/home? Yes/No

(b) If No, in which way?

4. Information on Educational Proficiency

4.1 What is your opinion about the performance of SC/ST girls in college examination in comparison to the general students?

Good/poor/very poor

4.2 Do you think that their mental calibre is poorer than other students?

(a) As good as other students;

(b) Slightly poorer;

(c) Much poorer.

4.3 If their performance is poor, what is in your opinion the reason for their low academic caliber?

(a) They are basically inferior in intelligence;

(b) Their comprehension is poor;

(c) Their experience at home and in school has not

equipped them properly them properly;

(d) Poverty is the cause of their low calibre.

5. Opinion about Govt. Policy

5.1 In your opinion are the reservation facilities prepared by Govt. for SC/ST students for admission are fair and useful?

(a) It is fair and useful for progress of SC/ST students;

(b) It is useful but not fair;

(c) It is not useful;

(d) It is not fair.

5.2 Are the reservation policies followed effectively in the institution? Yes/No

5.3 Are the scholarship schemes for SC/ST students beneficial and properly utilized?

(a) Yes, they are beneficial and properly utilized;

(b) They are not beneficial at all;

(c) They are beneficial but not utilized properly by students;

(d) The provisions are too liberal-the SC/ST students are being too much pampered.;

(e) Scholarship money doesn't reach in time.

5.4 Do the SC/ST students in your institution avail the scheme of free coaching classes provided to them?

(a) Very few students come for coaching;

(b) All the SC/ST students come for coaching;

(c) They join and then discontinue;

(d) No such coaching scheme.

5.5 If they do not avail the facility, what do you feel is the reason behind it?

5.6 Do you have any suggestion(s) for the educational development of SC/ST girls?

Annexure-I(D)
INTERVIEW GUIDE

a. Who takes Decision in your family?

b. Your role in the Decision-making.

c. Ideal age of marriage.

d. Dressing pattern.

e. Selection of mate.

f. Superstition.

g. Witchcraft.

h. Apathetic attitude of general caste people.

i. Liquor consumption at home/during festival/ Do you support it.

j. Evaluation of 'self' after getting education (of respondents).

k. Patriarchal or matriarchal family.

l. Gender disparity.

m. Restriction from parents in going out of village.

n. Permission needed from community leaders.

o. Customs and traditions.

p. Do your teachers encourage you for study?

Higher Education of SC/ST Girls in Orissa : A Study of Participation and Attainment Social Matrix

	Objectives		Parameter		Complex Variable		Simple Variable	Source
1	To access and analyze the trends and disparities in enrollment of SC/ST girls students in Post Secondary Higher Educational Institutions.	1	Enrollment	1	Trends	1	Annual Enrollment of SC/ST girl students in institutions.	Documents from institutions (secondary source)
				2	Disparities	2	Annual Enrollment of General Category Students	- do -
2	To investigate the reason for the disproportional participation of SC/ST girls in higher education through a review of economic, social, cultural and institutional constraints.	1	Background information (Personal)	1	Bio-data	1	Name	Questionnaire
						2	Age	- do -
						3	Marital Status	- do -
						4	Caste	- do -
						5	Native Place	- do -
						6	Place of Residence	- do -
						7	Language Spoken	- do -
		2	Background Information (Family)	1	Family Size	1	No. of family Members	Interview schedule

	Objectives		Parameter		Complex Variable		Simple Variable	Source
				2	Family Status	1	Occupation of parents (Father and Mother)	I.S.
				3	Family Economy	1	Annual Income of Parents	I.S.
				4	Educational Background of Family	1	Education of Parents (Father and Mother)	I.S.
		3	Economic Constraints	1	Family Income	1	Income of Parents (Father and Mother)	I.S.
				2	Source of Support for Education	1	Family or Relations	I.S.
				3	Amount available for education	1	Money Received from Home	I.S
						2	Sufficiency of Funds	I.S.
						3	Bank Account	I.S.
						4	Economic Obligations	I.S.
						5	Savings	I.S.

	Objectives		Parameter		Complex Variable		Simple Variable	Source
				4	Part time Employment	1	Govt. Office/School, Private Office/School, Private Tuition, No Employment	I.S.
				5	Financial Position	1	Comfortable, Moderate, Difficult	I.S.
		4	Social Constraints	1	Family Objection	1	Person Objecting to Study	I.S.
						2	Means of Overcoming Objection	I.S.
				2	Time Available for Study	1	No. of Hours in a Day	I.S.
				3	Time Devoted for Household work	1	No. of Hours in a Day	I.S.
				4	Time needed for Study	1	More Time	I.S.
						2	Reason for not Getting Time	I.S.
				5	Staying in Hostel	1	With Same Caste Girls with Other Groups	I.S.

	Objectives		Parameter		Complex Variable		Simple Variable	Source
				6	Friendship with Other Caste Students	1	Information about Two Best Friends	I.S.
				7	Behaviour of Classmates	1	Influence of Caste on Behaviour	I.S.
				8	Association with Politics	1	Any Member of Family in Politics	I.S.
						2	Going to Cast Vote	I.S.
				9	Participation in College Functions	1	College Election	I.S.
						2	College Sports	I.S.
						3	Cultural Progra-mmes and Pujas	I.S.
				10	Decision about Career	1	Choice of Career	I.S.
						2	Person taking Decision	I.S.
				11	Family Type	1	Patriarchal Matriarchal	Interview Guide
				12	Age of Marriage	1	Age of Girls	I.G.

	Objectives		Parameter		Complex Variable		Simple Variable	Source
				13	Change of Priority in Marriage	1	Importance Given For Mate Selection	I.S.
				14	Gender Disparity	1	Preference to Education of Brothers	I.G.
				15	Social Alienation	1	Different from Community Members	I.S.
		5	Cultural Constraints	1	Different Culture	1	Name of Caste	I.G.
				2	Language Problem	1	Language Spoken at Home	I.S.
				3	Restriction in Leaving own Village	1	Restriction	I.G.
				4	Permission Needed From Community	1	Permission	I.G.
				5	Customs	1	Tradition	I.G.
				6	Dress Pattern	1	Particular Dress	I.G
				7	Celebration of Festivals	1	Celebrated in Home	I.S.
						2	Celebrated in Hostel	I.S.

	Objectives		Parameter		Complex Variable		Simple Variable	Source
				8	Lack of Interest in Outward Activities	1	Recreational Activities E.G. T.V. Movies Sports Cultural Programmes	I.S.
				9	Inter-Caste Marriage	1	Approval to go for Inter-Caste Marriage	I.S.
		6	Institutional Constraints	1	Choice of Institution	1	Only College Around	I.S.
						2	Special Facility for SC/ST Girls	I.S.
						3	Admission not Available Elsewhere	I.S.
						4	Nearer to Home	I.S.
				2	Choice of Course	1	Relatively Easy	I.S.
						2	Favourite Subject	I.S.
				3	Discontinuation in study	1	After HSC	I.S.
						2	After Plus 2	I.S.
				4	Difficulty in admission	1	Entrance Test	I.S.

	Objectives		Parameter		Complex Variable		Simple Variable	Source
						2	Providing admission fees	I.S.
						3	Adjustment to new surroundings	I.S.
						4	Any others	I.S.
				5	Difficulty in Institution	1	Understanding lessons	I.S.
						2	Approaching the teachers	I.S.
						3	Teachers' attitude	I.S.
						4	Friends' attitude for discussion in study	I.S.
				6	Availability of books	1	Purchase old books from friends Borrow books from friends Library Arrangement	I.S.
				7	Visiting Library	1	Frequency	I.S.
				8	Accommodation in hostel	1	Adequate seats	I.S.
				9	Inadequacy of scholarship	1	Amount of scholarship	I.S.

	Objectives		Parameter		Complex Variable		Simple Variable	Source
				10	Disbursement of scholarship	1	Time of disbursement	I.S.
3	To investigate the impact of special hostel facilities provided to SC/ST girls on their pursuit of higher education	1	Special Hostel facilities	1	Accommodation in hostel	1	No. of seats	I.S.
				2	Preference for hostel	1	Better opportunity	I.S.
						2	Discussion about studies with friends	I.S.
				3	Library facility in hostel	1	Enough books	I.S.
						2	Reading room	I.S.
						3	Help in choosing books	I.S.
				4	Management of Hostel	1	State Govt. College/ University Private Organisation any Other	I.S.
				5	Newspaper	1	Availability	I.S.
				6	Computer Facility	1	Availability	I.S.

	Objectives		Parameter		Complex Variable		Simple Variable	Source
				7	Friendship	1	Friendship with Other Caste Students	I.S.
						2	Relation with Their Family	I.S.
				8	Sharing Rooms with Others	1	Caste of Roommates	I.S.
				9	Security in Hostel	1	Security Measure	I.S.
				10	Dining Hall Facility	1	Inter-Caste Dining	I.S.
				11	Food Served in Hostel	1	Students' Opinion	I.S.
				12	Special Hostel Facility	1	Students' Feeling	I.S.
4	To study the attainment of SC/ST girls in higher educational institutions with regard to their performance vis-à-vis performance of girl students of other castes in different examinations.	1	Attainment of SC/ST girls with regards to performance in college.	1	Examination Result	1	Examination Result of SC/ST Girls in 5 Consecutive Years	College/ University records

	Objectives		Parameter		Complex Variable		Simple Variable	Source
						2	Comparison of Result with That of General Caste Girls	-do-
				2	Aspiration and Self Evaluation	1	Career Aspiration	I.S.
						2	Self Evaluation of Performance in Studies	I.S.
						3	Meeting the Teachers And Seeking Their Guidance	I.S.
				3	Preference for Service	1	Choice of Jobs	I.S.
				4	Attainment In Sports And Ncc	1	Excel in Field of Sports	I.S.
				5	Attainment in Extra Curricular Activities	1	College Election	I.S.
						2	Participation in Cultural Programmes	I.S.

	Objectives		Parameter		Complex Variable		Simple Variable	Source
		2	Awareness about Policy of Reservation	1	Opinion about Usefulness of Reservation Policies	1	Reservation of Seats in all Educational Institutions	I.S.
						2	Reservation of Jobs in Govt. and Public Sector	I.S.
				2	Opinion about Reservation in Private Sector	1	Opinion	I.S.
		3	Change of Attitude	1	Criteria for Choice of Mates	1	Economic Status Social Status Caste Education Looks any Other	I.S.
						2	Inter-Caste Marriage	I.S.
5	To examine the current policies of govt. for promotion of educational development among girls of SC/ST communities, their implementation and their efficacy in achieving the desired goal.	1	Examination of Current Reservation Policies in Education	1	Facilities Provided	1	Reservation of Seats	I.S.

	Objectives		Parameter		Complex Variable		Simple Variable	Source
						2	Post Metric Scholarships	I.S.
						3	Freeship and Stipend	I.S.
						4	Special Hostel Facility	I.S.
						5	Provision of Books	I.S.
						6	Provision of Special Coaching	I.S.
						7	Others	I.S.
6	To recommend policy changes and other remedial measures for increasing access of SC/ST girls to Higher Education.	1	Suggestions for Policy Change and Remedial Measure	1	Suggestions from Students	1	Seat Reservation	I.S.
						2	Adequacy of No. of Hostels	I.S.
						3	Facilities for Special Hostel	I.S.
						4	Timely Disbursement	I.S.
				2	Suggestions from Heads of Institutions	1	Difficulty in Implementation	I.G.

	Objectives		Parameter		Complex Variable		Simple Variable	Source
				3	Suggestions from Govt. Officials	1	Difficulty in Actual Implementation	I.G.
				4	Suggestions from Established Personnel after Higher Education	1	Problems Faced	I.G.
						2	To Overcome Barrier	I.G.
						3	To Increase Access of SC/ST Girls	I.G.
				5	Suggestions from Parents	1	Satisfactory Implementation of Schemes	I.G.
				6	Suggestions from Community Leaders	1	To Motivate More Girls to Receive Higher Education	I.G.

BIBLIOGRAPHY

1. Bhandari, R.K. (1982) – "Educational Development of Women in India", Ministry of Education and Culture, pp. 93-95.
2. Chanana, K. (2002) – "Treading the Hallowed Halls: Women in Higher Education in India", in 'Economic and Political Weekly' 17-24 March, 2000.
3. Chanana, Karuna (2001) – "Secondary to Higher Education: Focus on Women" – in 'Interrogating Higher Education' – Rawat Publication, p. 239-255.
4. Chanana, Karuna (2001) – "Accessing Higher Education: The Dilemma of Schooling Women, Minorities, SCs and STs in contemporary India in 'Interrogating Women's Education', p. 301.
5. Chanana, Karuna (2001) – "Accessing Higher Education" in 'Interrogating Women's Education', p. 310.
6. Chanana, Karuna (2001) – "Women's Higher Education, Recruitment and Relevance" – in 'Interrogating Higher Education', p. 263.
7. Chatterjee, H. (1975) "School Drop out Among Harijan Children: Cause and Care" – New Delhi, Cultural Institute of Research and Training in Public Co-operation.
8. Chatterjee, S.K. (1990): "Special facilities for Educational Advancement of the Scheduled Castes" in 'Educational Development of Scheduled Caste' – chapter 4, p. 103-126.

9. Chitnis, Suma (1974) – "Literacy and Educational Enrolment among the Scheduled Castes of Maharashtra" – Tata Institute of Social Science.

10. Ghose Mallick S.K. and Ghose Mallik Amita (1990); "Mode of Subsistence and Response to Elementary Education in Some Tribes of Orissa – in 'Tribal Transformation in India' – Vol. IV, pp. 195-201.

11. Kailash V. (1982): "Tribal Education and Occupation: Dynamics of Impact and Change" – pp.15-20.

12. Kalabati (1975) "Educational Status of Rural Girls", Pp.29-43.

13. Karba Lalita (1991): "Scheduled Caste Girls: Educational backwardness and Prospects" published by Mittal Publication, New Delhi.

14. Lakshmaih T (2001) – "Whiter Education for Tribals" – Social Welfare-April, 2001-pp.23-24.

15. Lal Shyam (1987): "Constitutional Safeguards and Five Year Plans for the Educational and Economic Development of the Tribals" – in 'Education Among Tribals' – published by Rupa Books International.

16. Manna, Sarita (1990): "The Fair Sex in Tribal Culture: Problems and Development" Chapter 6 (Education) – pp.186-206.

17. Mathur, N.N.G. (1991) "Strategy Evaluation and Conditioning of Tribal Education – in 'Problems of Tribal Education: Past, Present and Future'.

18. Mishra, B.C. (1996) in "Education of Tribal Children" published by Discovery Publishing Home, pp.147-160.

19. Nambissan GB. and Sedwal, M. (2001) – "Education for All : The Situations of Dalit Children in India" – in 'India Education Report' edited by R.Govinda Published by N.I.E.P.A. pp.72-86.

20. Pasayat, Chitrasen (1995): "Literacy Situation among Tribal Families in Orissa" – in 'Contemporary Society : Tribal Studies' – Vol. II – Chapter 23 – pp. 228-239.

21. Priyam M. Saxena, S. and Kumar, K: "A new Right for the Poor" in 'Frontline', June-7, 2002, p.76.

22. Ram Sharma, S. (1984): "Incentives for Scheduled Case and Scheduled Tribe" – In 'Women and Education' – Vol.V, Chapter 11, pp.125-133.

23. Ram Sharma, S. (1984): "Need for Technical and Vocational Education for Scheduled Caste Women" – in 'Women and Education' – Vol.V – pp.250-274.

24. Ram Sharma, S. (1984): "Status of Higher Education for Women" – in 'Women and Education' – Vol. IV, Chapter 8, pp.122-132.

25. Rath, R. (1974): "A Research Project on the Study of Scheduled Caste/Scheduled Tribe Students in Orissa" Department of Psychology, Utkal University, Orissa.

26. Rehaman, M.M.: Biswal, K.K. (1994): "Women and Education" in 'Education, Work and Women' – Chapter 2, p. 29.

27. Sahay, Sarita (2002) – "Tribal Women in the New Profile; Annual Publication – pp. 20-21.

28. Satya Sundaram, I. – "The Dalits: Rights and Empowerment" – in 'Social Welfare', January, 2000- pp. 30-33.

29. Shah, B.V. (1979) –"Education and Social Changes among Tribals in India".

30. Shah, Veena (1992): "Tribal Education : Perspective and prospects" – Chapter 2, pp.12-35.

31. Shah, Vimal P. (1984) and Patel Tra : "Research Problem" in 'Social Context of Tribal Education' pp.1-8.

32. Shils, E. (1961) – The Intellectual between Tradition and Modernity: The Indian Situation, Mouton, Hague.

33. Sinha, A.K. (1985) – "University Education among the Tribals: Chhotnagpur a Case Study" – in the Seminar Report on "National Integration and Tribal Development" in the Centre for advanced Study in Anthropology, Ranchi University.

34. Suguna, B. (1992): "Women in Higher Education: Issues and Challenges – Journal of Institute of Education, Pune – Vol. XI, No. 4- pp. 119-125.

35. Sujata, K. (2001) : "Education among Scheduled Tribes" – 'India Education Report', edited by R. Govinda, NIEPA Publication (pp. 87-95).

36. Tribhuban, U.D. (1977): "A Study of Educated Scheduled Caste Women in an Urban Setting" – Pune University.

37. Tripathy, S.N., Padhy, D.N.(1995) : "Education for Tribal Women" in 'Tribal Women in India' – pp. 126-134.

38. Xavier, Lewis : "Changing Nature of Higher Education" in 'Social Action' – Vol. 50, No. 4, pp. 375-378.

INDEX